THE GLASGOW ALMANAC
An A-Z of the City and its People

Stephen Terry

Neil Wilson Publishing · Glasgow

Neil Wilson Publishing Ltd
303 The Pentagon Centre
36 Washington Street
Glasgow
G3 8AZ

0141 221 1117
0140 221 5363
info@nwp.co.uk
www.nwp.co.uk

A catalogue record for this book is available from the British Library.

ISBN 1-903238-63-3

Typset in Sabon
Printed in Finland by WS Bookwell

Contents

Introduction
Glasgow, a city and its people

Settlements have existed in the Glasgow area for 10,000 years but the city originates from St Mungo's monastery, founded at Cathures in 543, at the site of the Cathedral. The name Glasgow first appears in the 12th century, possibly deriving from Cathures and Deschu villages (Saltmarket) amalgamating into Cleschu, later Glaschu, 'dear green place' in Gaelic. The original Cathedral of 1136, established Glasgow as a religious centre and it became an educational one with the university's founding in 1451.

In the 18th century Glasgow profited enormously from the tobacco trade but that ended when the American War of Independence started in 1776. Cotton and other imports then allowed Glasgow to thrive and it became a booming manufacturing centre for chemicals, paper, glass and china. Local coal and iron mining fuelled heavy industries like shipbuilding and locomotive production in the 19th century, establishing Glasgow as the second city of the British Empire. The city's population boomed as Highland Scots, the Irish, Jews, Italians and East European immigrants arrived to satisfy the job market.

Many surrounding districts were brought into the city but increasing overpopulation created slums resulting in many ancient buildings being demolished to make way for Glasgow's famous tenements. The Depression and economic downturn made Glasgow a 'depressed area' by the 1930s and it never really recovered with heavy engineering all but gone by the 1970s.

Today it thrives primarily from the service, tourism and retail sectors of the economy and has regained its international reputation, becoming European City of Culture (1990) and UK City of Architecture and Design (1999).

Glasgow's Coat of Arms

Here is the bird that never flew
Here is the tree that never grew
Here is the bell that never rang
Here is the fish that never swam

Glasgow's Coat of Arms has been made up from at least three other seals dating back to the 13th century. All four symbols are present on the Glasgow emblem because of deeds carried out by the city's patron saint, St Mungo.

In 1270, the Bishop of Glasgow's seal displayed the fish, so used because of the story of Queen Langueth, who was given a ring by her king but who had then given it to her soldier lover. On discovering that the queen had done this, the king stole the ring from the soldier, threw it in the river and demanded the queen show it to him on pain of death. The queen sent the soldier to St Mungo who told him to fish in the river and when he did he caught a fish with the ring in its stomach, so saving the queen's life.

The bird, was a robin that was killed. St Mungo prayed and brought it back to life.

The tree was originally a hazel branch. St Mungo had fallen asleep whilst guarding a holy fire and it was extinguished. He prayed over the branches which then burst into flames.

The bell is said to have been gifted to St Mungo by the Pope and appeared on a Chapter of Glasgow seal.

By the 15th century, all four symbols were displayed together on a Chapter of Glasgow Seal but not until 1647 did the seal begin to resemble today's Coat of Arms.

CHAPTER 1
Architecture

Architects

Burnet, John James (1857-1938)

Many of Glasgow's most stunning Edwardian buildings were the work of John James Burnet. Born in Glasgow in 1857, he followed in his father's footsteps as an architect in the city. He trained with his father's firm but also spent some time studying with the famous architect Jean-Louis Pascal at the premier art school in France, the École des Beaux-Arts.

It was here that he practised in the 'Beaux-Arts Style', a very grandiose and academic style of architectural design. Burnet returned to Glasgow and became a partner in his father's firm in 1879. The previous year he had won a competition to design the Royal Glasgow Institute of Fine Arts building on Sauchiehall Street. The building was sold in 1912 and was destroyed by fire and demolished in the early 1970s.

Burnet's work is still evident in some of Glasgow's most prestigious buildings. He is responsible for the creative design of both the impressive Charing Cross Mansions and the Savings Bank building and further down the Clyde at Govan, the Elder Library. His architect's firm concentrated a lot of their work in Scotland but they also opened an office in London.

He planned and designed the King Edward VII Galleries that was added to the British Museum between 1905 and 1914. During this period he also built the Kodak House in London's Kingsway which was a pioneering display of exposed steel-frame construction.

Hamilton, David (1768-1843)

Glasgow-born architect David Hamilton was to become one of the dominant men of his profession in the city in the early years of the 19th century. Born in 1768, he started working as a mason before turning to a career designing many of the city's architectural masterpieces. He worked as an assistant to Robert and James Adam on their Glasgow buildings, including the Trades House (1794) and he combined his own artistic flair with their influences.

Hamilton was renowned for his magnificent gothic-style churches such as the Campsie Parish Church in Lennoxtown, which was built in 1812. He was also responsible for the masterful Kincaid House (1812) and the following year in Fife, the Crawford Priory. But probably his best-known works were in the neo-classical style. In Glasgow one of his first architectural projects was the construction in 1802 of the new Hutcheson's Hospital on Ingram Street facing onto the Trongate. It replaced the old hospital established in 1639 by the philanthropic lawyers George and Thomas Hutcheson.

He was later commissioned to build the Royal Exchange which was completed in 1829. One of his most outstanding and visually impressive pieces of work is the massive Nelson Obelisk erected on Glasgow Green in 1806 (which was struck by lightning almost immediately after its construction).

Changing styles to Jacobean designs, Hamilton went on to produce Dunlop House in 1833. And on a much larger scale with a more Norman influence, Hamilton designed Lennox Castle in partnership with his son, James.

By the end of his life he was considered the grandfather of Glasgow architecture.

Mackintosh, Charles Rennie (1868-1928)

The end of the 20th century saw an influential revival of interest in the work of Charles Rennie Mackintosh.

One of 11 children, he was born in Glasgow in 1868. As a weak child with a club foot he spent a lot of time outdoors to improve his health and developed a passion for drawing flowers, landscapes and architecture. Leaving Allan Glen's School at 15, he was apprenticed to local architect John Hutchison but studied at Glasgow School of Art in the evenings.

At the School of Art he and his friend Herbert McNair collaborated with the sisters Margaret and Frances Macdonald to develop a distinctive Art Nouveau style. Margaret, an artist in her own right, married Mackintosh in 1900. Their work became known as the 'Glasgow Style' and they produced artefacts in glass, metal and textiles, which found a greater reception in Europe than in Britain and they exhibited in Glasgow, London, Vienna and Turin.

At 24, Mackintosh worked for architects Honeyman and Keppie who won the competition to design the new Art School building in 1896. Mackintosh's design was accepted and construction began in 1897. Considered his greatest achievement, the now famous Glasgow landmark was completed in 1909. Most of his work, including the design of Kate Cranston's famous Willow tearooms, dates from this period. In 1913 he left the company and tried, without success, to establish his own company.

Despite being an international decorative arts centre, Glasgow had few clients for Mackintosh and he and Margaret moved to Suffolk in 1914, then to London the following year, before moving to France in 1923.

After contracting cancer of the tongue he returned to London and died there in relative obscurity in 1928.

Sellars, James (1843-1888)

One of the most accomplished architects in Scotland during the 19th century was James Sellars. Born in Glasgow in 1843, the son of a house factor, Sellars was apprenticed into architecture when he was 14. His first major success was in 1871 when he designed the Stewart Memorial Fountain. It was built by master sculptor John Mossman and erected in Kelvingrove Park in 1872, honouring Lord Provost Stewart's part in bringing the waters of Loch Katrine to the city.

With the public acclaim he received Sellars was soon inundated with commissions. Much of it came from the great building boom of the 1870s, and included Kelvinside Hillhead Parish Church (1876) and his most famous work, St Andrew's Halls (1877). The boom ended abruptly in 1878 with the City of Glasgow Bank crash but fortunately for Sellars, his contracts continued.

He completed the New Club building in St Vincent Street (now James Sellars House) the following year and went on to build other landmarks including the Victoria Infirmary and the House of Fraser department store in Buchanan Street. His final success came in 1888 when he was appointed architect for the hugely successful International Exhibition in Kelvingrove Park. However, it is believed he stood on a nail at the construction site and the resultant wound became gangrenous. He died later that year and was buried in Lambhill Cemetery where eight years before he had designed the triumphal entrance arch.

In 1890 Sellars' assistant John Keppie unveiled an Egyptian-style granite monument in his honour.

Thomson, Alexander 'Greek' (1817-1875)

As one of the most significant architects of Victorian Britain, Alexander Thomson's undeniable influence promoted Glasgow as one of the great architectural cities of the world. The 17th of 24 children, Thomson was born in Balfron, 15 miles north of Glasgow. His family moved to Glasgow in 1825 and Thomson's first job was in a lawyers' office.

His draughtsman's skills soon attracted attention and he was taken on as a trainee architect with Robert Foote and John Baird, becoming their chief draughtsman from 1845 to 1849. He then partnered another, unrelated, John Baird before establishing A&G Thomson, with his brother George, in 1856. Thomson was a true city architect, designing everything from tenements to mansions and churches to warehouses.

Highly regarded among his contemporaries, he was inspired by the classical Greek style, giving rise to his nickname. He also incorporated Roman, Egyptian and Indian motifs, often in the same creation. Ironically, he rarely left Scotland and never ventured overseas but by establishing his Travelling Scholarship he indirectly allowed Charles Rennie Mackintosh his first chance to study abroad.

Although Mackintosh has received more public acclaim, Thomson's importance was finally recognised by the end of the 20th century, when one third of his work had already been destroyed in Glasgow.

In 1861, Thomson moved into one of his own creations, Moray Place, where he lived until his death in 1875. He is buried in the Southern Necropolis, a short distance from one of his finest creations, the now-derelict Caledonia Road Church.

Wilson, Charles (1810-1863)
Prolific during the 19th century, Charles Wilson was born in 1810. The son of a builder, he served his apprenticeship under the grandfather of Glasgow architecture, David Hamilton and stayed with the company for 10 years.

He was a major contributor to some of Hamilton's most famous achievements including the conversion of the Cunningham Mansion into the Royal Exchange, now the Gallery of Modern Art. However, in 1837 Wilson left Hamilton and went on to accomplish a most remarkable career. Many of his magnificent projects survived the demolition purges of the 20th century, including Kirklee Terrace, the first of its kind to be built for the city's professional middle classes.

Wilson was also placed in the unique position of being asked to design a whole area of Glasgow. He was responsible for much of what is still standing today around Woodlands Hill, such as Park Circus and Terrace and many of the buildings that overlook Kelvingrove Park.

Although many of his famous architectural designs were constructed in the West End, he was also responsible for many landmark buildings in the east of the city. His most notable creation was the massive five-storey, 210ft-high, Duke Street Cotton Mill, built in 1849 and later to become the Great Eastern Hotel.

Charles Wilson died in 1863 and was buried in the Southern Necropolis in the Gorbals, just a few yards away from the cemetery's entrance archway that he designed.

Buildings
191 Ingram Street.
Arguably the most lavishly restored Victorian building in Glasgow is No 191, Ingram Street. This 'A' listed building was constructed in 1841 by David Hamilton on the site of the 18th century Victoria Mansion. Hamilton designed the new building, facing down Virginia Street, for the Glasgow and Ship Bank which merged with the Union Bank in 1843. Between 1876 and 1879 the building's rear was extended and lavishly refaced by architect John James Burnet to become the new entrance on Ingram Street. The free-standing classical figures at second-floor level are by master sculptor John Mossman.

Hamilton's facade was used as the frontage of the Princesses Theatre in the Gorbals (now the Citizen's) but has since been destroyed.

The Union Bank moved to St Vincent Street in the late 1920s and in 1931 the building had been converted to justiciary courts. Now Lanarkshire House, it served as an overflow court for the Sheriff Court (housed in the County Buildings), the High Court (Justiciary Courts, Saltmarket) and even the Court of Session sat there. In 1986 the Sheriff Court moved to the Gorbals and after the Justiciary Court's extension was completed the High Court ceased to sit there.

By 1997 Lanarkshire House lay empty but after major redevelopment it reopened in 1999 as the Corinthian, one of Glasgow's most up-market nightspots. Its renovation involved removing the court's false ceilings, revealing the spectacular 26ft-high glass dome in the former teller's hall to the rear, designed by James Salmon I in 1853.

Baird Hall

Baird Hall on Sauchiehall Street in Glasgow has been used for several purposes since it was built more than 60 years ago. It was originally the Beresford Hotel which was built to help accommodate the many thousands of visitors that Glasgow expected for its Empire Exhibition of 1938. Architects Weddell & Inglis worked on a contemporary design that would complement the architectural theme of the exhibition which was held at Bellahouston Park. Bellahouston was chosen because it was flatter than Kelvingrove – the site for the city's three previous major exhibitions.

Work started on the Beresford Hotel in 1937 and was completed the following year in time for the exhibition which attracted more than 12.5million people between May and October. Apart from the two semi-circular towers that extend on either side of the main entrance from the first floor right up to the 10th, the most striking part of the whole structure was its colours. The central fins between the towers were red and the rest of the exterior was covered in black and mustard yellow earthenware and porcelain tiles. Sadly these bright colours have now been covered over by layers of uniform yellow paint.

The building continued to operate as a hotel until 1952 when it was leased to ICI which used the premises as office accommodation. In 1964, the building was sold to the University of Strathclyde renaming it Baird Hall and converting it for use as student accommodation. In 2003 the building was sold for redevelopment into private residential flats.

Baronial Hall

Nothing now remains of the 16th-century Baronial Hall which was situated near to the site of the Citizen's Theatre in the Gorbals on the south side of Glasgow. In the early 1500s the land was leased from the Bishops of Glasgow to John Elphinstone and passed down through the family. In 1563, George Elphinston, who dropped the 'e' from his surname, acquired the lands of Blythswood in the west end of Glasgow.

Sixteen years later the family was granted a feu holding of the land in the Gorbals by Bishop Boyd. George's son, also George, acquired an old chapel attached to the disused lepers hospital that had been established there during the 14th century. The chapel was converted for use by the family and Elphinston built a C-plan Baronial Hall and mansion and a fortified, castellated tower.

Elphinston was knighted by James VI in 1594, elected Provost of Glasgow in 1600 and later became a member of the Scottish parliament. But in 1634, financial constraints forced him to sell the Gorbals estate to Viscount Belhaven who extended the mansion. However, the land of the Gorbals was purchased by Glasgow in 1650 and in 1677 the tower and mansion were leased to the Marquis of Montrose.

In later years the tower was used as a prison and the chapel became a court house and was also used as the parish school. The mansion fell into disrepair and was demolished. Later the tower followed suit but the chapel survived until 1870.

Blythswood Square

Blythswood Square is the only square in the whole of Glasgow that was constructed in the same style as Edinburgh's New Town. It was originally called Garden Hill after William Hamilton Garden who promoted the development of the project before he went bankrupt and had to take off to America.

The plan was taken over by William Harley, who was responsible for founding a bath house nearby which gave Bath Street its name. Construction of the square was started in 1823 by architect James Gillespie Graham who modified the original set of plans created by James Craig who had laid out Edinburgh's New Town many years before. Work was completed in 1829.

All four terraces were originally set out in three bays over three storeys, in a neo-classical style, overlooking the central garden. However, it was done on a much smaller scale and was more open-ended than that which can be seen in Edinburgh. Today, all the terrace facades have been modified, most notably the complete reworking by James Miller of the eastern terrace for the former RSAC club between 1923 and 1926. On the northern side at No 5, is an inserted doorway by Charles Rennie Mackintosh.

However, the most infamous door in the square is that of No 8. This was the family home of the 19th-century designer of the McLellan Galleries, James Smith. His 22-year-old daughter, Madeleine Hamilton Smith, was sensationally tried, but released on a 'not proven' verdict, for the murder of Pierre Emile L'Angelier by arsenic poisoning.

Buchanan Street

Buchanan Street, regarded by many as the finest individual street in Glasgow, was the first to be pedestrianised, prohibiting vehicle access in 1975. It officially came into being in 1763 when maltster turned successful tobacco merchant, Andrew Buchanan, bought some land to the north of Argyle Street. Considered crazy for buying land so far out on the outskirts of the town, he nevertheless built his mansion there.

A few years later Buchanan opened up the plot of land behind his home into a street and by 1786 four houses had been built alongside the thoroughfare. Buchanan's business failed in 1788 but the work continued under trust until the road had been extended to present-day Gordon Street. The city fathers extended it still further by the turn of the century. However, during the early 19th century, the splendid houses had given way to three and four-storey terraces and the first shops were established on the ground floors. By the end of the century it had become the fashionable Victorian shopping centre in the city.

There was a determination to keep the trams out of the street but winning this fight only led to heavy congestion by the ever increasing numbers of cars and buses. During much of the 20th century Buchanan Street was the main traffic artery through the city and was also well known for its murmurations of starlings. With pedestrianisation in the 1970s calm befell the street and it has once more become the fashionable place to shop in Glasgow.

Ca d'Oro building

The Ca d'Oro building at the corner of Union Street and Gordon Street in the centre of Glasgow started off as a furniture warehouse.

It was one of the first buildings in the city to have been constructed using a cast-iron framework. This palazzo-style building has immense cathedral-like windows and its exterior was originally decorated extensively with gilt. It was designed by John Honeyman and construction was completed by 1872. It was believed that the name Ca d'Oro was derived from the 'Golden House' in Venice on which Honeyman's design was modelled. But it is equally likely that its name comes from the famous restaurant that opened there in 1927, more than half a century after it was constructed. The restaurant was added to the building by J Gaff Gillespie who was responsible for the rather unsightly mansard roof which to many eyes spoilt the overall elegance of the Italian design.

As well as being a warehouse and shops, the Ca d'Oro was also famous as a venue for weddings in Glasgow: it was *the* place to be married in Glasgow during the inter-war years. And even after WWII it remained popular until the 1950s when Alexander 'Greek' Thomson's Grosvenor building further along Gordon Street became in vogue. In 1987 the building was gutted by fire but restoration work was completed by 1989 with the addition of two bays to the building's Union Street elevation.

For many people the fire was a blessing in disguise because the mansard roof was not replaced. Since restoration the ground and basement floors of the building have been used for retail purposes.

Central Station and Hotel

Glasgow's Central Station Hotel is probably one of the most overlooked pieces of the city's architecture. A huge monument to Victorian station hotels, it is hemmed in on all sides so that its true splendour is hard to take in from the street. Occupying the north-west corner of Central Station where Gordon Street meets Hope Street, the building has survived the rigours of the city's pollution for almost 130 years. Its construction came after the City of Glasgow Union Railway refused to allow the Caledonian Railway the use of its bridge over the River Clyde for St Enoch Station. Caledonian was then forced to buy several city blocks to construct its own station.

After the station opened in 1879 the company decided to build a hotel on the opposite side of Hope Street from the station. However, the plans were revised and architect Sir Rowand Anderson constructed the hotel adjoining the station, rivaling the St Enoch Station Hotel, completed a few years before. Work started in 1882, three years after the station was completed, and nearly three years later, two more than planned, it was finished. Its most outstanding feature is the 17th century-style Swedish clock tower.

The hotel was considerably extended down Hope Street by architect James Miller between 1899 and 1908 with the doubling in size of the station during the same period. The hotel's interior was greatly changed around this time but has remained relatively untouched since, a reminder for today's guests of the history of this grand hotel.

Dixon Halls

Dixon Halls were built as a point of defiance against Glasgow. During the 19th century, these burgh halls on the south side of the city lay at the extremities of Glasgow where the urban sprawl was always threatening to swallow them up. But the bailies of Govanhill and Crosshill were determined to stave off the inevitable with funding donated by William Smith Dixon, who owned the famous Dixon's Blazes iron foundry nearby at Polmadie.

Architect Frank Stirrat won the design competition for the building and work started in 1878. It was completed the following year in the Scottish Baronial style. Unlike most buildings, it was built at a 45 degree angle across the corner of Dixon Avenue and Cathcart Road, with the burgh boundaries dissecting it. Tall and narrow, it had a clock tower and the roof was peppered with turrets and crowstepped gables.

In keeping with its purpose of keeping Glasgow out, there were two entrances, one for each burgh, which led to the courtrooms on the ground floor. There were also two sets of stairs leading up to the hall. However, one staircase has since been blocked off and the grand, open, timbered ceiling of the hall has been masked by false ceilings. The halls opened in 1879 and to many were seen as a great snub to Glasgow. But the city had the last laugh in 1891 when the two burghs were successfully annexed and became districts of Glasgow. The halls have been a day centre since 1978.

Egyptian Halls
The Egyptian Halls in Union Street was the second last of Alexander 'Greek' Thomson's masterpieces of architectural design. Although renowned for his Greek-style buildings, many of his creations involved many aspects of other cultures. So in the case of this building it is not odd to find that he chose an Egyptian line to predominate this magnificently proportioned terrace.

Work started in 1871, the construction being carried out by builder James Robertson and was complete by 1873, just two years before his death. The building is on four levels, supported by cast-iron columns, with numerous repeating bays giving the impression it could continue for ever. Each level is different in style and shape, sculpted with beautiful stone work and extensive use of glass. Their design ranges from the plate-glassed shop fronts on the ground level to the 'eaves gallery' with its Egyptian colonnade set in front of continuous glass, hiding the sloping attic rooflights.

Over the years some restoration work to the building has taken place but only the shop-fronts have been altered to any degree. It is still the finest example of the warehouse-style on Union Street, with the possible exception of the Ca d'Oro building at the junction of Gordon Street.

Today, the Egyptian Halls is the earliest of 'Greek' Thomson's buildings to survive in Glasgow – his very last piece of architecture in Bath Street was pulled down some years ago.

Grecian Buildings
The Grecian Buildings on Sauchiehall Street is one of the most unique, if not outstanding, of the structures created by Alexander 'Greek' Thomson. This commercial project was one of the few occasions where he was asked to design a building at the corner of a road. This allowed him to not only create an inspirational front elevation to his work but also to express a depth as well.

Constructed in 1865, the Grecian Buildings, despite its name, is dominated by an Egyptian style. Built on a modest scale, with only three levels, he chose to use a telescopic effect where each level diminishes in stature as you look upwards. The large plate-glassed windows of the ground floor were restored in 1988 but still retain an original character while the upper floors contrast well with each other. The first floor has tall window frames set almost flush with the facade while the uppermost eaves gallery has deeply recessed windows.

The overall appearance of the building was considered to be highly experimental and even revolutionary in its day. The Grecian Buildings helped establish Thomson as one of the great original thinkers in architectural circles during the second half of the 1900s.

Great Eastern Hotel
This is one of the largest and most impressive of all the buildings ever constructed in the east end of Glasgow. It is one of the great relics of the city's

Victorian industrial era when Glasgow was one of the most important manufacturing areas in Europe. The hotel was originally the Duke Street Cotton Mill, owned by the Alexander family.

Not only was it the grandest of all the spinning mills in the city but it is the only one that is still standing today. The cotton industry at this time was still relatively prosperous, having filled a gap in the merchants' market since the collapse of the tobacco industry after the American War of Independence. The cotton mill was designed by the famous Glasgow architect Charles Wilson and his five-storey 210ft-high building was completed in 1849 but, unlike many others during that period, was designed to be fire-proof.

It was not the first of its kind in the city however, that record goes to Houldsworth's Anderston Cotton Works, built in 1804 but demolished in 1968. The cotton industry, just like the tobacco industry, eventually declined because of outside influences, in part again due to unrest in America, this time the Civil War. In 1907 the cotton mill was renovated by architect Neil Duff who maintained its fire-proofing, using wrought-iron trusses and corrugated-iron shuttering.

When the conversion work was completed the old mill became a hostel for homeless working men, and in 1995 was acquired by a local housing association for conversion into flats.

Grosvenor Building

This outstanding building in the city centre's Gordon Street often goes unobserved because of the modern ground floor shop-fronts.

And the grand entrance of Central Station directly opposite also distracts pedestrians from looking up. The building was originally the work of Alexander 'Greek' Thomson and his brother George. It was the first and very successful attempt by the AG Thomson partnership into the design of the highly lucrative warehouse-style buildings in the city.

The building owes its elaborate design to the fact that it was built to satisfy the architects rather than follow guidelines laid down by any prospective owner. It was constructed on the site of a United Presbyterian church and George Thomson, a member of its congregation, persuaded the church to sell the site to fund the building of a new church – Thomson's famous St Vincent Street Church (1857-59).

The three-storey warehouse was built between 1859 and 1861 but it burned down three years later and was rebuilt over the next two years to the same design. Between 1902 and 1907, additional upper floors topped by twin baroque domes were added by architect JH Craigie. This accommodated the sumptuous banqueting hall of the Grosvenor Restaurant, from which the building derived its name. But the banqueting hall and magnificent staircase were destroyed by fire in 1967 and subsequently replaced with offices between 1971 and 1974. The chandeliers survived and were hung in the Trades' Hall in Glassford Street.

Grosvenor Terrace

Grosvenor Terrace in the west end of the city marks the start of a tree-lined boulevard that runs west along Great Western Road from its junction with Byres Road and Queen Margaret Drive. It was built in 1855 by architect John Thomas Rochead and for many it is his greatest achievement in the city.

The grand frontage is of an unmistakable Venetian palatial design and its most striking aspect is the repetitive nature of its composition. The three-storey north-facing terrace is made up of 83 identical bays stretching for about a quarter of a mile. Each has a huge semicircular-headed window, separated by classical columns set out in the standard hierarchical order of Corinthian above Ionic above Doric. Only the 10 slightly protruding bays at either end prevent the image of an infinite line of glass and stone.

It became one of the most desirable properties at the height of bourgeois living during the Victorian era. The eastern end of the terrace was converted into the Grosvenor Hotel in 1971 by Reo Stakis. Eight years later it was destroyed by a fire which raged out of control for more than six hours in the ninth week of a fireman's strike. However, the front was faithfully recreated by T M Miller using a reinforced steel and concrete frame, clad with glass reinforced concrete detailing taken from the original.

Hatrack building

One of the most architecturally stunning and unusual structures in Glasgow's city centre is the Hatrack building at No 142-144 St Vincent Street. This remarkable piece of architecture is 10 storeys high but is incredibly narrow, measuring less than 30ft across. Its intricate Art Nouveau sculptured red sandstone facade has been described as the skeleton that keeps the glass in place. It was designed in this way to let as much sunlight in as possible into what is essentially a three bay width structure facing south.

The most beautiful piece of glasswork, and certainly the most easily seen from the street, is the rather small but beautifully designed ornate stained glass oriel window. The window, which depicts a stately galleon, is supported just above the entrance by what appears to be a dragon or some other mythical creature.

Looking inside, you can still see the decorative iron work that used to house a lifting cage but has now been replaced by a more modern lift. The contract to design the Hatrack was won by James Salmon, Son & Gillespie and it was designed by architect James 'Wee Trout' Salmon II, so called because of his diminutive size.

Work was started on the building in 1899 and was completed three years later. However, the most remarkable part of the building was at roof-top level. There used to be a whole series of finials extending from the roof cupola which is of course how the building originally got its name.

Henry Wood Hall

Henry Wood Hall in the west end of Glasgow is where many of Scotland's finest orchestras have practised and performed for more than 20 years. But the building was originally built for an entirely different purpose although music was also intended to be played there.

The hall, situated at the corner of Berkeley Square and Claremont Street, was originally the Trinity Congregational Church. It was built in 1864 by the renowned architect John Honeyman who is most famous for his Ca d'Oro building in the city centre, one of Glasgow's first cast-iron framework buildings.

The building's main entrance is directly below the tall spire which more than any other aspect of the structure, reveals its original purpose. There are also two large stained-glass windows which depict the 'Origins and Inspiration of the Protestant Religion' that were inserted in 1905 by the Stephen Adam Studio. But little original ornament remains of the interior which served as a place of worship for more than 100 years.

In 1978 the building underwent major renovation work by John Notman & G S Calder in order to provide the Scottish National Orchestra with a base in which to rehearse. The main hall is T-shaped, has a very high ceiling and is well lit.

As well as functioning as a rehearsal area for the SNO it serves as a concert hall where the BBC Scottish Symphony Orchestra and some smaller orchestral groups give public performances. The building is named after the world-famous London-born conductor Sir Henry Wood.

Holmwood House

The classically Greek styled Holmwood House in Netherlee Road, Cathcart, was the finest of Alexander 'Greek' Thomson's domestic commissions. It rivals in splendour Charles Rennie Mackintosh's most famous domestic work, Hill House in Helensburgh, which he built for the publisher Walter Blackie almost half a century later.

Building work started on Holmwood in 1857 and it was completed the following year. Thomson designed the small house for James Couper who was wanting to start a family. The house was built above the River Cart just up the bank from Millholm Paper Mills which Couper and his brother Robert owned. Designed to a villa style using many adaptations of the picturesque subtlety of a classical Greek dwelling, he decided upon a horizontal rather than a vertical design focus.

This emphasis has allowed the main rooms of the house to stand out and provides an uninterrupted break between the house and coach house which are linked by a wall. The Coopers died childless and the house has changed hands several times since it was first sold in 1909. Over the years many of the wood, plaster and marble features inside the house have deteriorated. However, after investigations by Historic Scotland into the original designs, conservation work has been ongoing by the National Trust for Scotland, having acquired the property in 1965. Apart from the house, restoration work is presently being carried out on the Victorian kitchen garden. Holmwood House is open to visitors between April and October.

Kibble Palace

Glasgow's famous hothouse, the Kibble Palace in the west end of the city was actually built at the house of engineer John Kibble at Coulport, Loch Long. In 1873 he donated his glasshouse to the Botanic Gardens, dismantling it and shipping it up the Clyde to its present day location. When it was rebuilt at the Botanic Gardens site, the main dome was increased in size and two wings were added to the sides of the smaller dome.

The glass enclosing the Kibble Palace covers an area of more than 2000 square metres, making it one of the largest glasshouses in Britain. Inside there is a huge collection of tree ferns from temperate regions such as Australia and New Zealand and many other plant species from tropical Africa, Asia and South America.

The Palace itself is the main building in the Botanic Gardens but there are also 11 other linked greenhouses displaying a wide variety of other species ranging from cacti to orchids.

Originally used as a Winter Garden, it was a venue for concerts and other important events and meetings in Glasgow. It did not become the home for its now internationally renowned collection of flora until 1881 when the Royal Botanic Institution took over the lease for the building.

And today, apart from plant lovers and people just looking for peace and relaxation, many couples choose to get their wedding photos taken in front of the exotic greenery and statues.

It is one of the best loved city attractions today.

The Knowe

The Knowe is the earliest and least known of Alexander 'Greek' Thomson's larger houses. Standing at the corner of Albert Drive and Shields Road in the Pollokshields area of the city, this private house nevertheless depicts the characteristics of his later work. The first stage of the house was built between 1852 and 1853 for the hatmaker John Blair. Over the next 20 years or so Thomson was commissioned to design several additions to this beautiful home.

During the period of its initial construction he was still using a double-style formula to his designs – both Greek and Roman – which is evident in many aspects of the exterior. Three years after completing the first phase he dropped the Romanesque style and almost all future work was carried out in a Greek style – his famous architectural signature. The first stage of the house was very small in comparison to today's final creation. Its interior was relatively unexceptional except for the magnificent staircase with its stained glass windows depicting Egyptian scenes.

Between 1855 and 1858 the north-east wing was added, replacing a smaller, short-lived earlier extension and in 1873 the coachhouse was altered to become the Lodge which was almost identical to the main house although in miniature. In 1899, nearly a quarter of a century after Thomson's death, the south-east wing accommodating the billiard room was constructed.

It was designed by J. McKellar in sympathy with Thomson's external style but with an Art Nouveau interior.

Langside Halls

Langside Halls on the south side of Glasgow was originally constructed in the city centre more than 150 years ago. It was erected in Queen Street in 1847 for the National Bank of Scotland. It was designed by the architect John Gibson and the intricate stone-work detailing was carried out by John Thomas of London.

Over the next half century the building sat in a fine square of business chambers until 1901 when the corporation decided that the space would be better used as a warehouse. Rather than demolish this impressive structure however, it was decided to transfer it over to Langside. It was dismantled carefully and every stone was transported across the river to its new position at the eastern corner of Queens Park near Shawlands Cross. The rebuilding work was undertaken by the city engineer Alexander Beath McDonald.

Construction started in 1902 and by the following year it was completed and opened as a suite of halls for use by the general public. With great care the exterior was reconstructed in the original Palladian style complete with the swags of fruit and royal coat of arms flanked by figures depicting Peace and Plenty. And in keeping with the original design, the bearded faces on the keystones were faithfully set in place, representing the Clyde, Thames, Severn, Tweed and Humber rivers. The grand interior of the building was also faithfully reproduced although not from the original which had been largely transformed by James Sellars in 1856.

Lion Chambers

One of the first buildings constructed using reinforced concrete in Scotland was the Lion Chambers in Hope Street. This revolutionary new technique allowed this eight-storey, 90ft-tall building to be slotted into a space that was only 33ft by 46ft.

It was built between 1904 and 1907 by architects James Salmon II and John Gaff Gillespie for the lawyer William G. Black, an amateur artist and member of the Glasgow Art Club.

The building originally housed a printing works in the basement and shops and law chambers with pre-cast busts of judges at the oriel windows. The upper floors were set aside for artists' studios.

The architects were also responsible for another of Glasgow's remarkably thin buildings, the Hatrack in St Vincent Street, whose 10 storeys are squeezed into a 30ft-wide space.

The Lion Chambers' walls are only four inches thick, dimensions unheard of until the development of reinforced concrete, the norm in today's construction. Their slenderness was made possible by the Hennebique system, a technique developed by two French engineers LG Mouchel and TJ Gueritte. The contractor for the building was The Yorkshire Hennebique Contracting Company, based in Leeds.

The building is supported by a space-saving framework of only 21 columns measuring 13 inches to 8 inches square that run continuously the whole height of the structure. Its design was inspired by two earlier buildings in nearby Buchanan Street, the Britannia Building which itself was modelled on the Athenaeum building of the 1890s.

McLennan Arch

The McLennan Arch standing in front of the High Court building at the entrance to Glasgow Green originally sat above the entrance to the Assembly Rooms in Ingram Street. Supported on a massive stone plinth, it was the centrepiece facade of the building designed by Robert and James Adam which was completed in 1796. It was the first of the large-scale classically pretentious buildings in the city.

However, in the 1880s it was decided to build an extension to the rear of the General Post Office on George Square which was used as a sorting office. This required the demolition of the Adam building. But the two wings which had been added by Henry Holland managed to survive until 1911.

Prior to its destruction, the arch was saved by Bailie James McLennan, JP, who bought it so that it could be retained and preserved for the people of Glasgow.

In 1894, city architect John Carrick re-assembled the arch in Jail Square but in 1922 it was rebuilt at the southern end of Charlotte Street at one of the entrances to Glasgow Green.

McLennan's Arch eventually started to tilt and it was dismantled for a third time before it fell down. Eventually in 1991 work started on its reconstruction in its present location and it was finished the following year.

The central arch, which was originally a window, made a fitting triumphal gateway for the runners to pass under on the home stretch of the Glasgow Marathon.

Castles and Mansions
Aikenhead House

Sitting right in the centre of King's Park is Aikenhead House, the magnificent early 19th century mansion of the tobacco merchant John Gordon. It was constructed in 1806 on the site of a much earlier 17th century house.

The merchant's home was most likely built to the design of architect David Hamilton who is regarded as the grandfather of Glasgow architecture. Among Hamilton's many famous achievements are Hutcheson's Hospital on Ingram Street and the former Royal Exchange, now the Gallery of Modern

Art at Royal Exchange Square. Hamilton was also responsible for the massive Nelson Obelisk in Glasgow Green, Camphill House in Queen's Park and Gorbals Parish Church.

The later additions of the extensive wings to Aikenhead House, added in 1823, are certainly Hamilton's work and it is quite possible he had the main part of the house re-cast to blend in with his elegant, stylishly simple new design. In the middle of the flower lawn to the front of the house, stands a most unusually shaped sundial. Classed as a listed structure, the sundial originally stood in the formal garden of Douglas Castle in South Lanarkshire.

In 1930, the city of Glasgow acquired the ownership of the house and the surrounding land and turned it into a public park. Aikenhead House was restored by the City and for a time was used as a municipal museum. However, in 1986, the two-storey central block and both the one-and-a-half storey wings of the house were converted into 14 residential flats.

Auldhouse Castle

Auldhouse Castle was built in the 17th century on the ancient lands of the High Stewards of Scotland. Often described as a mansion rather than a castle due to its small size, it stands to the south of Auldhouse Park on the south side of Glasgow. The land was granted to the Maxwells in 1344 along with many other estates in the area.

This L-shaped tower is the only surviving building on the site, believed to have been built by George Maxwell, minister of Mearns, or his son John, minister of Eastwood and the High Kirk of Glasgow.

There is a lintel over the kitchen fireplace that is dated 1631. After John's death, the next Auldhouse Maxwell to inherit the castle along with the lordship of Pollok was another George, famous for persecuting witches. In 1676 he became ill with a fever while visiting Glasgow. The sickness was put down to witchcraft and eventually a widow was accused after an effigy of George with pins in it were supposedly found in her cottage. She and four of her family were quickly found guilty of heresy and were taken to Paisley where they were strangled and burned. George soon recovered but died later that year.

After his son died without leaving an heir, Auldhouse and the surrounding lands passed to the Maxwells of Blawarthill and since then the castle has passed through many hands. It has been used as children's home and was recently converted into private flats.

Bishop's Castle

Nothing remains today of the Glasgow (or Bishop's) Castle. It used to stand to the south of Glasgow Cathedral in what is today the central square. The castle may have been built around the time the cathedral was rebuilt during the 12th century but it does not appear in official records until 1258.

Although a Royal castle, it was used as a stronghold for the Bishop's of Glasgow during the Wars of Independence. The English occupied it for a brief period until around 1296 when it was recaptured by William Wallace. But five years later it came again under the control of Edward I and a garrison was put there for its defense. However, it was routed by Wallace in one of Glasgow's few official battles – The Battle of the Bell O' The Brae – a fight mentioned in Blind Harry's epic tale.

During the 15th century Bishop John Cameron built the five-storey tower and further fortifications were added later until its grandeur led to its being called the Bishop's Palace. But by the 18th century the castle was in a ruinous state.

Part of the remaining castle structure was used as a place of execution in the last quarter of the 18th century. The last vestiges of the castle were removed to make way for the construction of the original Royal Infirmary building in 1792. The only evidence of its existence today is a stone from the castle which bears a brass engraved illustration located in Cathedral Square.

Bedlay Castle

Bedlay Castle, like many ancient buildings in Scotland, is haunted but some of its ghosts have no earthly connection to the building.

The castle dates from two periods. The eastern half, with its rectangular keep and square tower, is from the late 16th century. It was built by Lord Robert Boyd of Kilmarnock, who was given the estate by kinsman Bishop James Boyd in 1580. He sold it in 1642 to the lawyer James Robertson, later Lord Bedlay, who not only gave the castle his name but added the western section with the two round towers.

However, some of the ghosts inhabiting this privately owned building a few miles south east of Kirkintilloch, supposedly date from many centuries before the castle was built.

The estate was originally owned by the diocese of Glasgow but was forfeited for a time until being returned to the Church after David I came to the Scottish throne in 1124. Fifty years later Bishop Jocelyn built there and by 1350 Bishop Cameron lived there. However, he died under mysterious circumstances and it has been reported that heavy footsteps and the occasional glimpse of a large, heavily bearded man in ecclesiastical robes can be seen wandering around the castle.

Some people suggest that the ghost is actually James Campbell of Petershill who bought the castle in 1805. Spectral forms were seen during his stay at the castle after he built a family mausoleum there. But the ghosts disappeared when it was relocated to Lambhill Cemetery.

Camlachie Mansion

Camlachie mansion was built in 1720 on the estate of Wester Camlachie, at that time on the extreme eastern boundary with Glasgow. It was built for tobacco merchant James Walkinshaw of Barrowfield, his grandfather having bought the land half a century before.

The Walkinshaw's, one of the most influential families in Glasgow at that time, had laid out the nearby village of Calton in 1705, then known as Blackfaulds. The Camlachie mansion itself was not grand, being only two-storeys but nevertheless it was by far the grandest in the area. However, the family lost their estates in 1723 for their support of the Jacobite cause. Lady Barrowfield continued to reside in the mansion until 1734 when she sold it to merchant John Orr who had bought the Calton from Glasgow three years before.

The mansion's most famous visitor arrived in 1749. General James Wolfe, then a lieutenant colonel in the army, was posted to Glasgow but as there were no barracks at that time he was given the use of the mansion by Orr. Wolfe was still very young, only 22.

It would be another decade before the hero of Quebec led his famous but fatal victory against France on the Plains of Abraham, giving Britain control over Canada.

Camlachie mansion became locally known as General Wolfe's House and was used by a fabric manufacturer and tenements were later built onto it before it was demolished. The name lived on in the nearby pub, the General Wolfe, which survived until the 1980s.

Camphill House

There are many grand old houses situated within the grounds of Glasgow's numerous parks but Camphill House is fairly unique in that it was an addition to an existing park. Today Camphill House is located near to the boating pond in the western end of Queen's Park on the south side of the city.

The park itself was opened to the public in 1862 after much controversy over its location, some miles outside the city boundary.

But with the expansion of Glasgow's borders during the 1890s, Queen's Park was eventually brought into Glasgow. And in 1894 the city decided to buy the neighbouring Camphill estate with the intention of incorporating it into the existing park.

The house itself dates back to the beginning of the 19th century. Although an exact date of its construction is not recorded, building work was certainly carried out between 1800 and 1818 when the house was completed.

The house was built for the cotton manufacturer Robert Thomson but the architect for this magnificently elegant four-square classical house is unclear. It is most likely that architect David Hamilton was responsible for its design. Camphill House has many similarities in style to Aikenhead House in Kings Park whose remodelling work was carried out by Hamilton.

Two years after the house was incorporated into the park it became a museum and in recent times was a museum of costume. However, during the 1990s Camphill House went under another transition and is now residential flats.

Castle Toward

Castle Toward was built in the early 19th century for the wealthy Glasgow entrepreneur and cotton and textile merchant Kirkman Finlay.

Born in the Gallowgate, Finlay bought the land on the Cowal peninsula on the Firth of Clyde in 1818 while still MP for the Clyde Burghs and Lord Provost of Glasgow. The design of the magnificent castle was passed to David Hamilton who started work on this castellated mansion in 1820. Completed the following year, the castle got its name from the ruined 15th century Toward Castle close by.

It had been the stronghold of the Lamont clan until it was besieged by the Campbells in the 17th century, intent on destroying their rivals. After the siege ended in 1646, Toward Castle was abandoned.

Hamilton's castle, with its many towers is considered to be one of his finest works. However, much of what is seen today was added in the early 20th century.

After Finlay's death in 1842, the estate passed through several owners until the 1920s when it was taken over by the famous Coats family who had made Paisley the thread-making capital of the world.

It was this family that added several more towers and extended the original mansion, keeping so close to the original style that it is impossible to determine which is the oldest part from the outside. The building has been used as a residential outdoor educational centre for more than 50 years.

Castlemilk Castle

Nothing now remains of the 15th-century Castlemilk Castle.

The site of the castle now stands surrounded by the housing estate of the same name on the south side of Glasgow.

It was built by the Stewarts of Castlemilk, from Dumfriesshire. They were feuded the land by the Hamiltons of Rossavon after it was forfeited in 1455 by the Douglas family who themselves had taken ownership of the estate after the Wars of Independence.

The small rectangular keep was completed in the late 15th century.

It is believed that in 1568, the night before the Battle of Langside, Mary Queen of Scots slept there. However, this claim is one of many made of her last place of shelter before losing the subsequent battle which forced her to flea to England.

A few years later, in 1579, the Stewart family moved permanently from their lands in Dumfriesshire to the castle, bringing the name of Castlemilk with them. But it wasn't until the 18th century that the new name appeared with any official status in the parish records.

During the 18th and 19th century the small castle was extensively added to, becoming a splendid castellated mansion. Upon the death of the last laird in 1938, the estate was sold to Glasgow.It was converted into a children's home and opened 10 years later.

Known as Castlemilk House, it continued to serve as a home until 1969 when it was closed.

Despite a great public protest the magnificent building was demolished in 1972.

Cathcart Castle

At the southern end of Linn Park stands the remains of the 15th century Cathcart Castle. Only a few stones at ground level remain of what was a five-storey oblong keep, built in 1450 by Alan Cathcart, the first Lord Cathcart.

The cliff-top site overlooking the River Cart was most likely the location of a much older earth and timber fortification but there are no surviving records to confirm this.

For almost a hundred years the castle remained in the hands of the Cathcart family. Then in the 1540s the third Lord Cathcart moved to Ayrshire and the Semples of Lochwinnoch took over the property.

In 1568 it is believed that Mary Queen of Scots stood on a hill, Court Knowe, near to the castle where she witnessed the defeat of her army at the Battle of Langside.

For the next 200 years the castle remained in Semple family hands. They left the castle around 1740 and within 10 years the building had fallen into a ruinous state and was uninhabitable. By the turn of the 19th century William Shaw, 10th Baron Cathcart, gained Royal favour for services to the Crown and he bought back the castle in 1812. However, in 1927, the castle was acquired by Glasgow Corporation which allowed its condition to deteriorate still further. In 1979 the front wall of the castle collapsed and the following summer it was pulled down, leaving only a few stones to mark where it had stood for nearly 600 years.

Crookston Castle

Crookston Castle was built about 1400 on the site of a much older defensive timber structure dating back to the 12th century. Towards the end of the 1160s, the land where the castle stands on the southern bank of the Levern water, was given to Robert Croc of Neilston by the High Steward of Scotland. He built the original fortification on top of the knoll and excavated the oval ditch and bank defences.

The land changed hands many times over the next 200 years until 1400 when Sir Alexander Steward constructed the second and current Crookston Castle. Today it stands ruined, surrounded by Pollok housing estate but it was originally a three-storey keep with four towers, one at each corner. Only one remains intact.

In 1489 the Earl of Lennox rebelled against James IV who bombarded the castle with the famous large cannon, Mons Meg, from Edinburgh Castle, leaving it in a condition much as it is today.

During the 1560s, it is believed Mary Queen of Scots became betrothed to her second husband, Henry Stewart, Lord Darnley, who owned it at that time. But by the 16th century the castle was deserted.

It changed ownership many times until 1757 when Graham Duke of Montrose sold it to the Maxwell's of Pollok who partly restored it in 1847 to commemorate Queen Victoria's first visit to Glasgow.

Sir John Stirling Maxwell gifted it to The National Trust for Scotland, which he helped found, in 1931. It was the trust's first property.

Darnley Castle

All that remains of Darnley Castle is part of a tower and an adjoining room. Situated to the south of Nitshill Road, the castle was the ancestral home of the Stewarts of Darnley who became the Earls of Lennox in 1488 after Duncan, the existing earl, was executed by James III.

Henry Stewart, Lord Darnley, returned from exile in England in 1565, and asked his cousin Mary Queen of Scots to marry him while staying at his Crookston Castle home. It is reputed he was nursed back to health by Mary under the ancient sycamore that stands across the Nitshill road from Darnley Castle. Darnley became Mary's second husband but was murdered in 1566 by a group that included the Earl of Bothwell, Mary's third husband. Darnley's father Matthew Stewart became Regent to Henry's son James VI in 1571 but was murdered later that year by some of Mary's supporters.

In the 17th century Darnley Castle was in the possession of Ludovick Stewart but in 1679 he was heavily in debt and lost much of the estate. Just over a decade later the castle was purchased by the Duke of Montrose who let it fall into ruin. And when the Maxwell's of Nether Pollok owned the estate, most of what remained was demolished.

What survived has been a doocot, farm and mill buildings and was later converted into The Mill restaurant and has been the Ashoka At The Mill since 2000. The modern parts of the building are painted white.

Farme Castle

Nothing now remains of the 15th century Farme Castle to the east of Farme Cross in Rutherglen on the south side of Glasgow. The castle was a simple three-storey keep that was built on the Farme estate, extending originally from Dalmarnock to Cambuslang. It was granted to Walter the Steward by Robert the Bruce in the early part of the 14th century but later passed into the hands of the Douglas family.

By 1482 it was owned by the Crawfords and the castle became known as Crawford's Farme. However, by the middle of the 17th century it changed hands again, first to Sir Walter Stewart of Minto, then the Flemings and then the Dukes of Hamilton.

During the 18th century it was occupied by an industrialist, James Farie, whose collieries were nearby. Farie, however, did not own these mines, they were rented from the Duke of Hamilton who retained ownership of the entire estate. The Farie's of Farme continued to live in the castle and surrounding additions that eventually formed a courtyard and castellated mansion.

In 1917, one of the colliery managers who was living on the property at the time, removed one of the castle's old ceilings. Underneath an old timber ceiling revealed ancient inscriptions alluding to the Stewarts, dated 1325, suggesting the castle had incorporated a much older structure.

The castle was eventually used to store old mining equipment before it was demolished during the 1960s along with several red sandstone tenements that stood nearby at Farme Cross.

Garscadden House

Garscadden House was one of the great mansions on the outskirts of Glasgow that survived until the 20th century before being swept away by the ever-expanding city. It stood to the south-west of Bearsden, north of Garscadden Road in present-day Drumchapel. The mansion house was incorporated into a 15th century tower on the estate.

The land was originally owned by Patrick Fleming of Biggar in 1369 which later passed to Sir Robert Erskine. In 1444 it was in the hands of the Galbraith's of Gartconnel and several families thereafter until 1723 when it was owned by artist Henry Colquhoun of Kilermont. He built the grand mansion, later known as Garscadden House, which was expanded in 1747.

Colquhoun was known to his drinking companions as the laird of Garscadden, each of them customarily addressing themselves by the names of their estates. A group of them were drinking in Law in Lanarkshire when the laird of Kilmardinny remarked on how pale Garscadden looked. Another laird replied that he had been dead for two hours but he had not wished to spoil the good conversation. This story is reputedly where the phrase 'as gash as Garscadden' originally derives.

In 1939 the estate was purchased by the City of Glasgow. In 1951 the construction of the city's third peripheral housing scheme of Drumchapel was started.

Garscadden House was converted into service flats in 1950. But it was gutted by fire in 1959 and was eventually demolished. Tower blocks now stand on the site of the mansion house.

Garscube Estate

One of the last of the great country estates on the outskirts of Glasgow was Garscube. Situated between Maryhill and Killermont to the north-west of the city, it incorporated much of the land surrounding the headwaters of the River Kelvin and Allander. Garscube Estate was granted to Umphredus de Kilpatrick in 1250 by the Earl of Lennox and later passed to Sir John Colquhoun. In 1687, he sold it to John Campbell of Succouth when Colqhoun moved to his estates near Luss on Loch Lomond.

Ilay Campbell, John's great grandson, studied law at Glasgow University during the 1750s. He became highly regarded in legal circles and in 1789 became Lord President of the Court of Session and also Rector of Glasgow University. Two years later, when he stepped down from the university position he was honoured with a baronetcy. In 1808 he retired from legal life and lived at Garscube until his death in 1823. His son, Sir Archibald, later decided to pull down the estate's house and build a new one. He employed architect William Burn who used his own loose style of Baronial design to create a magnificent country mansion which was completed by 1827.

In 1921, Glasgow Corporation purchased 72 acres of the estate which was turned into Dawsholm Park. And in 1948, Sir George Campbell sold most of what remained, including Garscube House, to Glasgow University for its world-renowned veterinary science department. Garscube House became lecturers flats, but in 1954 dry rot forced the building's demolition.

Haggs Castle

Of all the museums in Glasgow the only one that was specifically designed with children in mind was Haggs Castle in Pollokshields. Bought by Glasgow Corporation in 1972 it underwent major renovation work and was opened in 1976.

It provided an educational and enjoyable experience for children who were encouraged to interact with exhibits, dress in period clothing and play old fashioned instruments. A Victorian-style herb garden and shrubs were planted to help the young visitors learn more about what it must have been like to live in the 19th century. But the castle itself is much older.

It was built by John Maxwell of Pollok in the 16th century. Work started in 1585 and was completed in 1587. It was the family's main residence until 1595 when it became a dower house. Haggs Castle remained occupied until 1753 when it was abandoned and by 1840 it was a ruin with only a smithy remaining on the ground floor. A decade later, with suburban houses being built nearby, the castle was repaired and became the house of the Maxwell's factor. By the turn of the 20th century a northern staircase and wing were added.

At the end of WWII the property was converted into flats.

It was then bought by the Corporation who owned it until the late 1990s when it was sold and became a private residence once more and despite the work carried out over more than 400 years many of the original features and stonework remains today.

Hutcheson's Hall

Looking north up Hutcheson Street is one of the most elegant buildings in the city centre – Hutcheson's Hall. It was built between 1802 and 1805 to replace the much older Hutcheson's Hospital which had been demolished to make way for Hutcheson Street. The original hospital was built by George and Thomas Hutcheson, the philanthropic bankers. Upon George's death in 1639, his fortune passed to his brother with the provision that he build a hospice to care for impoverished old men. Thomas died two years later, the year the hospice was completed. Another stipulation to the Hutcheson's trust was that it would provide schooling for poor boys. The trust used money raised from selling land to build houses in part of the Gorbals, now Hutchesontoun, to build the new hall after the hospice was pulled down.

David Hamilton built it to a 17th-century style, complete with a steeple similar to the original hospice tower. Major internal reconstruction was carried out by John Baird in 1876 who heightened the first floor hall and added an impressive staircase.

Today two statues of the Hutcheson brothers, carved by James Colquhoun in 1649, stand in alcoves in the hall. They were originally placed on the hospital tower before moving to either side of the new building's entrance. They are the oldest portrait statues in Glasgow. Today the hall is a visitor centre and the National Trust for Scotland's Glasgow and West of Scotland headquarters. The Trust purchased the building in 1982.

Kelburn Castle

Kelburn Castle is the oldest castle in Scotland still occupied by the same family. The Boyles have lived there since 1140 when a Norman Keep was built above the beach at Largs.

Kelburn means mountain stream in Gaelic but the de Boyvilles, who later changed their name to Boyle, were Knights who came to Britain from Normandy with William the Conqueror in 1066.

A grander castle with two towers was built around the keep in the 1580s and by the end of the 17th century the Mansion House was added.

In 1703 David Boyle, who was Rector of Glasgow University, became first Earl of Glasgow after persuading other peers to abandon the Jacobite cause and vote for the Union.

During the 18th and 19th centuries the family had acquired large estates in Ayrshire, Paisley, Dunbartonshire, Fife, Northumberland and the greater part of Cumbrae. They built Episcopal churches all over Scotland, including Cathedrals in Perth and Cumbrae and as a result ended up in debt by more than a million pounds. Most of the lands were lost but David Boyle of Stewarton, later 7th Earl of Glasgow, sold his own lands to buy back the Kelburn Estate.

Unlike other families who sold their estates in the 20th century, the present Earl, Patrick Boyle, continues to live in the castle and is devoted to its restoration. At the castle entrance is the family's double-headed eagle crest taken from a Norwegian standard at the Battle of Largs in 1263, which resulted in the removal of the Norse presence in Scotland.

Kelvingrove House

The first museum in the West End Park was housed in Kelvingrove House. The house was originally a classical mansion built in 1783 by architect Robert Adam for the Glasgow merchant Patrick Colquhoun. However, when the grounds were bought by the Town Council in 1852 it was decided the building should be converted to an industrial art museum. Almost 70 acres of land surrounding Kelvingrove House on the eastern side of the River

Kelvin was purchased at a cost of nearly £80,000.

Work started on the conversion of the building and by 1871 it was opened to the public. As well as displaying industrial art Kelvingrove Mansion Museum was also home to an aquarium, natural history section and other miscellaneous items generously donated by its patrons.

Sadly the museum was to have a short life span. The contents soon outgrew the size of the building and it was decided that the house should be pulled down after the opening of its much grander and larger neighbour – Kelvingrove Art Gallery and Museum.

The site was also required for the coming 1901 Exhibition Concert Hall but an extension to the mansion, which had been added in 1876, was retained briefly to house the Japanese Pavilion during the exhibition.

Afterwards it was home to the Jeffery Library until 1911 when it too was pulled down to make way for an international exhibition. Many of the artefacts from the Kelvingrove House collection are still retained by Kelvingrove Art Galleries and Museum.

Mearns Castle

Mearns Castle, a 15th-century rectangular keep is now part of a church. Lying to the east of Newton Mearns in Glasgow's south side, this three-storey castle was built in 1449 by Lord Herbert Maxwell of Caerlaverock. It stands on the site of a timber and rubble fortification constructed by the Knight, Roland de Mearns.

The land was originally owned by the Pollok family but through marriage belonged to the Maxwells by 1300 who retained it until around the 16th century.

It passed into the hands of Lord William Herries, a catholic, but he was forced to give it up by James VI in 1589. Later the castle was occupied by the Earl of Nithsdale who in 1648 sold it to Sir George Maxwell of Pollok. In 1676 Sir George became ill with a fever while visiting Glasgow. His condition was put down to witchcraft. Six people were subsequently accused which resulted in five of them being strangled and burned.

Several other families owned the castle over the years but it was eventually allowed to fall into a ruinous condition. But in the 1970s it was bought by the Church of Scotland who repaired it and used it for the congregation of Maxwell Church while a new building was built next to the castle.

The original church had been established in 1848 further south, near the River Clyde, but had to be closed to make way for the construction of the Kingston Bridge.

Partick Castle

Nothing remains today of the once splendid Partick Castle. It was constructed in 1611 on elevated ground on the west bank of the River Kelvin. Standing on land that was originally the site of an ancient manor house owned by the Bishop's of Glasgow, it was an L-shaped tower-house very much in the Scottish style of the period. It was more than 30ft high and consisted of two storeys as well as a garret and vaulted basement level.

Mason William Millar of Kilwinning built the castle for the eminent Glasgow philanthropist and benefactor George Hutcheson. George, together with his brother Thomas, were responsible for establishing Hutcheson's Hospital, now Hutcheson's Hall in Glasgow's merchant city, as well as many other charitable Glasgow institutions.

Partick Castle was just one of several family homes in and around the Glasgow area owned by George and his wife Elspeth Craig.

Little is known of what happened to the property after George's death in 1639. However, in the late 18th century it is believed to have been owned by tradesmen who rented out the upper floor as a dance hall.

By the mid-19th century the house had fallen into disrepair and most of the stones had been taken to build other properties nearby.

What little remained of the castle was demolished and a foundry and laundry were established on the site in its place.

Today only the tall chimney of the laundry remains, surrounded by a scrapyard, marking the spot where the old castle once stood.

Pollok House

The 18th century Pollok House stands near the site of three previous buildings constructed by the Maxwell family who owned the Pollok estate and grounds for more than 700 years. The family's first home was built along the banks of the White Cart River in the 13th century. A second fortified house was built slightly higher up, which remained in occupation until the mid 16th century. The third home of the Maxwell's was the Laigh, or Low Castle, which was built in the 14th century, part of which can still be seen in the stable court of the present house.

In 1737, the idea to build a new house came after second Baronet, Sir John Maxwell, consulted the famous architect William Adam, father of James and John. Work eventually began on the house in 1747, a year before William died. It is believed John took over the project but it remains a mystery as to how much, if any, of the original design was adhered to. The building was eventually completed in 1752.

Major extensions to the house were carried out by the 10th Baronet, Sir John Stirling Maxwell, between 1890 and 1908. Pollok House was given to the City of Glasgow by Anne Maxwell Macdonald in 1966. As well as the splendid period furniture, silver and glassware, the house contains the finest privately owned collection of Spanish paintings in Britain. The management and running of Pollok House was taken over by the National Trust for Scotland in May 1998.

Provan Hall

Provan Hall is arguably the oldest dwelling house in Scotland. It is one of only two domestic buildings, the other being Provand's Lordship, to survive in Glasgow since the middle-ages. There is no accurate record of when the hall was built but it was certainly between 1460 and 1480.

When it was built it became the country residence of the Prebendary of Barlanark, who in 1488 was crowned King James IV. He sided with France against England and was killed at Flodden in 1513. His lands were eventually sold to Canon William Baillie in 1565. His daughter, who had married into the Hamilton family, inherited the property and it remained in that family until 1667 when it was bought by Glasgow Burgh.

In 1727, an inn was built across the courtyard from the hall which was used as a rest-stop for the Glasgow to Edinburgh mail coach.

Most of the estate's land was sold in 1729 and in 1778 Glasgow merchant Dr John Buchanan bought Provan Hall and its remaining four acres of land. It remained in his family until bachelors Reston (whose ghost haunts the building) and William Mather died of pneumonia in 1934. Local businessmen maintained it until 1938 when it was taken over by the National Trust For Scotland.

In the 1970s Glasgow District Council agreed to upkeep Provan Hall which is now surrounded by Auchinlea Park in Easterhouse. More than 7,000 people annually visit Provan Hall's education centre with its small museum and exhibition area.

Provand's Lordship

The oldest house in the city is Provand's Lordship, standing opposite the Cathedral in the oldest part of Glasgow. It was built in 1471 on what is now the High Street by Bishop Andrew Muirhead during the reign of King James III. The Provand's Lordship building is actually two separate structures built at different times. The oldest part is at the front overlooking Cathedral Square and is built on three levels with three rooms to each floor which are almost identical in size and shape.

During the 17th century additional rooms were built to the rear and are connected to the original structure by a staircase. It has been called the Provand's Lordship only from the late 19th century when it was accepted as being connected to the Cathedral through the Prebendary of Barlanark.

But the house, originally called the Hospital of St Nicholas, was founded to care for 12 old men by Bishop Muirhead. Andrew Muirhead was Bishop of Glasgow Cathedral from 1455 to 1473 and a much worn coat of arms can still be seen on the southern gable of the house.

In the early 1900s, the house was restored by the Provand's Lordship Society, specially set up for the task, and in 1927 entrepreneur collector Sir William Burrell helped provide many original period furnishings dating back to the time it was built.

Later additions to this historic landmark where Mary Queen of Scots once slept, have included the addition of a medieval herb garden to the rear.

Rutherglen Castle

The ancient castle of Rutherglen was one of the most important buildings in Scotland. It was built in the 13th century, about 100 years after Rutherglen became a Royal Burgh, some 500 years before Glasgow was granted the honour. Situated to the north-west of where Castle Street meets King Street, it had several large towers and heavily fortified walls that were more than 5ft thick.

During the Wars of Independence it played an important role for both sides. It was here in 1297 that a truce was signed and it was subsequently occupied by Edward II. But in 1309 Robert the Bruce laid siege to the castle and recaptured it. For a brief period it was retained by Scotland as a royal residence and also played host to meetings of parliament before once again falling into the hands of the English.

However, in 1313 it was once more in Scottish possession after it was liberated by Edward Bruce, Robert's younger brother, who became King of Ireland three years later. The castle remained in Scottish hands until the 16th century by which time only the great tower remained. Its final owners were the Hamiltons of Elliston who were at that time the lairds of Shawfield and supporters of Mary Queen of Scots.

A year after her defeat by Regent Murray at the Battle of Langside in 1568, the castle was burned. The last remnants of the castle's foundations were removed in 1759 so that vegetables could be grown on the site.

Shawfield Mansion

Nothing now remains of the magnificent 18th century Shawfield Mansion. Built for Daniel Campbell of Shawfield between 1711 and 1712, it was the finest mansion in the city, situated at the top of Stockwell Street, facing along the Trongate.

Its architect was Colen Campbell, a prominent lawyer at the time. After the success of Shawfield Mansion he turned full-time to architecture and designed many other buildings, mainly south of the Border.

Daniel Campbell was MP for Glasgow district of Burghs. However, he not only voted for an increased tobacco tax but committed the folly of voting in a new Malt tax in 1725. Campbell decided to stay at his country retreat a few days before the new tax was imposed – a wise move as on that day an outraged Glasgow mob ransacked his mansion. But the Government forced Glasgow to pay out an enormous compensation to Campbell of more than £6,000 with which he bought the islands of Islay and Jura and became Campbell of Islay.

Campbell sold his wrecked mansion to the McDowalls of Castle Semple and Garthland. They must have restored it because in December 1745, Bonnie Prince Charlie stayed there while retreating from England after his army met significant opposition at Derby. The mansion was sold in 1760 to the tobacco lord John Glassford of Dougalston. Glassford died in 1783 and his son Henry sold it in 1791. The following year it was demolished to make way for laying out Great Glassford Street, now Glassford Street.

Sherbrooke Castle

Probably the greatest example of the Baronial mansion in Glasgow is Sherbrooke Castle in Pollokshields on the south side of the city. It was built in 1896 for John Morrison, one of the most important building contractors in Glasgow during Victorian and Edwardian times.

Morrison established a partnership with Thomas Mason in 1876. Among the many buildings that they were the main contractors for were the Royal Princesses' Theatre, now the Citizen's, built in 1878, and the City Chambers, constructed during the 1880s.

Morrison's castle was designed by architects Robert Sandilands and John Thomson, the eldest son of Alexander 'Greek' Thomson. It was built on the top of a rise, well above road level and when it was finished it was a classic example of the overly-grand style of the decadent middle-classes of the day. Its overall effect was baronial in the extreme, every aspect of the design taken to its farthest extent. The immense square tower is the most eye-catching and remains one of the best-known landmarks in Pollokshields today.

The grand central staircase with all the main rooms leading off on three sides is the most dramatically impressive aspect of the interior. During WWII the castle was occupied by the Royal Navy and as a consequence it was the only property in the area to retain its iron railings – the rest were removed and melted down for the war effort. After the war the castle was turned into the Sherbrooke Castle Hotel, a function it still serves.

Stobcross House

During the early part of the 18th century the Anderston area of Glasgow established itself as one of the first industrial villages on the outskirts of the city. But the origins of this weaving village that thrived during the industrial revolution dates back a further two centuries. It was then occupied by the Andersons of Stobcross who farmed the land that was owned at that time by the Bishops of Glasgow. The family derived their name from a wooden cross, or stob, that marked a junction on the main Glasgow to Dumbarton road. By the beginning of the 18th century the Andersons had accrued enough wealth to build a mansion named Stobcross House, with crow-stepped gables in the Scottish style.

Around the 1720s James Anderson feudalized some of the Stobcross estate to establish a weavers' village. He benefited from rentals and the weavers gained by not having to pay to join the Glasgow Weavers' guild, the village being located just outside the city boundary. The village was called Andersons-town but in 1735 the family sold their lands to merchant John Orr of Barrowfield, who had just bought Calton village on the other side of Glasgow.

Stobcross House was allowed to fall into a ruinous condition and it was demolished in 1875 to make way for the Queen's Dock. In the 1980s the dock was filled in using the rubble from the demolished St Enoch's Hotel to construct the SECC. The Clydeside Expressway marks the avenue that led up to the mansion.

Statues and Monuments

An Clachan Memorial

One of the most unassuming monuments in Glasgow is the An Clachan Memorial in Kelvingrove Park in the city's west end. An ordinary rounded boulder with An Clachan Memorial inscribed, it stands by a footpath on the eastern bank of the River Kelvin, just north of the Prince of Wales bridge of 1895.

This bridge replaced a timber one built for the prince's visit to lay the foundation stone for Glasgow University's new building on nearby Gilmorehill. The stone marks where the An Clachan, or Highland Village, exhibit stood during the 1911 Exhibition. This exhibit was placed in the Entertainment section and its mock-up design was regarded by many, certainly the Highlanders, as somewhat unrealistic. The only authenticity came from the people who staffed the Cultural display – they were all Gaelic-speaking Highlanders.

But it was fitting the Highlanders should have a place in any Glasgow exhibition because of their long association with the city. They first arrived during the early 1700s and as their numbers increased an inn called the Black Bull opened on Argyle Street to cater for their arrival.

In 1827 the Glasgow Highland Society was formed and 40 years later a Gaelic-speaking church was opened on Queen Street. Many came seeking work as the population growth was making it harder to earn a living from the land. But in the early 19th century, they arrived in droves during the notorious Clearances, forced off their crofts so that the landowners could profit from sheep and cattle farming.

Cameron Memorial Fountain

One of the smallest memorial fountains in Glasgow is situated at the western corner of Charing Cross. The Cameron Memorial Fountain is one of the few relics in the area to be untouched by the sweeping changes that took place during the construction of the M8 motorway.

This elaborate drinking fountain was erected in 1896. Designed by architects Clarke and Bell in an impressive Baroque style, the base is in pink Peterhead granite while the upper section is sculpted terracotta by the Doulton company.

Two sides of the fountain display bronze plaques bearing a portrait and an inscription to the long serving Liberal MP for Glasgow. Cameron was born in Dublin in 1841, the son of John Cameron, a newspaper proprietor who owned papers in both Dublin and Glasgow. Charles studied to become a doctor but between 1864 and 1874 edited his father's *North British Daily Mail* in Glasgow. But in 1874 he was elected MP for the city and held various political posts in Glasgow until 1900. During this period he achieved many reforms including the abolition of imprisonment for debtors, the adoption of the sixpenny telegram, introduced the Inebriates Act and was involved in bringing in many liquor licensing laws.

He was also a great supporter of the Highlanders plight around this time and as chairman of the Federation of Celtic Societies he fought for many land reforms for the crofters. In 1904 he was elected president of The Cremation Society of Great Britain. He died in 1924.

Cameronian War Memorial

One of the most emotive and inspiring statues in all of Glasgow is the War Memorial near the south west corner of Kelvingrove Art Galleries and Museum in Kelvingrove Park. It is a bronze statue of a group of charging soldiers of the Cameronians (Scottish Rifles), designed by I Lindsay Clark. Erected on the site in 1924 it commemorates the 10 million people who lost their lives during the Great War, the war to end all wars. But it is specifically dedicated to the Cameronian regiment which was one of the most famous Scottish regiments in the British Army. Originally called the 26th Cameronians, it was raised in a single day in 1689 under the Earl of Angus.

The name 'Cameronians' was used in honour of one of the most notable and extreme Covenanters, Richard Cameron. His Sanquhar Declaration of 1680 declared war on Charles II as an enemy of God.

The regiment did not become known as The Cameronians (Scottish Rifles) until 1881 when it was amalgamated with the 90th Perthshire Light Infantry, which formed in 1794.

The regiment served in every major war until it was eventually disbanded in 1968 after winning a remarkable number of Victoria Crosses and producing an unusually high number of generals. It was also unique in the army in producing two Commanders-in-Chief and two Field Marshals.

A history of the regiment is on display in the building that used to be the Duke of Hamilton's riding school, at Low Parks Museum in Hamilton, South Lanarkshire.

Carlyle, Thomas

Thomas Carlyle's statue in Glasgow's Kelvingrove Park was erected in 1883 next to a public toilet, two years after the great historian and literary critic's death. The wits of the day said it allowed people to see it at their own convenience but the toilets have long gone and with them the joke.

Carlyle was born in Ecclefechan, Dumfriesshire, in 1795, in the Arched House, built by his master mason father and uncle, which is now a museum to his life. Educated in the village and Annan grammar school, at the age of 13 Carlyle made the three-day walk to study to become a minister at Edinburgh University. But in 1814 he returned to his old grammar school to teach mathematics. He also taught in other schools but in 1818 was back in Edinburgh where he developed dyspepsia.

He also met Annan-born clergyman Edward Irving, later charged in London with heresy which led to the Catholic Apostolic Church's formation.

Carlyle's first literary successes were his translations of great German works by the likes of Goethe and Schiller in the 1820s.

Carlyle married Jane Baillie Welsh, a descendent of John Knox, in 1826 and in 1834, when Sartor Resartus was published, they settled in London. In 1837 he published his finest work, *The French Revolution*, after re-writing the first volume which a chambermaid had used to light a fire. Other great works include *Past and Present* (1843) and *Frederick The Great* (1858-65) but he wrote little after his wife's death in 1866.

Doulton's Fountain

One of the most splendid fountains ever erected in Glasgow was Doulton's Fountain. It was originally constructed from moulded terracotta bricks as a show piece outside the Indian Pavilion during the 1888 International Exhibition in Kelvingrove Park.

Donated to the city by the world famous china manufacturer Sir Henry Doulton, it was he that arranged for the red terracotta fountain to be re-located in 1890.

The complex design of the fountain was a magnificent tribute not only to the people of Glasgow but reflected the glory of all the British Empire as it was towards the end of the 19th century. At the pinnacle of the sculpture stood Queen Victoria and below her were figures that represented all the people within her dominion.

However, a year after the fountain was put in Glasgow Green, the statue of Victoria was struck by lightning. But the Doulton company came to the rescue once more and arranged for a replica to be handcrafted, returning the fountain to its former glory.

Sadly, the fountain has not had a happy history. Over the years the fragility of the terracotta combined with the less than friendly Glasgow weather has eroded the fountain structure. And what weather and time has failed to destroy, wanton vandalism has more than made up for.

However, there is some good news – the fountain is included in a multi-million pound package to re-establish the Green as a thriving area in the east end of the city.

Elder, Isabella

The statue of Isabella Elder, one of Glasgow's greatest benefactors, was erected in 1906. Setting aside Queen Victoria's statue, erected more than half a century before, this statue was the first one in the city to honour a woman.

This seated bronze statue on a granite base was designed by MacFarlane Shannon and faces the Govan shipyard her husband, John, started in 1852 – Randolph, Elder and Company, which became Fairfields before being taken over by Kvaerner.

Isabella was a remarkable figure considering she was brought up during the Victorian age, a time when a woman's brain was considered far too delicate to be troubled with strenuous thought. She strived to overthrow this chauvinistic attitude of women's inferiority and on her husband's premature death in 1869, almost single-handedly ran his shipyard for a time. And keen to give something back to Govan, she provided funds for many projects, including the Elder Cottage hospital and Elderpark Library, built in Elder Park, gifted to Govan as a memorial to her husband in 1885.

But one of her greatest achievements was in establishing a medical education facility for women. She bought North Park House in the West End (now the HQ of BBC Scotland) and in 1890 established Queen Margaret College. Five years later the medical building by John Keppie and Charles Rennie Mackintosh was completed. The college later joined with Glasgow University and today, in the grand ceremonial Bute Hall, Isabella Elder's image can be seen depicted in a stained glass window.

Fire Service memorial

At the eastern end of Glasgow's famous 'City of the Dead', the Necropolis, there stands a memorial to those who lost their lives in two of the city's worst fires of the 20th century.

This tall granite monument is dedicated to the 19 brave men who died in 1960 and another six who were killed in 1972. On one side of the monument reads, 'In proud and loving memory of the officers and men of the Glasgow Fire Service and the Glasgow Salvage Corps who perished in the Cheapside Street Fire 28th March 1960'.

The fire service lost 14 and the salvage corps lost five after a blaze at a bonded warehouse, holding a million gallons of whisky and rum, exploded.

The other tragedy happened on August 25, 1972, when six firefighters lost their lives while extinguishing a blaze at Kilbirnie Street in the Kingston area on the south side of the River Clyde. Sadly, Glasgow is no stranger to such losses.

Such was the frequent occurrence of fires that for much of its history Glasgow was known as the tinderbox city. One of the worst fires in its history occurred in 1652, 14 years before the Great Fire of London. The fire, which started in the High Street, managed to destroy one third of the city. As a result, six years later all dangerous factories were moved outwith the boundaries. Several candle factories re-established themselves in some fields to the west, which became known as the 'Candleriggs', a name the area still retains today.

Gladstone, William Ewart

The statue of the Liberal reformer and Prime Minister William Ewart Gladstone was erected in George Square in 1902. Designed by William Thorneycroft, the standing bronze statue was originally positioned in front of the City Chambers. However it was moved to allow the Cenotaph to be built in its place in the early 1920s.

The statue depicts Gladstone in the robes of the Rector of Glasgow University to which he was elected in 1877. There are two bas-reliefs which show the Prime Minister in the Commons and at home in Cheshire chopping down trees.

Gladstone was greatly admired by Glasgow's merchants for his successful part in the Free Trade movement which allowed them to buy cheap goods from all over the world. He was honoured with the freedom of the city in 1865.

Gladstone, born in Liverpool in 1809, studied at Oxford before entering Parliament in 1832 as a Conservative. After serving in several junior ministerial posts he left the Tory Party to join the Liberals and in 1867 became their leader. The following year he became Prime Minister for the first time, holding the post for the next six years. During this time he established many social reforms as well as introducing elementary education and the Irish Land Act in 1870. He was re-elected Prime Minister three more times, 1880-5, 1886 and again in 1892 when he introduced two bills for Irish Home Rule, both of which were defeated.

He resigned as premiere in 1894 and died four years later.

McCall, Alexander

The monument to one of Glasgow's most famous policemen, Alexander McCall, is the first work thought to have been produced solely by Charles Rennie Mackintosh.

This tall Celtic cross makes use of all the traditional interlacing design, in contrast to Mackintosh's architectural style found on much of his later work. Situated in the southern part of Glasgow's famous City of the Dead, the Necropolis, this white granite memorial was sculpted by Peter Smith, a mason with the Mossman firm. McCall's profile was cast in bronze and inset into the cross which was unveiled not long after his death in 1888 in memorial to one of Glasgow's longest serving Chief Constables.

McCall was born in Ayr in 1836 and held the Glasgow police force's most senior position for more than 18 years and died in office.

His most famous case occurred in 1866 while he was still a superintendent. It involved the forging of bank notes by Glaswegian photographer John Henry Greatrex. McCall discovered that Greatrex had recently sold a lithograph machine. On examining it, McCall realised it was the same machine that was used to manufacture the forged notes newly in circulation at that time. He pursued Greatrex to London and when he fled to the US, McCall followed and eventually arrested him in New York. After standing trial in the High Court in Edinburgh in 1867, Greatrex was given 20 years penal servitude. It was this exceptional piece of detective work that helped secure McCall's promotion three years later to the force's top job.

Orange, King William of

Sitting astride a horse with a moving tail outside Glasgow Cathedral sits the controversial figure of King William of Orange. But when the statue was first erected in 1734, the tail could not move.

James MacRae, a poor washerwoman's son from Ayr, gave the statue to the city when he returned from India, having made his fortune with the East

India Company. It was the very first statue in Glasgow and originally stood in front of the Tolbooth at Glasgow Cross but was later moved farther along Argyle Street where it remained for 189 years.

When it was eventually removed from there, the excuse given was that it was impeding the flow of traffic. But another story at that time was that at Hogmanay, a drunken reveller mistook the statue for a real person and tried to get on the back of the horse to give the rider a wee dram from his bottle. Unfortunately, he didn't know his own strength and in trying to pull himself up onto the saddle, pulled half the tail off the horse. This was too much for the drunk to comprehend so he fled, leaving the tail where it fell. A sober citizen found it and returned it to Glasgow Corporation. The half-tailed statue was removed and spent three years in a sculptor's yard. In 1923 it was moved to Cathedral Square with the tail fixed back on with a ball and socket joint.

So now King Billy's horse swishes its tail whenever it gets windy.

Pearce, Sir William

The statue of Sir William Pearce was built as a memorial to one of the great engineers who helped make the River Clyde the world's greatest shipbuilding area.

It was erected in 1894 in Govan on the south side of Glasgow six years after his death. Designed by Onslow Ford, the bronze statue on a tall granite base is today known locally as the 'Black Man' after many years of discolouration by the weather. It stands on the southern side of Govan Road, opposite the Pearce Institute which was donated as a community centre to Govan by Sir William's late wife Lady Dinah in 1906.

Pearce was born in Kent in 1833 and served at Chatham's Royal Dockyards. He moved to Glasgow in 1863 to be general manager of Robert Napier's Lancefield yard in Govan. But six years later he joined the nearby Randolph, John Elder & Co yard at Fairfield and in 1878, nine years after Elder's death, he was in charge of the then named John Elder & Co. He built several luxury liners including the 5,000 ton Arizona for the Guion line.

In 1885, when Elder's became Fairfield's, Pearce became Govan's first MP and the year after rescued the struggling *Glasgow News*, renaming it the *Scottish News*. But it folded in 1888, the year Pearce paid for the removal of the Old College's High Street entrance to Glasgow University's new west end location. It was remodelled as a lodge and named after Pearce who died the same year.

Peel, Robert

The statue of Robert Peel was erected in George Square in 1859. Highly regarded in Glasgow, the standing bronze statue on a granite base of the Tory leader was designed by John Mossman.

Robert Peel, who was born in Lancashire in 1788, was elected Lord Rector of Glasgow University in 1836 the year after his first term serving as Prime

Minister had ended. But his popular acclaim in the city among the working and middle classes was mainly derived from his repeal of the hated Corn Laws shortly after the Irish Potato Famine. The move withdrew the economic and agricultural protection provided to the ruling classes under the Act but this highly popular move among the lower classes cost him his job.

He had led the country for five years up to 1846 but when he abolished the Act, many in his party were unimpressed and a split was created within the Conservative party and Peel was forced to resign as Prime Minister. Peel remained in Parliament for the next four years until he died after a riding accident. But his lasting fame had come many years before during his second term as Home Secretary. He established the Metropolitan Police force in 1829 which gave rise to the nicknames 'bobby' and 'peeler'.

Contrary to popular belief, Peel's police force was not the first professional police force in Britain. The very first organised policing body in the country was created in Glasgow almost 30 years before Peel established the London force.

Roberts, Lord
Looking out over the valley of the River Kelvin from the vantage point of Park Gate stands a monument honouring the famous soldier Lord Roberts.

Unveiled in 1918, the bronze equestrian statue by Harry Bates depicts him astride a horse with attendant figures of Victory and War below. It was erected by the city who had been inspired by Frederick Sleigh Roberts' series of inspiring speeches made in 1913, urging the establishment of a citizen's army prior to the start of WWI. The statue is a replica of one erected on the Maidan in Calcutta in 1898, honouring his military service and achievements in the sub-continent.

Roberts was born in Cawnpore, India, in 1832 and after military training at Sandhurst, England, he returned to India where he served with distinction during many conflicts. For his work in helping to quash the Indian Mutiny of 1857-58, he was awarded the VC. He was commanding officer of the British Army during the Second Afghan War and became the commander-in-chief in India from 1885 until 1893. In 1892 he was created a baron. Three years later he was promoted to the rank of Field Marshall and was commander of the army in South Africa during much of the Second Boer War. In 1901 he was created an earl and viscount.

Over the next three years Roberts served as the last commander-in-chief of the British Army, the office subsequently being abolished.

He died in 1914 while visiting troops in France after the outbreak of WWI.

Scott, Sir Walter
The first monument to the great Scottish poet and writer Sir Walter Scott was erected in Glasgow in 1837, five years after his death. Dominating George Square, the standing stone statue is mounted on top of an 80ft-high Grecian Dorian style column. The statue was designed by John Greenshields who died two years before it was erected.

Many people thought he had made a mistake in its design because the plaid Scott wore was draped over his right shoulder and not the left. However, it was pointed out later that Scott was wearing a shepherd's plaid which in the borders was normally worn on the right, not the left as the highlander's custom dictated.

Scott was born in Edinburgh in 1771, the ninth of 12 children. He studied at Edinburgh University to become a lawyer. He was admitted to the Bar in 1792 before embarking on a writing career in 1796. Much of his work was re-creations of old border tales. *The Minstrelsy of the Scottish Border* was his first published work in 1802 although he had published other works anonymously before. His ballads made him one of the most popular Scottish writers of the age. Over the years he wrote some of the greatest historical novels, romantic poetry and novels ever produced. Among his most famous and best known are *The Lady of the Lake* (1810), *Waverley* (1814), *Rob Roy* (1817), *A Legend of Montrose* (1819) and *Ivanhoe* (1819).

He was created a baronet in 1820 and died in 1832.

St George and the Dragon

One of the least known statues in Glasgow is that of St George and the Dragon. The statue is made from stone and depicts the saint mounted on a horse killing the dragon with a lance.

Today it is located near St George's Cross underground station. However, the statue has only been there since 1988. Before then it was mounted on the corner of the roof of the St George Co-operative Society building nearby before the statue was given to the city. This explains why the statue appears to be unfinished on one side – the side that would have originally been against the building and therefore not visible to the public eye.

St George himself has no real connection to Scotland at all. He is believed to have been a soldier, martyred in Palestine during the 4th century. His most heroic tale was recounted in the Golden Legend, which tells of a dragon that lived in what is now Libya. The local people had to appease the beast by sacrificing maidens. One of the women selected was their Princess. On hearing of her imminent fate George raced to her rescue, killing the dragon with his lance. He then converted the locals to Christianity, distributed the King's reward to the poor and rode away.

St George was not recognised as England's patron saint until the reign of Edward III, who created the Knights of the Garter around 1348, officially titled Knights of the Order of Saint George.

Thomson, John

One of the great monuments to academic achievement in Glasgow is situated in Glasgow's famous City of the Dead – the Necropolis. As you enter the cemetery from the Bridge of Sighs, the stone stands to your left.

It was erected in 1847 by Dr James Thomson in memory of his third son John, a medical student at Glasgow University, who died when he was 20.

James Thomson came to Glasgow from Belfast in 1832 to take up the chair of mathematics at the university. He died two years after his son John, but his eldest son, also called James, continued the family tradition at Glasgow by becoming its professor of Civil Engineering in 1873. He held the position until 1889, three years before his death.

The final name that appears on this commemorative stone is inscribed on the base of the monument. William Thomson, the second son of James, also became a professor at the university in 1846, having enrolled there at the age of 10, gaining him a place in the Guinness Book of Records. William took up the mathematics chair when he was 22 and became the most famous of the three sons. He established the second law of thermodynamics and the Kelvin scale for measuring absolute zero. He was also responsible for laying the first submarine Atlantic cable which revolutionised communications between Europe and America.

William is better known to the world as Lord Kelvin. He died in 1907 and was buried next to Sir Isaac Newton in Westminster Abbey.

Victoria, Queen

The statue of Queen Victoria was originally erected at the west end of St Vincent Place in 1854 to commemorate her first official visit to the city five years before. However, it was moved to George Square and mounted on a new pedestal in 1866 at the same time of the unveiling of the statue of her husband Prince Albert. Queen Victoria, like Albert, is mounted on a bronze equestrian figure.

Both the statue of the Queen and her consort were designed by Baron Marochetti of Vaux, who was also responsible for the statue of the Duke of Wellington at Royal Exchange Square.

When Queen Victoria first visited Glasgow she was 30 years old. She had been crowned Queen of Great Britain and Ireland in 1838 upon the death of her uncle, William IV. Victoria married her cousin, Albert, in 1841, when they were both 20 and together they produced four sons and five daughters. During much of her reign she took an active and sometimes influential interest in the policies of her government, but was careful not to favour any particular party. When Albert died in 1861, she retired from public life and spent a good deal of time at Balmoral Castle.

During her reign, Britain's power and prosperity rose considerably. She was created Empress of India in 1876 and upon her death in 1901, Queen Victoria had succeeded in achieving the longest reign of any monarch in British history.

Wallace the fire dog

Whenever the fire brigade rushed through the streets of Glasgow a hundred years ago, Wallace the fire dog raced ahead, leading the way to the fire. For nearly a decade Wallace was first at the scene despite being absolutely terrified of fires. But he would only move away from the heat and smoke after the firefighters arrived.

He was present at all the big fires, including the spectacular burning of the Trongate Waxworks in 1896. When the fire bell sounded at the station house he would leap from his basket and always seemed to know the direction to go, with the horse drawn fire trucks never far behind.

Wallace's career started in 1894 after he followed the firemen back to the Central Fire Station on College Street after running alongside the fire truck at the city's annual lifeboat procession. He became the station's mascot after repeatedly returning and his owner agreed he should stay. In 1900, Glasgow Corporation paid his dog licence in recognition of his work.

A pair of boots were made to protect his front paws from the rough cobbled streets but, sadly, in September 1902, Wallace passed away peacefully in his sleep. The firemen had known something was wrong because the previous day Wallace failed to get out of his basket for the first time in his career when the alarm sounded.

Wallace's body was preserved and is on display at Central Headquarters, Port Dundas Street, with the special boots he never wore.

Watt, James

One of the few statues to remain in its original setting in Glasgow is the one commemorating the great inventor James Watt.

The statue to the man who is credited for starting the industrial revolution, was erected at the south-west corner of the square in 1832. It was the second monument in the square, the first being of the famous soldier Sir John Moore, which is believed to be cast from bronze cannons. Watt's statue, also made of bronze, was designed by the sculptor Sir Francis Chantry.

Thankfully he decided to ignore his original brief, choosing to have Watt sitting rather than astride a horse. The only connection Watt ever had with horses was that he was the first person to use the term 'horse power' for rating the output of engines.

The other recognition of Watt's importance in the city is a plaque at a large boulder in Glasgow Green close to the Nelson monument. It is believed that this is the spot where, in 1764, he was sitting when he conceived the idea for his separate condenser that dramatically improved the workings of the steam engine.

Watt, the son of a merchant and councillor, was born in Greenock in 1736. He came to Glasgow in 1754 to work as a mathematical instrument maker at the University. His capacity for invention continued throughout his life. As well as producing efficient steam engines Watt also invented an air pump, the steam jacket and a smokeless furnace before his death in 1819.

Wellington, Duke of

One of the most famous statues in Glasgow is that of Arthur Wellesley, the 1st Duke of Wellington. However, it is probably best known for the ever present traffic cones that are placed on top of the great military leader's head and that of his horse, as quickly as the authorities remove them. So frequent is the occurrence that it would be highly unlikely for any visitor to the city to be able to take a picture of the statue without its modern day headgear.

The statue was first unveiled to the people of Glasgow in 1844. It was designed by Baron Marochetti of Vaux and the substantial cost of £10,000 was paid through generous public subscription.

The 'Iron Duke' and his horse are cast in bronze and sit on top of a solid granite plinth. Standing in front of the Gallery of Modern Art in Royal Exchange Square, it looks across Queen Street and down Ingram Street. On the side of the granite plinth four bronze panels have been mounted. The two larger ones represent the battles of Assaye and Waterloo. Waterloo was the most famous of all the Duke's military campaigns in which he secured the end of the Napoleonic war in 1815. The two smaller bronze plaques depict 'The Return of the Soldier' and 'Peace and Agriculture'.

Prime Minister from 1828-1830 and again in 1834, the Duke died in 1852, eight years after the statue was erected in his honour.

CHAPTER 2
Education

Schools, Museums and Societies

Allan Glen's

The first technical school in Scotland was Allan Glen's in Glasgow, established by the wealthy wright Allan Glen who was born in Pollokshaws in 1772 and buried in the Southern Necropolis in 1850.

He left £21,000 to found a fee-paying school for boys of 'respectable parents of the industrious classes'.

The first school building was constructed on North Hanover Street on land belonging to Glen and was opened in 1853. At first the education was restricted to the three Rs but in 1876 it expanded to subjects of a more technical nature, the first elementary school to do so in the country. In 1882 it came under the governorship of the new Glasgow and West of Scotland Technical College, an amalgamation of Anderson's College and other technical institutions that would eventually make up Strathclyde University. By 1912, Allan Glen's was a financial burden on the college and was passed to the control of the School Board of Glasgow. It moved premises to North Montrose Street in 1926 but in 1958 it was decided to build a new school to the north of Cathedral Street.

Built by the City architect's education department between 1961 and 1963, it formally opened in 1965 with modern laboratories. But the city's co-educational and non fee-paying policy eventually ended Allan Glen's.

It closed in 1989 and the building was taken over by the College of Commerce. Among the school's most famous pupils were Charles Rennie Mackintosh, actor Duncan Macrae and industrialist Sir Andrew McCance.

Elder Park Library

Like many landmarks in Govan, Elder Park Library was a bi-product of the shipbuilding industry. The library was built in the south-east corner of Elder Park, which had been gifted to Govan by John Elder, the famous Clyde shipbuilder, in 1885.

Elder, a great innovator in shipbuilding, started Fairfield's shipyard, now Kvaerner Govan, in the 1850s and built it into the largest private shipbuilders in the world before his death in 1869.

The library, along with the former Elder Cottage Hospital nearby, was paid for by his widow Isabella.

Both buildings were designed by Sir John James Burnet between 1902 and 1903. The famous Glasgow architect designed the library in a continental Baroque style but retained some elements of his own characteristic detailing. The most striking aspect of the building was the large dome above the entrance which protrudes from the front of the building and is supported by a simple but elegant series of columns. But despite this grandeur, the actual entrance is far from splendid, being stuck away to the side. In keeping with the library's benefactor, above the entrance columns there are figures of a draughtsman and shipwright on either side of the Govan coat of arms. The rear of the building was extended and remodelled in the 1920s and the interior of the building was beautifully repanelled and opened up between 1959 and 1962. But the busts of John and Isabella Elder have been retained in the hall in keeping with the building's original character.

Glasgow Humane Society
Thousands of lives have been saved since the founding in 1790 of the world's oldest practical life saving body, the Glasgow Humane Society.

It was established three years after Glasgow merchant James Coulter donated £200 to start a lifeboat service to rescue drowning people and recover bodies.

A small house was built on Glasgow Green for the society's volunteers to stay while on call. It was extended in 1867 but was replaced in 1937 with a new house opposite the suspension bridge, designed by architect J Thomas King.

For more than 60 years the society relied on volunteers to carry out its work as well as pay the ferry workers for every body recovered. In 1859 George Geddes was appointed as the first full-time officer. Geddes had been a volunteer since the 1840s, having been drawn to the work at the age of 11, after he saved a drowning woman in the Clyde. He continued to save lives until his death in 1889 when his son, also George, took over, working until 1932 when he was killed during a rescue. His replacement, Ben Parsonage, had already been working with the society for many years. He spent the rest of his life living in the house on the Green with his family and became the longest serving member in the society's history, 61 years, until his death in 1979. He saved almost 1,500 people and pulled out more than double that number of bodies from the rivers of Greater Glasgow.

And in keeping with the society's unofficial tradition, Parsonage's son, George, took over and continues to serve the society on a part-time basis.

Glasgow University
Glasgow University is the fourth oldest in the UK after Oxford, Cambridge and St Andrews. Founded officially in 1451 by Pope Nicholas V, it was originally situated on the High Street in the east end of the city and remained there for more than 400 years.

In the 1860s, the Glasgow Union Railway Company wanted to buy the old college buildings and land for a new station. With the money from the sale, the university transferred to the West End at its present location on Gilmorehill, opening in 1870. English architect Gilbert Scott designed it close to the old college style and with its construction, Glasgow University became the country's largest public building since the Houses of Parliament were built a decade before.

Its splendour was many years in the creating with the spire's construction finished by 1883 and the west quadrangle was finally completed in 1929. The teaching hospital, the Western Infirmary was opened in 1874. Bute Hall, where graduation ceremonies are held, was finished in 1877 after funds were donated by the Marquis of Bute.

In 1892 women were admitted to the main university, eight years after the opening of Queen Margaret College on the other side of Kelvingrove Park. A great part of student life is the Union and the men's was founded in 1885 and the women's in 1906.

But it was not until 1980 that the men's union finally admitted women as members, the Queen Margaret Union having been mixed sexed for many years.

High School

The High School of Glasgow is the oldest in the city and one of the oldest in Britain, dating back to the 12th century. Started in the Cathedral almost 200 years before the university was established, the Grammar School of Glasgow as it was known then, was under the control of the Church. However, the school does not officially appear in any records until the middle of the 15th century when it was under Glasgow burgh control. It was now situated further down the High Street at present-day Nicholas Street. The curriculum had little changed over the previous five centuries, Latin and Greek grammar being of primary importance.

By the end of the 18th century it moved to the north of George Street but relocated again to John Street in the 1820s. It became the High School in 1834 and by 1872 its running was transferred to the new Glasgow School Board. It transferred the school to premises on Elmbank Street vacated by Glasgow Academy.

The biggest change in the school's history took place during the 1970s. In 1970, the High School ceased to be a fee-paying school in keeping with the education board's guidelines. Over the next few years it resisted further change by the board but in 1976 it ended its long history and closed. However it reopened in the same year as an independent educational trust school. It amalgamated with Drewsteignton School in Bearsden at a newly built Anniesland complex next to the old school's playing fields.

John Smith & Son Booksellers

Probably the oldest independent bookseller in the world, John Smith & Son Bookshops was founded in Glasgow in 1751.

Born in 1724 in Strathblane, Stirlingshire, John Smith, the youngest son of the Laird of Craigend, fought at the Battle of Laffeldt in Flanders in 1747 and was wounded in action.

By 1751 he had established a small book shop, John Smith and Son on St Vincent Street, having already started three other shops in the city. He set up Glasgow's first circulating library, following the example of Lanarkshire-born poet, Allan Ramsay, who established the first one in Britain in 1725.

Smith's circulating library proved to be very popular and successful. It maintained the largest collection in the city for more than 70 years. At its peak there were several thousand volumes listed in Smith's catalogue. But it was from his successful, small one-room bookshop that his company gained an international reputation, as stockists of academic books for universities.

John Smith outlived three wives and on his death in 1814, the business was carried on by his two sons, John Smith II and John Smith III.

The company currently comprises of more than 20 shops based in Scotland, England, Ireland and Botswana, most of them located on university campuses.

Kelvingrove Art Gallery and Museum

For more than 100 years Kelvingrove Art Gallery and Museum has displayed some of the world's finest masterpieces.

As Glasgow's most prestigious art gallery it has exhibited paintings by artists including Rembrandt, Picasso, Monet and Van Gogh.

Probably its best-known exhibit was Salvador Dali's masterpiece Christ of St John of the Cross.

The arrival of this painting in 1952 almost single-handedly rejuvenated public interest in the museum. It was relocated to the St Mungo Museum of Religious Life and Art when it opened in 1993.

At Kelvingrove there are four main exhibiting halls, Natural History and Zoology, Archaeology, History and Ethnography, and Decorative and Fine Arts. An extensive temporary exhibition area displays many collections on loan from institutions world-wide.

As one of the best civic collections in Britain today it depicts the natural world and the history of man and his accomplishments through the ages.

Purpose built, the museum first opened in 1902 after a design competition for its construction was won by eminent architects John W Simpson and E J Miller Allan. Glasgow Corporation acquired the site which was originally part of the grounds of the now demolished Kelvingrove House mansion, built by world famous Scots architect Robert Adam in 1783.

The Art Gallery and Museum collections originally came from many separate collections donated by private citizens as well as art works transferred from the McLellan Galleries. The museum was closed in July

2003 and is currently undergoing a £25.5million refurbishment, which is due to be completed in March 2006.

Martyrs' Public School

The Martyrs' Public School in the Townhead area of Glasgow was built more than 200 years after the execution of the men it commemorates. Designed by Glasgow's world-famous architect Charles Rennie Mackintosh, it was named after three Covenanters, executed for their beliefs in 1684.

James Lawson, James Nisbet and Alexander Wood were killed on the spot that the school now stands. Formerly known as Howgatehead, a century later it became the official hanging site in Glasgow, taking over from Gallowmure in the Drygate in 1765. After six hangings at Howgatehead, executions moved a short distance to the east to the ruined Bishop's Castle in 1784.

Now Parson Street, the site was also where Mackintosh, born in 1868, stayed for the first six years of his life. Mackintosh was the senior assistant in architectural firm Honeyman and Keppie during the construction of the school between 1895 and 1898. Many of the ideas Mackintosh incorporated into the Scots Renaissance building were later expressed in a grander fashion in his famous Glasgow School of Art and Scotland Street School.

Best viewed from the pedestrian bridge that links Parson Street with the Royal Infirmary, the most outstanding features are the three rooftop ventilators disguised as small domed turrets. And although constrained by the requirements laid down by the school board, he also managed to add many Art Nouveau touches, notably around the doors, stairwells and windows. No longer used as a school, the building was taken over by the Forum Arts Trust in 1983.

Mitchell Library

Glasgow's Mitchell Library, with a collection of more than one and a quarter million books, is the largest public reference library in Europe. The creation of the library was made possible after the death of Stephen Mitchell in 1874.

A local tobacco baron, Mitchell was very much for education and had encouraged the employees of his company to attend night classes. And he even set up his own classes to help educate the youngsters working for him.

He bequested £67,000 to the council to set up a public library that he hoped would enrich the lives of the public and of the city in general. He stated in his bequest: 'Books on all subjects not immoral shall be freely admitted to and form part of the library and no book shall be regarded as immoral which simply controverts present opinions on political and religious questions.'

The library opened in 1877 in Ingram Street in the city centre and as the collection grew it moved in 1891 to new premises around the corner in Miller Street. In 1911 it moved to its present site at North Street near Charing Cross and has continued to expand, taking over St Andrew's Halls and eventually the whole city block.

Today, a staff of around 100 librarians run the library but due to limited space only one tenth of the huge collection is on display to the public. Every year, half a million people visit the library which has an annual running cost of more than £3m.

Museum of Transport

Scotland has a long history in the world's transport industry and has produced some of the finest ships, trams, railway locomotives and cars the world has ever seen.

In 1964 Glasgow opened the Museum of Transport rather fittingly in the old depot on Albert Drive, Pollokshields, where the very last tram completed its final journey two years before. Unlike many museums it was a delightful and exciting experience for children when it opened because you could climb up into many exhibits and pretend you were the driver of the tram or train. And parents enjoyed it because it made education fun and at the same time was a trip down memory lane.

The museum is a tribute to all forms of transport and shows how technology has changed over the last few hundred years. Shipping made Glasgow world famous and the shipyards made scale models of their vessels.

The museum has in its collection models of the 'Three Queens', the *Queen Elizabeth*, *QE2* and *Queen Mary* as well as warships, sailing ships and Clyde ferries.

Motor cars from the humble Hillman Imp to the luxurious Rolls Royce are on display as is the world's oldest surviving pedal cycle.

You can wander down a reconstructed 1938 street or see what the old underground stations were like.

Even the anti-nuclear protesters' caravan at Faslane can be seen at the museum's new and much larger premises behind the Kelvin Hall where it was relocated in 1987. It is as popular today as it was 40 years ago.

People's Palace

The best loved building in Glasgow, The People's Palace, opened more than 100 years ago but only after a great debate over whether art and culture would benefit poor people.

Working-class people were thought to be uninterested in art until Councillor Robert Crawford, chairman of the Health Committee as well as the city's galleries and museums, argued successfully to get the project off the ground. He argued that the dirtiest people in the city had not campaigned for public baths but when the council provided them they were the first to make use of them. Crawford won his argument and Lord Rosebery opened the People's Palace on January 22, 1898. He proved the critics wrong and to this day the museum is still a popular place for Glaswegians, young and old, to visit and learn about their city.

When it opened it was not just a museum but a music hall, winter gardens, reading room and a place where people could come and meet friends. The museum was built on Glasgow Green in the East End which the council had bought and turned into a public park by 1857 but for hundreds of years it had been used as common grazing for livestock and washing clothes in the Clyde. The history of the museum is part of the history of Glasgow and remains as popular today as it was when it first opened.

Piping Centre

One of the most unusual changes in the use of a building in Glasgow is the conversion of a church into a bagpipe museum.

Cowcaddens Church, facing down Hope Street from McPhater Street, was built between 1872 and 1873. Designed by architects Campbell Douglas and Sellars for the Free Church of Scotland, it comprises both Italian and Greek styles with a very elegant Tuscan tower at the south west corner. The overall appearance of the church has more than a hint of Alexander 'Greek' Thomson's celebrated works at Caledonia Road Church in the Gorbals and his St Vincent Street ecclesiastical masterpiece.

In 1968 the religious function of the building was discontinued and the building deteriorated until it was barely more than a shell. However, the Piping Trust, an organisation established to promote the study of the Highland bagpipe, decided to rescue what remained of the once beautiful church. After securing funding and sponsorship deals of almost £4million to reconstruct the building, the Piping Centre opened in 1996.

Bagpipes are renowned throughout the world as Scotland's musical instrument but originated in the Middle East 4000 years ago. They evolved into their most popular form in Scotland from the 16th century, eventually achieving their modern three-drone pipe appearance by the early 18th century. Today the Piping Centre has earned an international reputation for the teaching of this famous instrument. The centre also boasts a unique museum dedicated to the pipes, as well as containing a conference venue, hotel, bar and restaurant facilities.

Royal Highland Fusiliers Regimental Museum

One of the most specialised museums in the city is the Royal Highland Fusiliers Regimental Museum on Sauchiehall Street.

From the outside it looks almost like another shop but inside it is packed with information and memorabilia of military history of this famous regiment.

The Royal Highland Fusiliers (Princess Margaret's Own Glasgow and Ayrshire Regiment) is unique in that it is the only regiment that carries three colours. And it is distinguished as having been awarded the greatest number of battle honours of any Scottish regiment. But the regimental name is a relatively new one dating back to 1959 when it was formed by the amalgamation of two other famous Scottish regiments.

The first of these was the Royal Scots Fusiliers which dates its origins to Mar's Regiment, created in 1678. And the other, the Highland Light Infantry,

Glasgow's own, the last to be based at Maryhill barracks until the amalgamation, traces its origins to the 73rd Highland Regiment, originally Macleod's Highlanders in 1777. These infantry units have been formed from men of Glasgow and Ayrshire who have been enlisting for more than 300 years.

The displays in the museum reveal a whole range of artefacts ranging from medals to weaponry as well as maps and pictures of some of the great battles in which these men fought. Among the wars in which they served are the American War of Independence, Crimea, South Africa, Indian Mutiny, siege of Gibraltar and all the major conflicts of the 20th century.

Scotland Street School

Scotland Street School at Kingston was built by the famous Glasgow architect Charles Rennie Mackintosh.

Work started in 1904 and was completed in 1906 when it opened its doors for infants and later primary school children. Still later it provided secondary education up until it closed in 1979.

Mackintosh's design was severely restricted by the stipulations laid down by the Govan School Board but he did manage to add some stunning architectural detail to the exterior. The most dramatic features of the building are the two staircase turrets which are almost entirely made out of glass. Mackintosh wanted to decorate the inside of the stairwells with black tiling but this was refused him because his budget did not cover interior design. Nevertheless the bright light streaming in through the glass must have left quite a wonderful impression on the Govan children used to the more dingy closes of their tenement flats.

Today school parties can visit the old school and see how the history of education has changed over the last 150 years. The children can also dress in period clothes and be taught in traditional school rooms of the Victorian, Edwardian, inter-war and mid-20th century period and compare them to modern teaching methods.

For adult visitors it is a chance to take a nostalgic look back at their own educational era with old black and white photographs, inkwells and the headmaster's desk. And after a quiet reminiscence they can be glad that it is all mercifully behind them.

Springburn Museum

Springburn Museum depicts the changes of the area from its humble beginnings as a weaving village through to its rise as the world's greatest steam locomotive manufacturer.

This remarkable museum opened in 1986. Situated in Springburn Library in the north-east of Glasgow, it was the city's first independent community museum and is run by volunteers and relies heavily on local donations. Its exhibits change on a regular basis as more and more material is donated by local residents, reflecting the areas ever changing landscape, both socially and environmentally.

The main thrust of the museum is its rise from a small village in 1840 to a thriving industrial centre of more than 30,000 people by the turn of the 20th century.

At its height, Springburn had four great railway works – Cowlairs, St Rollox, the Hyde Park and Atlas Works, employing more than 9,000 men. The massive output of steam locomotives from these yards to countries all over the world amounted to almost one half of all the engines produced on the planet as a whole. Completed locomotives would be taken by road down to Finnieston at the River Clyde. There they would be loaded onto ships by the massive 175ft-high hammer-head Finnieston Crane with its 175-tonne lifting capacity.

The crane is all that remains today of the once great might of Springburn's global engineering influence.

Sadly, Springburn reacted too late to the change from steam to diesel and electric engines and today nothing remains of its once great locomotive industry.

St Mungo Museum of Religious Life and Art
The only public museum in the world that devotes itself to religion is in the oldest part of Glasgow. The St Mungo Museum of Religious Life and Art, situated at the top of Castle Street at the corner of Cathedral Square was opened in 1993. It is housed in a purpose built building that was designed to blend with and complement its surroundings.

The museum is named after Glasgow's patron saint - who first established his Christian monastery around 543 – near the site of the museum. However, although it is named after a Christian saint the museum's purpose is not to promote one religion over any other. It contains many priceless artefacts depicting the six major religions practised around the world today – Christianity, Hinduism, Buddhism, Islam, Judaism and Sikhism.

Its most famous exhibit is the world acclaimed masterpiece by the painter Salvador Dali – *Christ of St John of the Cross* (1951). This painting had been displayed in the Kelvingrove Art Gallery and Museum since 1952 but was relocated to Glasgow's newest museum as a very special attraction for its opening.

Another of its most popular attractions is the Japanese Zen Garden, the only authentic one of its kind in the United Kingdom.

But the museum is not just a place to display religious objects.

Set out in three main halls, Art, World Religions and Religion in Scottish History, the museum examines different religious beliefs in an everyday sense as well as in a spiritual way.

Stirling's Library
The building in the centre of Royal Exchange Square has been used for many different purposes over the 200 odd years since it was built.

It was originally the mansion house of the wealthy tobacco lord, William Cunninghame of Lainshaw, who built it in 1778 on what was then farm land. In 1817 it was bought by the Royal Bank of Scotland which used the building for the following 10 years until it moved to new premises to the west of the then developing square.

Major reconstruction work was started on the mansion house by architect David Hamilton who designed the huge double portico of Corinthian pillars. He also added the large newsroom hall to the rear of the house which had previously been a garden. The building was transformed over five years and became the Royal Exchange with renovations finally completed in 1832. In 1880 the mansard storey was added and became the home of Glasgow's first telephone exchange.

However by the early 1950s Glasgow District Libraries took over the property and it was used to house Stirling's Library, originally a collection of books bequeathed to Glasgow by merchant and town councillor Walter Stirling in 1791. Stirling gave the city his house on Miller Street to house the books but over the years the collection was moved around the city.

After nearly 50 years occupying the Royal Exchange building, Stirling's Library was returned to Miller Street to make way for the Gallery of Modern Art which opened in 1996. In 2002 the Miller Street library was moved back to the basement of the gallery and is now called theLibrary at GoMA.

People
Anderson, John

John Anderson was one of the great pioneers of education in Scotland. Born in Roseneath, Dunbartonshire, in 1726, his grandfather was the first minister of St David's (Ramshorn) Church in Glasgow, now owned by Strathclyde University – which Anderson founded.

But Anderson's career did not begin in academia. At the age of 19, he helped defend Stirling against the Jacobite army, an experience that led to his future military interests. His education started at Glasgow University some years later and in 1755 he was appointed the chair of Oriental Languages. Two years later he became Professor of Natural Philosophy and his work on the development of the Newcomen engine helped James Watt invent his condenser that revolutionised steam power.

Anderson's military expertise was called upon again in 1759 to develop Greenock's defences against the French. His recoiless field gun design failed to impress the British Army but the French accepted it when he visited France in 1791.

But Anderson's great passion was teaching, especially with the working men who attended his innovative evening classes.

His radical support of the students' petition to the government over the apathy of many professors led to his idea of founding an 'alternative university' as a place of useful learning. Instructions for its establishment were carried out after his death in 1796.

Over the years it has been called many names including Anderson's University, Anderson's Institute and Anderson's College and eventually in

1964 it became Strathclyde University. Before then it was the oldest technical school in Britain.

Boyd-Orr, John

John Boyd-Orr was one of the first people to make major changes to the state of the world food problem. Born in Kilmaurs, Ayrshire in 1880, he studied at Glasgow University before serving in WWI earning the Distinguished Service Order and the Military Cross.

During the 1920s, at the Rowett Research Institute, he conducted experiments in feeding milk to school children. Results showed that poor inner city kids who received milk grew at a comparable rate to children of wealthier families. Helped by politician and ex-university friend, Walter Elliot, his research resulted in free milk being provided in schools.

Boyd-Orr also looked at relationships between health and wealth, showing that income was an important factor for society's health problems. He also studied animal dietary needs and agricultural practices, developing the basis for modern scientific farming techniques in Britain.

During WWII he became MP for Scottish Universities and after the war he became the first director of the United Nations Food and Agriculture Organisation. He was intentionally pessimistic over the state of the world food crisis to highlight it's problems and therefore get something done, rare for the UN at the time. His work in Scotland was utilised worldwide in alleviating some nutritional problems faced by many poor countries.

Dedicated to ridding society of malnutrition, he was awarded the Nobel Peace Prize in 1949. In the same year he was created 1st Baron Boyd-Orr. He died in 1971 and as a memorial tribute, Glasgow University named its new biology building after him.

Campbell, Thomas

Glasgow-born poet Thomas Campbell was responsible for founding a movement to remove the power of the church in dictating who could get a university education.

In 1825, Campbell wrote a letter to *The Times* that inspired many notable figures of the day to establish a 'free-thinking' university in London. The University of London was established the following year allowing people from all religious backgrounds the right to attend university. Before 1826 you had to be a member of the Church of England to be allowed entry to Oxford or Cambridge, the only two English universities at that time.

A journalist and poet, Campbell was the 11th child born into a wealthy Glasgow tobacco merchant's family in 1777. In 1797 he went to Edinburgh to study law. But while there he became more interested in the reading and writing of poetry. While travelling in Europe in 1800 he wrote articles and poems of the Battle of Hohenlinden, the epic battle that helped secure Napoleon Bonaparte's position as France's head of state.

Settling in London in 1803, he continued his literary career contributing to many publications including *The Edinburgh Encyclopaedia*. He published his *Specimens of the British Poet* in 1819 and from 1820 to 1830, edited *The New Monthly Magazine*.

Among his best known poems are 'The Battle of the Baltic', 'Hohenlinden', and 'Ye Mariners of England'.

But outwith the literary world, Campbell is probably best remembered for his part in establishing a fairer university education system. He died in 1844.

Cochran, William Gemmell

One of the greatest statisticians to come out of Glasgow used his mathematical knowledge to improve agriculture, health, education and even the effects of bombing in WWII.

William Gemmell Cochran was born in Rutherglen in 1909. His academic career started after he won first prize in a bursary competition in 1927 which provided him with the funds to study at Glasgow University. Graduating in 1931 with an MA in mathematics and physics he won a scholarship to take his Ph.D. in mathematics at Cambridge University.

While there he realised that a more practical line in his studies was needed so he attended courses at the School of Agriculture. In 1934, before finishing his higher degree he was offered a post at Rothamsted Experimental Station and spent the next five years there working on experimental designs and surveying techniques.

In 1939 he moved to America to take up a statistician's post at Iowa Statistical Laboratory where he worked on graduate training programmes. But in 1943 he transferred to Princeton where, until the end of the war he worked on probability studies of naval warfare and bombing raid strategies. After WWII he returned to set up graduate programmes at the North Carolina Institute of Statistics.

From 1949 until 1957, Cochran was employed at the world famous Johns Hopkins University, where he developed statistical applications for efficient medical practices. From there he moved to Harvard to set up its statistical department and remained there until he retired in 1976. He died in 1980.

Collins, William

One of the world's great publishing houses was started by a Glaswegian in the early half of the 19th century.

William Collins was born in Pollokshaws in 1789. He started off his working career as a clerk in a cottonmill but in 1813 established a private school for poor children in Glasgow.

Collins persuaded the famous preacher Thomas Chalmers to come to Glasgow to become minister of the Tron Church two years later.

It was this association that eventually allowed him, with Chalmers' financial backing, to establish his own publishing company, William Collins & Co, in Glasgow in 1819. The company's initial success was in producing Chalmers' own books and other religious and scientific texts but Collins was soon publishing school books as well.

On his death in 1853, the firm was taken over by his son, William II, and the company continued to expand still further. Over the years it prospered and remained in family hands from one generation to the next right into the 20th century when William V took over. It is he that can really be credited for pushing the company into the international market.

He added to the already impressive list of authors, which included Henry James and Agatha Christie, by persuading Glasgow school teacher, Alistair MacLean, to publish his novel *HMS Ulysses*.

William died in 1976.

In 1990 William Collins & Co joined a New York publishing firm, founded by James and John Harper in 1817, to form the worldwide Harper Collins publishing company.

Foulis, Robert and Andrew

The Glasgow-born Foulis brothers played a major role in the intellectual enlightenment of Glasgow. Robert, born in 1707 and Andrew, 1712, were sons of Andrew Faulds, a local barber and brewer (they changed their name to Foulis in 1738 after a trip to Europe).

Robert trained as a barber in 1720 but later attended the university where he studied under his mentor, moral philosopher Francis Hutcheson. Andrew studied Humanity but their interest in classical books led to a tour of Europe in 1738, returning with a large quantity which they sold in London.

In 1741, Robert opened a bookshop at the university, 10 years before John Smith founded his famous shop. Hutcheson encouraged Robert into printing. The Foulis Press started in 1742, producing mainly very high quality classical and literary publications.

The following year he was appointed printer to the university and with Andrew they established an international reputation, especially for publishing the classics. Robert's interest in the arts led to a trip to Europe in 1751 where he purchased many masterpieces. These helped establish his university arts academy in 1753, 15 years before London's Royal Academy of Arts. But lack of funds resulted in the academy dying with Robert in 1776, a year after Andrew's death.

Andrew's son Andrew kept the Foulis Press going until financial difficulties forced its closure in 1800. The brothers were buried at the Ramshorn kirk old cemetery which is now outwith the walls, marked by a cross and the initials RF and AF on the pavement.

Glaister, John

John Glaister was one of the great pioneers of Forensic Science.

Born in 1856, he was educated in Lanark. His interest in forensics came after reading a report written by a former pupil William Smellie, the 18th century obstetrician. His parents wanted him to study law but after their death when he was 15, he was sent to Glasgow University by his uncle to study medicine.

He completed the course in four years. But he was too young to sit the final exams so he sat a diploma which allowed him to practice medicine until he was 21 when he could sit the degree examination.

After qualifying he set up a practice in Townhead before succeeding the eminent surgeon Sir William MacEwen in 1881 to become lecturer and later Professor in Medical Jurisprudence at the Royal Infirmary.

In 1899 he became Professor of Forensic Medicine and Public Health at Glasgow University where he modernised the department, providing specialist laboratories and a student library and museum.

He wrote the first edition of his definitive work *Medical Jurisprudence* in 1902 which is still a standard text today.

His practical as well as theoretical approach to forensics made him an expert witness in many criminal cases and led to his becoming a household name.

During the notorious Oscar Slater murder trial in 1909, he provided the only evidence that linked Slater to the murdered woman.

But it proved unjustifiable and Slater's death penalty was reduced to life imprisonment.

Glaister died in 1932.

Graham, Thomas
One of the world's most famous and important chemists was Thomas Graham. Born in Glasgow in 1805, the son of a wealthy merchant, he studied an Arts degree at Glasgow University, graduating in 1824 and then enrolled in Divinity at his father's insistence.

But Graham had developed a great passion for Chemistry and moved to Edinburgh ostensibly to continue his ecclesiastical studies but in fact joined the medical school. When his father learned of the deception he cut him off without a penny so he turned his hand to tutoring and journalism in both Edinburgh and Glasgow to support himself financially.

By 1830 he was elected Professor of Chemistry at Anderson's University in Glasgow. During this time he made most of his important discoveries, developing Graham's Law of Diffusion, which explained the movement of gases. He later became the founder of colloidal chemistry which explains how substances such as emulsions mix together and is popularly regarded today as the founder of physical chemistry. He was made a Fellow of the Royal Society in 1836.

The following year, having retained the chair at Anderson's University for seven years, he decided to accept an offer of the Chemistry chair at University College, London. He continued his experiments in London, breaking new ground in theoretical and practical chemistry and in 1841 he founded the Chemical Society of London.

In 1855 he became the Master of the Mint and it was Graham that introduced the bronze coinage that is still in use today.

He died in 1869.

McCance, Sir Andrew

The man who planned and implemented the Ravenscraig steel works also helped establish Glasgow's second university.

Metallurgist Sir Andrew McCance was born in Cadder, near Glasgow in 1889 and was educated at Morrison's Academy, Crieff.

He completed his secondary education at Allan Glen's School in Glasgow before going to London to study at the Royal School of Mines.

In 1916 he finished his formal education, graduating from London University with a BSc in 1916. He then went to work for the great autocratic Scottish industrialist, William Beardmore at the Parkhead Forge as an assistant manager. But in 1918, he moved on and set up special steels and alloys manufacturing at the Clyde Alloy Steel Company. When Colville's Ltd, the steel manufacturers, started up he became a member of the board and as General Manager and Director of the firm, he was directly involved in the formation of the Colville Group in 1936.

His skill and knowledge of the steel industry continued and after receiving a Knighthood in 1947 his plan to build a large steel works at Ravenscraig was eventually accepted. Much respected in his specialist field, he became Chairman of the Royal Technical College and in this capacity he supervised the establishment of the Royal College of Science and Technology in Glasgow.

In 1964, the Royal College and the Scottish College of Commerce were merged and re-named by Royal Charter, the University of Strathclyde with a building named after McCance.

He retired in 1965 and died in 1983.

Murray, David

One of the greatest recorders of Glasgow's history was the historian and lawyer David Murray. Born in 1842, Murray first became interested in history and literature at the age of eight. He started collecting books, manuscripts and newspaper cuttings and any other material that took his interest, especially anything relating to Scotland, in particular Glasgow.

He studied at Glasgow University from 1858, qualifying with an MA in 1863. Although he left university to become a lawyer, he retained a strong association with it, being elected to several senior positions in later years.

When the university decided to move premises in 1870 from the High Street to Gilmorehill, Murray was asked to write about it.

Memories Of The Old College Of Glasgow became a complete anthology with anecdotal stories added to bring the book to life.

He wrote many other books, including *Museums, Their History And Their Use* (1904) and *Early Burgh Organisation in Scotland* (1924) – the first volume tracing Glasgow's origins.

However, although much of his life was steeped in looking to the past, he was also known for his forward thinking. He was an early advocate of the vote for women and pressured for women to be allowed to become lawyers, his own firm taking on the first female apprentice in 1917.

On his death in 1928, he bequeathed his entire library to Glasgow University. It comprised of more than 14,000 volumes, including many of the earliest examples of Glasgow printing, many by the Foulis brothers.

Owen, Robert Dale

One of the great social reformers, anti-slave campaigners and politicians in American history was Glasgow-born Robert Dale Owen.

Born in 1801, he was the grandson of David Dale who had started the first workers' welfare reforms at his New Lanark cotton mills in 1784. Robert Dale Owen grew up at the mill with his father Robert Owen who was a pioneer of the cooperative movement.

In 1825, he emigrated to America with his father where they set up a socialist community at New Harmony, Indiana. He edited the New Harmony Gazette until 1827 when he became associated with Dundee-born controversial reformer Fanny Wright.

They established the experimental community of Nashoba, Tennessee, where they educated and emancipated freed slaves bought by Wright. But the project was short-lived and they travelled to Europe before returning to New York in 1829 where Owen became editor of the radical Free Inquirer.

Entering politics, he served on the Indiana legislature from 1836-1838 and while serving in the US House of Representatives, introduced the bill in 1838 which created the world-famous Smithsonian Institution. He was US Ambassador to India between 1855 and 1858 and three years later at the outbreak of the American Civil War, he urged an end to slavery in a highly influential letter to President Lincoln.

Owen turned to writing and published *The Policy Of Emancipation* (1863), *The Wrong Of Slavery* (1864) and a novel *Beyond The Breakers* (1870). His autobiography *Threading My Way* was published in 1874, three years before his death.

Quarrier, William

William Quarrier, who set up his revolutionary orphanage near Bridge of Weir, was no stranger to poverty. Born in Greenock in 1829, the second of three children, his mother moved them to Glasgow when he was five, after his father died from cholera.

When he was seven, Quarrier was working 70 hours a week in a Glasgow factory but a year later he started a shoemaker's apprenticeship. And by the time he was 23 he had his own successful business.

But personal prosperity never blinded him to the poverty of others.

In 1864 he set up the Shoeblack Brigade, providing shoe shine kits, uniforms, a basic education and a place to stay for boys who would otherwise have been sleeping rough. It proved successful and he expanded the scheme to include newspaper and delivery boys.

Determined to avoid copying the existing vast impersonal institutions, Quarrier established his first home in 1871 in Renfrew Lane and soon opened several more, culminating in the City Orphanage in James Morrison Street.

When Nittingshall Farm, near Bridge of Weir, came on the market, Quarrier saw a chance to realise his dream which would eventually become the famous Village, named after him. The first two cottages opened in 1878, each housing about 20 children with their 'parents', the man teaching the boys his trade, while his wife trained the girls.

He also set up an employment scheme with Canadian farmers for over 7,000 children, many ending in adoption.

Quarrier died in 1903 but Quarrier's still helps disadvantaged children and also adults.

Ramsay, William

Glasgow has produced many eminent scientists over the years and chemist William Ramsay was no exception. Born in 1852, Ramsay studied under the pioneering chemist Robert Bunsen in Heidelberg from 1871.

He was Professor of Chemistry at Bristol from 1880 to 1887 before moving to University College, London, holding the chair until 1912.

During his professorship at London, he predicted that nitrogen in the atmosphere was contaminated by an unknown heavy gas.

In 1894, working with English chemist John William Rayleigh, they removed oxygen and nitrogen from the air revealing another gas, later named argon, which makes up one per cent of the atmosphere.

Ramsay's next discovery was to have much greater implications for the human race. By separating the lightest gas, helium, from the mineral cleveite, he went on to show that this gas was continually produced during the radioactive decay of radium. This new understanding of how chemical elements behaved in relation to each other helped formulate a knowledge which would later play a vital role in manipulating nuclear reactions.

Continuing his research into the properties of the radioactive emissions of radium, he discovered the final noble gas, called radon. Ramsay went on to discover more gases such as krypton and xenon. He also discovered one of the most useful gases that man has harnessed – neon – and also wrote many technical books including *Modern Chemistry* (1900) and *Elements and Electrons* (1913).

In 1904 he was awarded the Nobel Prize for Chemistry. He died in 1916.

Robertson, James Jackson

One of the major reformers who influenced Scotland's educational system during the middle of the 20th century was James Jackson Robertson. Born in 1893, he attended Kilmarnock Academy and Hutcheson's Grammar School in Glasgow before going to Glasgow University. After graduating with a degree in the Classics Robertson decided on a career in the teaching profession.

He progressed through the ranks of the secondary school education system until he was made head teacher at Aberdeen Grammar School in 1942, a position he held until 1959. His enlightened input into the educational establishment was highly regarded and many of his ideas were put into practice while sitting as a member of the Advisory Council on Education in Scotland.

Probably his most famous work was contained within his forward thinking report 'Secondary Education' published in 1947. It targeted the needs for educational reform in Scotland at that time and outlined plans for the next 20 years. Many of the report's insights are still well thought of today.

His influence extended in other directions within the education community nationally being appointed chairman of the Schools Broadcasting Council for Scotland as well as many other national bodies.

Not only was he honoured with an LLB from Aberdeen University but he was also made a fellow of the Royal Society of Edinburgh and the Educational Institute of Scotland. He was also made President of the Scottish Secondary Teacher's Association and is well remembered today for his skilful use of the English language.

Robertson died in 1970.

Smith, Adam

The research carried out by the world-renowned political economist, Adam Smith, took place while he was in Glasgow. Born in Kirkaldy in 1723 Smith went to Glasgow University when he was 14. He was greatly influenced by the famous professor of moral philosophy, Francis Hutcheson.

After graduating in 1740, he won the Snell Exhibition to Oxford where he spent the next seven years of his life but felt he learned little. He moved to Edinburgh where he gave public lectures before returning to Glasgow in 1751 to become Professor of Logic and the following year Professor of Moral Philosophy. In 1759 Smith published *Theory Of Moral Sentiments* which laid the psychological foundations of *The Wealth Of Nations*.

His years in Glasgow were 'by far the happiest and most honourable period' of his life. Through his membership of the Merchant's Club he developed his economic theories, testing them among the men of business.

In 1764 Smith became travelling tutor to the Duke of Buccleuch which set himself up financially for life. While in Europe he began working on his famous book and in 1767 returned to Kirkcaldy to dictate and rework it. He moved to London where *An Inquiry Into The Nature And Causes Of The Wealth Of Nations* was published in 1776 which advocated free trade and minimal state interference.

Despite frequent misrepresentation, it is still regarded as one of the most important books ever written.

In 1787 Smith was elected Lord Rector of Glasgow University.

He died in 1790.

Snell, John

Without the help of John Snell many famous Scots may never have achieved their status in the world's history books. Snell was born in a small village in Ayrshire and enrolled in Glasgow University in 1642. He studied there for a few years and then travelled south to fight for the King in the English Civil War. However, in 1654 Snell entered the service of Sir Orlando Bridgeman who became Lord Chief Justice of Common Pleas and later the Lord Keeper of the Great Seal.

Snell became his seal-bearer and continued in the role with his successor, the Earl of Shaftesbury. Already a man of means, Snell's fortune grew and he bought an estate in Warwickshire. He donated books and provided funds informally to deserving students at Glasgow University which gave him an honourary MA in 1662.

In 1677, two years before he died, Snell made a will establishing a trust in order to help Scottish students from Glasgow at Balliol College, Oxford. However, Snell laid down some strict conditions that beneficiaries should, among other things, not have to take Holy Orders while at Balliol. This proved difficult to conform to due to legal and other difficulties but eventually the first four Snell Exhibitioners were admitted in 1699.

Many famous people have taken up the scholarship since it started more than 300 years ago. They include the political economist Adam Smith, mathematician James Stirling, the first Scottish Archbishop of Canterbury Archibald Campbell Tait and the anatomist Matthew Baillie.

Stow, David

David Stow was one of the great pioneers of education in Scotland during the 19th century. Stow was born in Paisley in 1793. He moved to Glasgow where he became a wealthy textile merchant but developed an interest in the education of youngsters.

In 1816 he established the first of many teaching establishments that were to be his life's work. It was a Sunday evening school for the poor children in the Saltmarket. Twelve years later he set up a larger day school in Drygate and formed the Model Infant School Society.

Aware that the educational problems in the city also required suitably qualified teachers, Stow decided that a teacher-training facility would have to be set up. At first it was set up in conjunction with his society but in 1837 he moved it to Dundas Vale to Britain's first purpose-built teacher training facility – the Normal School for the Training of Teachers.

With the Disruption in 1843, Stow left the Church of Scotland to which his college was associated and two years later formed the Glasgow Free Church Normal College.

Stow was ahead of his time, advocating coeducation, playgrounds and the abolishment of corporal punishment. And his high standard of training became world-renowned with many English schools keen to take his graduates.

Stow died in 1864. In 1907 his college amalgamated with another teaching establishment. It moved in 1921 to the west of the city and became Jordanhill College of Education, which amalgamated with the University of Strathclyde in 1993.

Newspapers
Evening Times
Of the three Glasgow evening newspapers, only the *Evening Times* is still published. The other two, the *Evening Citizen* and *Evening News*, ceased publication in 1974 and 1957 respectively.

The *Citizen* was the first evening paper, first published in 1864.

Established as a family readership, it became known as the churchgoers' paper because it provided a list of Glasgow's Sunday services in its Saturday edition. Between 1914 and 1924 it was called the *Glasgow Citizen*, a trait shared by all the evening papers at one time or another when their distribution was within Greater Glasgow.

First published in 1915, the *Evening News*, a Tory paper, was the shortest lived, surviving just over 40 years. But it was one of the first papers in Britain to publish a special edition with a full list of the football results.

The *Evening Times* is the longest running of the three. Published since 1877, it had the largest circulation when the three papers were competing for readership. And over the last 20 years or so it has been a successful campaigner, tackling issues directly affecting the community.

The Herald
The Herald is the oldest English-speaking national newspaper in the world.

First published in January 1783, two years before *The Times* in London, it was originally called the *Advertiser*. Its first owner was printer John Mennons and it was a right-of-centre publication greatly favoured by Glasgow employers and businessmen. The paper only published once a week until 1793 when it appeared on Mondays and Fridays.

Mennons left the paper in 1802 and one of the new partners, Dr James McNayr, gave the paper a new title – *The Glasgow Herald and Advertiser*. Two years later it was called simply *Glasgow Herald*, a title it retained for 30 years until it became *The Glasgow Herald*.

From 1855 it also published on Wednesdays and since 1858 it has been a daily paper.

Over the years the paper has changed ownership many times and also its offices around the city. From 1836 until 1964 it had been under the ownership of George Outram & Co but an ugly takeover bid involving Hugh Fraser and William Thomson ensued. Five years later the battle was won by Fraser and his backers but within 10 years the paper had gone over to the Lonhro empire.

In 1992, the management made a successful £74million bid and it came under the control of Caledonian Newspaper Publishing and Glasgow was dropped from its title. *The Herald* was taken over by Scottish Television in 1996 which became Scottish Media Group the following year. *The Herald* and its sister papers, the *Evening Times* and the *Sunday Herald*, are now owned by the Newsquest media group.

CHAPTER 3
Entertainment

Festivals
1888 Exhibition
Glasgow's first major exhibition was urged on by civic rivalry between its industrial rival Manchester and its old adversary Edinburgh, which had hosted shows in 1887 and 1886 respectively.

In 1888, the Glasgow International Exhibition easily outshone both. It was the largest and grandest Britain had seen since London's Crystal Palace Exhibition in 1851.

Glasgow only had two sizable open spaces that could accommodate the exhibition at that time – Glasgow Green and the West End Park. The West End Park, now known as Kelvingrove Park, was chosen over Glasgow Green as many of the organizers resided in the area, highlighting the city's division between working and professional classes.

Following the style of Crystal Palace, the exhibition was focused under one roof, the main building enclosing a staggering 470,000 square feet. Although advertised as international, most of the displays focused on Glasgow's industrial might with much of the remainder coming from the Empire, in particular India.

Surrounding the main complex were many beautiful buildings, mostly made from wood, including a full-size replica of the long-gone Bishop's Palace.

The Prince of Wales opened the exhibition on May 8 and by the time it eventually closed its gates on November 10, a staggering 5,748,379 people had visited. The profits, which exceeded £46,000, were used to finance the building of Kelvingrove Art Gallery and Museum.

Of the countless major exhibits and displays at the show, only a few have survived. The terracotta Doulton Fountain that had stood outside the main building was moved to Glasgow Green in 1890.

1901 Exhibition
The second of Glasgow's great international exhibitions was held in 1901. It was conceived to inaugurate the Art Gallery and Museum in what is now Kelvingrove, built from the 1888 exhibition's profits.

Eager to reassert itself as the second city of the Empire, Glasgow chose 1901 as a challenge to the first great British exhibition, Crystal Palace, 50 years before. Spread over 73 acres, the exhibition had a greater international flavour – the main building being the temporary Eastern Palace with its imposing dome.

Beneath the dome stood an 18ft-high statue of Edward VII, the first erected in his honour.

However, Edward, who had agreed to open the exhibition while he was still the Prince of Wales, now declined. In his place, the Duchess of Fife opened the self-styled largest and most important exhibition staged in Britain, on May 2.

The Art Gallery housed the Fine Art section, featuring the work of the internationally renowned 'Glasgow Boys'. The industrial buildings were popular, as were the spectacular Russian Village, the model farm complete with a working dairy and a 3,000 seat concert hall. The most spectacular ride was the Canadian water chute, which plunged into the Kelvin.

Although the exhibition lacked 1888's novelty value, it managed to attract 11.5 million visitors before it closed on November 9. The profits were used to restore the park with the surplus going to the Art Purchase Fund to enhance the art gallery.

1911 Exhibition

The 1911 exhibition in Glasgow was unlike its predecessors in 1888 and 1901 in that it was designed to promote national appeal rather than exhibit internationalism.

The Scottish Exhibition of History, Art and Industry, like the previous two exhibitions, was set in Kelvingrove Park. It aimed to raise Glasgow to the cultural capital of Scotland, bidding to take the crown too long held by Edinburgh. When the exhibition opened on May 3, the weather was certainly very Scottish – it rained. It rained again on the last day, November 4 but for the 160 days in between, the weather was exceptional.

There was a multitude of attractions at the major buildings including the palaces of History, Industry, Art, the concert hall and the twin-towered Aviation pavilion. Smaller displays included recreations of traditional Highland villages and The Keep outside the 'Auld Toon' where the Saracen Fountain, now in Alexandra Park, was also to be found. As entertainment, there were many plays and amusement rides, the most exciting being the 130ft-high aerial railway across the River Kelvin. And of course, the now famous Glasgow institution – the Cranston Tea Rooms – designed by Charles Rennie Mackintosh – was also there.

The financial purpose of the whole exhibition was to help fund the establishment of a Chair of Scottish History and Literature at the University of Glasgow. Some 9.3 million visitors passed through its gates with a total of more than £15,000 allocated to the university.

1938 Empire Exhibition

The Empire Exhibition of 1938 was the most elaborate, extravagant exhibition ever held anywhere in the British Empire.

Glasgow needed a boost after the Depression and the exhibition aimed to promote peace and prosperity.

Although not central, Bellahouston Park, with greater flat areas, was chosen over Kelvingrove Park, the site of the three previous major exhibitions. More than 200 palaces and pavilions were designed and constructed under supervising architect Thomas Tait, designer of Edinburgh's St Andrew's House.

Costing more than £10 million and built in only 14 months, it was opened on May 3 by George VI. The famous 300ft corrugated silvered steel Empire Tower, or 'Tait's Tower', was built on a 3,000-tonne concrete foundation to avoid cutting down too many trees.

Engineering and manufacturing achievements were highlighted but other favourites included the model of Victoria Falls, a Highland village and a huge illuminated revolving globe. There were more than 20 eateries, catering for all tastes, and next to the exhibition, the amusement park was a huge success.

More than 12.5 million people visited before it closed on Saturday, October 29, during terrible weather. It failed to make a profit and with war the following year, plans to re-open it were shelved.

Tait's tower was demolished in July 1939. The war gave Glasgow temporary economic recovery but not through peace as the exhibition plans hoped to achieve. Only the Palace of Art remains.

Garden Festival

Glasgow has excelled at exhibitions and festivals since the first Empire Exhibition in1888, but 100 years later the city surpassed itself, putting on the internationally acclaimed Garden Festival.

Built on 100 acres of land-fill at the Prince's Dock on the southern bank of the Clyde, it attracted more than four million visitors in the 150 days it was open between April and September, 1988. More than 300,000 plants, shrubs and trees were planted in newly deposited top soil, much of which had been dredged from the river. The once desolate old dock was transformed into a landscaped dream of colours and smells surrounding and intertwining the six major themed areas. Many people visited more than once and some even went every day because there was always something new to see or had been missed on a previous visit. People strolled along the numerous paths or were transported by the narrow gauge railway, trams or the barge across the dock. Major attractions included the 240ft-high Clydesdale Bank Anniversary Tower and the Coca-Cola Rollercoaster. But for many visitors, it was not the displays, rides, restaurants or shops that drew them there but the wonderful atmosphere, provided by the people themselves, enjoying a great day out.

Parks

Alexandra Park

Alexandra Park was built to show there was no favouritism towards the south and west end of Glasgow for open green spaces in the second half of the 19th century.

The only other park in the east end at that time was Glasgow Green, the city's oldest park, so the City Improvement Trust purchased a 30-acre plot of land at Wester Kennyhill. Alexander Dennistoun of Golfhill sold it to the Corporation in 1868, with another five acres.

As with other parks in Glasgow, the physical work of creating Alexandra Park was carried out by the unemployed. The initial laying-out took place over the next two years with additional work being carried out from 1874 to 1875 when the lands of Easter Kennyhill were added. However the location of the park was set in some of the most polluted land to be found anywhere in Glasgow due to the concentration of so many heavy industry sites in the area. Of the many trees and shrubs originally planted, only the hardiest species survived while the others failed to flourish or died within a few decades. For many years to come the park was a very poor green place indeed.

At the western entrance to the park there is an octagonal gatehouse built by James Miller. And at the main entrance stands the magnificent cast-iron Saracen Fountain originally built by Walter Macfarlane's foundry for the 1901 International Exhibition in Kelvingrove Park.

Bellahouston Park

Bellahouston Park, on the south side has been an important venue for more than 100 years. It was first opened to the public in 1896. In 1899 the city's second municipal golf course (now an 18-hole pitch and putt) was established, following the success of the one in Alexandra Park, opened in 1895.

In 1938, the famous Empire Exhibition was held there, chosen over the more central Kelvingrove Park, which had been the venue for the three previous major exhibitions. Of the 200 palaces and pavilions that were built, only the Palace of Art remains which now serves as a sports centre. At the top of the hill a granite plinth marking the exhibition's official opening by George VI also remains, close to the site of the 300ft 'Tait's Tower' which was demolished in 1939.

During WWII an Italian prisoner of war camp was built in part of the park.

Two major events took place in the park in 1983, the Pipe Band World Championships and the historic visit of Pope John Paul II, both events drawing huge crowds. In 1996, Charles Rennie Mackintosh's 'House For An Art Lover' was completed from original drawings of 1901. It stands near a Victorian walled garden, part of Ibrox Hill House, built for Glasgow lawyer John Bennet in 1801, who acquired the land from the Hills of Ibrox, landowners since the 17th century.

The mansion was later owned by the McCalls of Govan and was demolished in 1913.

Botanic Gardens

The Botanic Gardens in the west end of Glasgow, like the city's oldest and most famous park, Glasgow Green, was a park long before the city opened it to the public in 1891.

Its original purpose was to provide botanical and medical experts from Glasgow University with a place to grow and study a huge variety of plants. The university bought the land between Great Western Road and the River Kelvin in 1839 to replace the site at Sauchiehall Street and Dumbarton Road that had been set up in 1817.

Maintaining the horticultural collection was the responsibility of the Royal Botanic Society of Glasgow, which had been established in 1819.

The Botanic Gardens officially opened in 1842. Access was free to society members with the public being allowed in on Saturdays for a shilling. Later, on certain occasions, the charge was reduced to a penny to make it affordable for the working classes to walk around and relax in the gardens.

In 1873 the Kibble Palace was donated to Glasgow by engineer John Kibble who shipped it up the Clyde from its original location at his house at Coulport, Loch Long. Eight years later the 2000 square metre glass structure, one of the largest glasshouses in Britain, came under the control of the society who took over the lease from Glasgow Corporation.

In 1891, the burgh of Hillhead, in which the gardens were situated, was annexed and brought into the city by the corporation and thrown open to the public.

Fossil Grove

By far the oldest tourist attraction in Glasgow can be found in the beautifully scenic surroundings of Victoria Park in the south side of the city. Fossil Grove is a 350 million-year-old window into the past situated in the west end of the park.

It was discovered by accident in 1887, the year after the park had been opened by Queen Victoria during her Golden Jubilee.

Workmen were digging a path through a disused whinstone quarry in the park grounds when they uncovered some unusual stone structures.

Unsure what they were, experts were called to examine the objects, some of them as large as 3ft wide. They quickly realised that they were the fossilized remains of ancient forests that had been preserved and protected by mud and shale.

Remains of trees from these forests produced the major coal seams during the Carboniferous Period, which would fuel Glasgow and Clydeside's success millions of years later.

The Carboniferous Period occurred from about 360 to 286 million years ago during the late Paleozoic Era of the earth's history.

The term 'Carboniferous' comes from Britain, referring to the rich deposits of coal that were first discovered here and also in northern Europe, Asia, and North America.

Rather than cover the fossils or move them to a museum, it was decided to protect them in-situ and today the visitor can view them under a protective glass cover from April to September.

Glasgow Green

Glasgow Green, the oldest public park in Europe, dates back to the 12th century when it first appears in official documents.

The first golf course in Glasgow was built there in the 18th century and for centuries it was common grazing land, a custom that continued until 1870.

Women washed their clothes in the Clyde for hundreds of years, even after the first of the famous 'steamies' was built on the Green in the 19th century. The Green was also used for many other chores, including the drying of salmon nets before the Clyde became too polluted.

Glasgow Green has also been central to much of the city's history. Regent Moray assembled his troops there before the Battle of Langside in 1568, which saw the defeat and capture of Mary Queen of Scots. Bonnie Prince Charlie used the Green in 1746, to rest his Jacobite army, shortly before it marched north to be slaughtered at Culloden.

More recently it has been the focus of many of the city's most important and controversial political demonstrations, including the traditional May Day marches. However, the Red Clydesiders' gatherings were forced to move to Queen's Park after the council deliberately planted inconveniently-placed flower beds. More recently the Anti-War march of 2003, saw more than 60,000 people gather there to march through the city to Finnieston.

The Glasgow Fair has been associated with the Green, both originating around the time that Glasgow was granted Royal Burgh status.

The Green has played host to numerous music festivals and has been the starting and finishing point for the city's internationally renowned marathons.

Greenbank Gardens

Greenbank Gardens is one of the most beautiful and tranquil places in the whole of Glasgow. Surrounded by an ever-encroaching urban area on the South Side, Greenbank is more than just a garden. It is an ideal place for a rapidly growing number of budding gardeners but it also serves as a place to relax and take in the atmosphere of more than 6,000 varieties of plants.

Greenbank actually consists of several gardens spread over more than 20 acres, including the summer, spring, cottage and foam garden. The foam garden consists of a magnificent water feature with a bronze water nymph. It was sculpted for the 1938 Empire Exhibition and lent to the 1988 Garden Festival and is now the centerpiece for the circular pond. The oldest garden, the 2.5 acre walled garden, has been around since the Georgian mansion was built in the early 1760s for the wealthy tobacco lord, Robert Allason. He had the house and gardens designed as a country retreat to escape the hectic city life.

The estate, originally more than 250 acres, has changed hands several times in the last two and a half centuries. Its last owner, William Blyth gave the land to the National Trust for Scotland in 1976. The family vacated the house in 1980. Both house and gardens are open to the public and its upkeep is aided by Friends of Greenbank Gardens, a voluntary independent charity formed in 1981.

Linn Park

Acquired in 1919, Linn Park on the south side was, like many other city parks, originally a private estate.

In 1965, it developed the first extensive nature trail system of any park in Glasgow, complementing the 212 acres of formal gardens, woodlands, golf course and equestrian centre. A nature centre was also set up in the old estate house in the heart of the grounds.

The Mansion House, called The Lynn, was built in 1828 as a country retreat for the famous soldier Colin Campbell, Baron Clyde. It was enlarged in 1852, using designs by Glasgow architect Charles Wilson.

There are two old bridges in the park, the oldest being Cathcart Old Bridge. A stone near the structure is dated 1674 but the existing bridge, with its two distinctively different spans, was probably built around the end of the 18th century. The other bridge is the oldest complete cast-iron bridge in Glasgow. A one-piece casting, it comprises of a single elegant span over the meandering White Cart River, and was built around 1835.

The remains of another structure is at the head of the park where the few remaining stones of the 15th century Cathcart Castle can be found. Close-by on a hill called Court Knowe, Mary Queen of Scots is believed to have witnessed her army's defeat at the Battle of Langside in 1568.

There are several cemeteries in the park and a crematorium, established in 1962.

Maxwell Park

One of the smallest parks in the city is Maxwell Park on the south side. Like several other local parks, it was established outwith Glasgow's boundary but was consumed by the rapidly expanding city during the industrial boom of the late 19th century.

The 21 acres of peat bog owned by Sir John Stirling Maxwell were donated to the Burgh of Pollokshields in 1878. In the same year, construction started on architect H E Clifford's Burgh Hall at the south-eastern side of the park.

The bog was drained to the lowest point to form a boating pond which became a popular skating rink in the winter and was used by paddle boats and model boat enthusiasts in the summer.

The Burgh Hall was completed in 1890, the same year the park officially opened but a year later the burgh was annexed by Glasgow and the park came under its control.

The park's most impressive features were the bandstand and the magnificent Hamilton Memorial Fountain. The fountain was erected in 1907. It was constructed by the Doulton company in the famous Italian white marble from Carrara in Tuscany as a memorial to John and Thomas Hamilton who hunted there when the land was still a bog. The French Renaissance-style fountain, with three-tiered basins and a hunting figure at the top, has sadly gone the way of many fountains in Glasgow, suffering from neglect and vandalism.

Other features such as the putting green, tennis pavilion and courts fell into disuse during the 1980s.

Queen's Park

The design for Queen's Park was drawn up by Sir Joseph Paxton in 1860.

Situated on the South Side, Pathhead Farm, owned by Neale Camphill, had been bought by the Glasgow Corporation three years before, despite being outside the city boundary. In 1862 it was opened to the public and was named after Mary Queen of Scots, not Queen Victoria, to commemorate Mary's final defeat in Scotland at the Battle of Langside, fought on the southern edge of the park in 1568.

Despite Paxton's elaborate proposals, many of his features were never used, including his winter garden and music hall, and the construction of a small loch. Today there are two ponds near the northern corner of the park, the smaller being for ducks while the larger was created for boating.

During the 1890s, the expansion of the city eventually brought Queen's Park inside its boundary and in 1894 the park was enlarged with the purchase of the Camphill estate to the west.

This additional land also took in the magnificent Camphill House. Dating from around the early 1800s, it became a museum in 1896 and exhibited many of the city's fine collection of costumes for many years until it was eventually converted into flats in the 1990s.

And near the centre of the park, at its highest point, there stands a flagpole where you can get one of the best views overlooking the city centre and beyond.

Ross Hall Park

Ross Hall Park is one of the most beautiful parks in the whole of Glasgow. Unlike many other open spaces in the city there are no recreational facilities whatsoever, the park being there purely for people to enjoy the landscaped splendour of the place. A small park of about 30 acres, set amidst the White Cart Water in the Crookston area on the South Side, it was taken over by the city in 1948.

Before then it was in private hands – part of the estate owned by the

Cowans of Hawkhead. The Cowan family built a large red sandstone Baronial mansion there in 1877. Around the turn of the 20th century the family decided to have the land surrounding their home landscaped and this they did to a lavish degree. The famous gardening firm of Pullman and Sons was given an almost blank-cheque commission to carry out the work in recreating the land. As well as laying out a garden with rare and exotic plants, the gardeners sculpted scenic walkways through the woodland areas, creating artificial ponds, waterfalls and a grotto. In 1908 the estate was sold to the Lobnitz shipbuilding family who continued the landscaping work still further. Very little has changed since then, even after the park came under Glasgow's control after WWII.

In 1983, the mansion house was converted for use as a private hospital with many additions being made during the 1980s which now obscure much of the old house.

People
Blake, George (1893-1961)
One of the great writers to depict life on the River Clyde was the writer George Blake.

Born in Greenock in 1893, Blake originally studied law at Glasgow University. During WWI he was wounded fighting at the Turkish peninsula of Gallipoli, the horrific battleground that saw the death of more than a quarter of a million men. Discharged from the military, he took up a career as a journalist in Glasgow. In the 1920s he moved to London and became the editor of the popular publication, *John O' London* as well as the *Strand Magazine*. He became the director of the publishing firm Faber and Faber between 1930 and '32. From 1932 he returned to Scotland for good, apart from a brief period during WWII when the Ministry of Information employed him.

His best known novel, *The Shipbuilders,* was published in 1935.

It painted one of the most accurate fictional portraits of life on Clydeside during the economic depression of the 1920s and '30s.

Blake wrote several books documenting the developments and changes taking place in the Clyde area producing *Down to the Sea* in 1937 and *The Firth of Clyde* in 1952.

He used his experiences of Greenock and Glasgow to create the fictional town of Garvel for the setting of his six novels about the lives of the Oliphant family. The series was popular and was later adapted for television.

Blake died in 1961.

Bone, Sir Muirhead (1876-1953)
Sir Muirhead Bone was a prolific artist whose etchings and engraving made him world-famous.

Born in Glasgow in 1876, Bone studied architecture at Glasgow School of Art but was self-taught as an artist. When he left art school he pursued a career as an etcher and watercolour artist and with his brother James published a book – *Glasgow in 1901*.

He contributed more than 50 small sketches and several full-page drawings including some of his well-known illustrations of the Clyde shipyards. In the same year, he moved to London to continue his work but in 1916 he was enlisted by the War Propaganda Bureau and became Britain's first official war artist. Dispatched to France during the Battle of the Somme he produced more than 150 drawings and when he returned to Britain he drew shipyards and battleships. Later he returned to France where he paid particular attention to capturing images of devastation and ruin.

After the war he returned to representations of architecture, portraits and landscapes, with a characteristic sense of realism and composition. In 1937 he was honoured with a knighthood and two years later with the start of WWII he became a war artist once more. During a long and prestigious career he produced more than 500 etchings, drypoints and lithographs, as well as thousands of drawings and watercolours.

Some of his best work is on display at the Imperial War Museum in London.

Bridie, James (1888-1951)

James Bridie was one of Scotland's most influential dramatists and was responsible for establishing the acclaimed Citizen's Theatre.

Born Osborne Henry Mavor in Glasgow, he was the son of the great pioneering electrical engineer Henry Osborne. He went to Glasgow University where he studied medicine and after graduating he entered general practice and as his career progressed he became a successful consultant . But he had an interest in the arts and theatre and started to write critical reviews. He also started writing his own plays under the pseudonym of Mary Henderson and in 1928 he had his first big show business break when the Scottish National Players performed his *Sunlight Sonata*. But it was *The Anatomist* which really began his professional writing career and his work was soon in great demand.

Other plays included *A Sleeping Clergyman* (1933) and during WWII, while serving in the Royal Army Medical Corps, *Mr. Balfry* was first performed in 1943. In the same year he founded the Citizen's Company and became their first president. Their first play was his own *Holy Isle*, performed in the Old Athenaeum Theatre in Buchanan Street. Two years later the company moved to the Royal Princesses Theatre in the Gorbals, later renamed the Citizen's Theatre.

James Bridie continued to write but also helped establish the Royal Scottish Academy of Music and Drama and became a member of the Arts Council and was an adviser to the Edinburgh festival.

Buchan, John (1875-1940)

The famous novelist, journalist, historian, poet and statesman, John Buchan, started his literary career in Glasgow.

Born in Perth in 1875, he moved to Glasgow at the age of 13 when his father Rev John Buchan was called to the John Knox Free Church in the Gorbals.

Buchan attended Hutcheson's Grammar School before going to Glasgow University in 1892 where he received a classical education.

During his undergraduate years he was a regular contributor to *Macmillan's* and the *Gentleman's Magazine*. Buchan continued his studies at Oxford before working in South Africa. On his return in 1901, he took up a career as a London lawyer but his great passion was still the written word.

He edited the *Spectator* for a time and also turned the fortunes of Nelson's publishing house with a series of pocket editions of great literary works.

During WWI he served in Intelligence, becoming director from 1916 to 1917 and after the war he entered politics. From 1927 to 1935 he was MP for Scottish Universities. He was later created a baron and as Lord Tweedsmuir was Governor of Canada until 1940.

He is best remembered for his books, of which he published more than a hundred. His most famous novel was *The Thirty-nine Steps*, published in 1915, the first of five charting the adventures of Richard Hannay. His biographies include *Montrose* (1928) and *Sir Walter Scott* (1932). His commendable autobiography *Memory Hold-the-Door* was published in 1940, the year of his death.

Carswell, Catherine (1879-1946)

Novelist and biographer, Catherine Carswell was born Catherine MacFarlane in Glasgow.

She attended Glasgow University but never matriculated despite it having been open to female students for several years. She studied English Literature under the famous scholar, critic and essayist Sir Walter Raleigh. Her first marriage in 1904 to Herbert Jackson proved to be a disaster after he tried to kill her in a fit of insanity and was committed to an asylum for life. She made legal history when she won her case to have the marriage annulled.

Pursuing a career in dramatic and literary criticism she wrote for *The Glasgow Herald* and developed a lasting friendship with DH Lawrence after writing a favourable review of his first novel *The White Peacock* in 1911.

In 1915 she married Donald Carswell and started writing her first autobiographical novel *Open the Door*, depicting the oppressive atmosphere within a middle-class Glaswegian family. It was published in 1920 and her second, *The Camomile*, was published two years later.

She turned to biography and is perhaps best known for her *Life of Robert Burns* (1930) which challenged the sentimental and idealistic view of the poet. It was greeted with much criticism by admirers of Burns but is now regarded as a landmark study.

Other biographies include *The Savage Pilgrimage: a Narrative of DH Lawrence* (1932). Her unfinished autobiography *Lying Awake* was published in 1952, six years after her death.

Friel, George (1910-1975)

The novelist George Friel was one of the 20th century's greatest modern Scottish writers.

Born in Glasgow in 1910 into a large family, he was educated at St Mungo's Academy and was the only one of seven children who went on to study at university. He attended Glasgow University before going to Jordanhill College where he trained to become a teacher.

He spent WWII in the Royal Army Ordnance Corps and returned to teaching in 1945.

Over the next few years he become disillusioned with the profession and began to concentrate on writing fiction.

He wrote many books including: *The Bank of Time* (1959), *The Boy Who Wanted Peace* (1964) and *Grace and Miss Partridge* which was published in 1969. However, in 1972 he produced a piece of work that has been described as one of the great Scottish novels. The powerful and ironic *Mr. Alfred MA*, based on Friel's experiences at the teaching 'chalk face', portrays the decay and erosion of the educational system through a lack of mutual understanding.

His final work, *An Empty House* was published the year he died, in 1975.

Fyffe, Will (1885-1947)

Will Fyffe, one of the greatest Scottish comic music hall legends became a household name after writing his most famous song about his adoptive city – 'I belong to Glasgow'. He had a special place in his heart for Glasgow and Glaswegians, despite being born on the east coast of Scotland.

Born in Dundee, he seemed destined for the stage, touring the length and breadth of Scotland with his father's theatrical company. His debut was as Little Willie in East Lynne and before he was 15 he had shown a tremendous agility for character portrayals across the spectrum of theatrical works. But he soon realised his greatest talent lay with comic characterisation. He devoted himself to music hall revues, bringing characters like Daft Sandy, the centenarian, the railway guard and the truly believable Glasgow drunk to an adoring audience.

The inspiration for his famous song came after a drunk in Glasgow's Central Station failed to recall to Fyffe where he was from but stated that at that minute he belonged to Glasgow, and Glasgow belonged to him.

Fyffe's celebrity spread, gaining top billing at the London Pavilion in 1921 and also further afield in America, with many feeling his popularity had surpassed Harry Lauder's.

During WWII he entertained the troops with such dedication that he was honoured with the Commander of the Order of the British Empire. Fyffe died in St. Andrews in 1947 and was buried in the old cemetery in Maryhill, Glasgow.

Garscadden, Kathleen (1897-1991)

Known to the nation as 'Aunt Kathleen', Kathleen Garscadden educated and entertained countless millions of children with her long running *Children's Hour* series.

Born in Glasgow, she was educated at Hutchesons' Girls Grammar School before going to London to train as a singer.

But early on, she decided to embark on a new career. Abandoning her hopes of becoming an opera singer, she became an announcer, pianist and singer at her father's own station before moving to the BBC in 1923.

There she was initially involved in concerts and the Woman's Hour and was dubbed 'Aunt Cyclone' for her weather forecasting. But after working on the world's first programmes to be made for school education she realised there was a need for a full time commitment to children's broadcasting.

Affectionately known as 'Aunt Kathleen', she worked as a presenter, broadcaster, programme organizer and producer throughout the 42 year reign of the extremely popular *Children's Hour* series. She tried to inspire her young audience with subjects ranging from religion to history but always made space for the traditions of Scotland as well.

During WWII she was instrumental in providing a broadcasting link between Scottish families and their evacuated children. Her long-running career with the BBC also aided the careers of other famous Scots stars, introducing Jimmy Logan, Stanley Baxter, Gordon Jackson and Moira Anderson to the world of broadcasting.

Loved by generations of children growing up with her programme, Kathleen Garscadden died in 1991.

Gibson, Sir Alexander (1926-1998)

Sir Alexander Drummond Gibson was one of the greatest orchestral conductors Scotland has ever produced. Exceptionally talented, he left his mark on Scottish classical music by founding the first professional opera company, the Scottish Opera.

He was born in Motherwell in 1926 and studied piano at the Scottish Academy of Music and continued his musical studies at Glasgow University. After military service during WWII, he won a scholarship to the Royal College of Music in London in 1948.

He formed and conducted a student orchestra at college and after continuing his musical training in Europe, he returned to join the famous Sadler's Wells Opera. Between 1952 and '54 he was the BBC Scottish Symphony Orchestra's associate conductor. In 1957 he became Sadler's Wells youngest ever musical director, conducting 26 operas and made his Covent Garden debut in the same year. Two years later, he returned to Scotland, becoming the SNO's first native-born Principal Conductor and Artistic Director.

He brought many new musical works to Scottish audiences, many of them before they were performed in London. Instrumental in forming Scottish Opera in 1962, he became its artistic director.

He was made CBE in 1967 and knighted in 1977. After an exceptional career, conducting all over the world, Sir Alexander eventually retired from the SNO in 1984 but returned many times as guest conductor until his death in 1995.

In December 1998, the Royal Scottish Academy of Music and Drama in Glasgow opened the Alexander Gibson Opera School in his memory.

Gordon, Harry (1893-1956)

Comedian Harry Gordon became one of Scotland's great all-round entertainers and was most famous for his comic character sketches created for his fictitious village of Inversnecky.

Harry Alex Ross Gordon was born in Aberdeen in 1893. From a young age he wanted to be an entertainer. When he left school, he went to work for a grain merchants but all his spare time was spent appearing in local amateur concerts. Eventually he picked up some professional work, turned full-time in 1912 and worked in many theatres in the north-east of Scotland. He served in the army during WWI but returned to the stage after the war and in 1924 bought the Beach Pavilion in Aberdeen. Gordon appeared there annually and made more than 100 radio broadcasts there, including *Harry's Half Hour* and *Gordon Gaieties*, until the theatre eventually closed in 1940. During this time he also appeared at many other venues throughout the country, including London in 1929, which proved to be one of his least successful venues.

But he became a huge star in Glasgow, at the Pavilion and King's, and established a record of 11 consecutive years (1937-48) with the Alhambra pantomime, seven with Will Fyffe. He also toured in the US in the 1940s.

But his greatest success was his long-running series of stand-up songs and monologues of many characters in his fictitious village, especially the Laird of Inversnecky.

Gordon died in Glasgow in 1956.

Graham, Alex (b. 1915) and Fred Basset

Always one step ahead of his owner, Fred Basset has spent more than 40 years trying to understand his masters mind, all thanks to the inspired talents of acclaimed Glasgow cartoonist, Alexander Graham.

Alex Graham has sketched thousands of cartoon strips of the lovable hound for the *Daily Mail* since Fred Basset first appeared in 1963. Over the years the cartoon strip has grown enormously popular, being syndicated all over the world, gaining a huge following in the USA.

Alex Graham was born in Glasgow in 1915. He attended the Glasgow School of Art, winning awards for portrait painting, but when he started drawing for the Scottish press his professional cartooning career really took off. His first cartoon strips appeared in the *Weekly News* in 1946 and the following year he broke into the national press in several publications. The very successful *Briggs the Butler* ran for 17 years in Tatler and inspired by his favourite sport, the strip, *Graham's Golf Club* featured in Punch.

Finally in 1963, Fred Basset hit the pages of the *Daily Mail* and his fame was secured as one of the most enduring and famous cartoonists Glasgow has ever produced.

Hanley, Cliff (1922-1999)

One of the wittiest and most informed observers of Glasgow life was the much loved novelist, dramatist, broadcaster and journalist Cliff Hanley.

Born in Glasgow's east end in 1922 he went to Eastbank Academy before starting a journalistic career in 1940. He soon proved to be more than a serious news reporter, showing a versatility that allowed him to write critical and witty articles on any subject.

But 'Wee Cliff' as he was affectionately known, spread his talents to all forms of the media at every given opportunity.

In the 1950s he was commissioned to write comedy scripts for Radio Scotland and in 1958 he published one of his finest books, *Dancing in the Streets*. A semi-autobiographical account of growing up in Glasgow, it was to be a theme that he would return to often.

Much of his work had a true sense of fun but there was also a gritty reality to his work.

As Henry Calvin he wrote crime novels.

Other Hanley books included *Love from Everybody* (1959), *A Taste too Much* (1960) and the Glaswegian family Highland holiday story, *The Hot Month* published in 1967.

But he is best remembered for writing the lyrics to an old pipe tune which became Scotland's other national anthem – 'Scotland the Brave'.

His worldwide acclaim led to his becoming Professor of Literature at York University, Toronto, from 1979 to 1980 and he was always in great demand for after dinner speeches.

Herriot, James (1916-1995)

The world's most famous vet was brought up and educated in Glasgow.

James Alfred Wight, better known as James Herriot, was born in Sunderland in 1916 and came to Glasgow with his family when he was a few months old. He attended Yoker Primary and Hillhead High before studying at Glasgow Veterinary College. He graduated in 1939 and the following year applied for a job in the Yorkshire Dales, a position that would lead to his international fame. He joined the practice of Donald Sinclair in the village of Thirsk, where he would spend the rest of his life.

He told his family of the weird and wonderful things that happened to him but it was not until 1966 that he was persuaded to put the stories on paper. After many rejections his first book was published in 1970 – *If Only they Could Talk* and two years later his most famous novel *All Creatures Great And Small* was published.

It formed the basis for the delightful long-running television series of the same name, first aired in 1977.

Other bestsellers include *It Shouldn't Happen To A Vet*, *Vet In A Spin*, *James Herriot's Yorkshire* and many compilations and children's books. But he always regarded himself as a vet and once said: 'If a farmer calls me with a sick animal, he couldn't care less if I were George Bernard Shaw.'

He received an OBE in 1979 and became a Fellow of the Royal College of Veterinary Surgeons in 1982.

Honeyman, Dr Tom J (1891-1971)

Doctor Tom J Honeyman was famous and indeed infamous for his purchase of Salvador Dali's Christ of St. John of the Cross for Glasgow in 1952. Director of Art Galleries and Museums from 1939, he was much castigated for the purchase as it used up the entire annual budget of £8200. But he was vindicated after charging an admission fee to view the painting in the 'Dali room' at the Kelvingrove Art Gallery and Museum.

Not only did this novel approach repay the cost of the painting in a matter of weeks but it boosted flagging public interest in the museum. And over the years the priceless painting has more than earned its keep from reproduction fees and still attracts thousands to its new home at St. Mungo's Museum of Religious Life and Art.

Honeyman did not start off his life in the art world.

Born in 1891, he studied medicine and had his own family practice in the east end. But his great passion was art so he moved to London and became an art dealer where he later persuaded Dali to part with his world-acclaimed masterpiece. However, Honeyman did many other things for Glasgow.

He was the first chairman of the Citizen's Theatre in 1943, the same year he became the second recipient of the St. Mungo Prize.

And Honeyman also persuaded Sir William Burrell to leave his collection to Glasgow. He resigned from his position with Glasgow's museums in 1954 and died in 1971.

Jackson, Gordon (1923-1990)

One of Scotland's best loved actors was Gordon Cameron Jackson.

Born in 1923 in Glasgow, his show business career started even before he left school.

His first performances were in BBC radio plays but when he left school at 15, he did not enter into the full-time acting profession straight away. For a couple of years he worked as an engineering draughtsman at the Rolls Royce factory before his first film casting as a young Scottish soldier in *The Foreman went to France* in 1941. He was cast in similar roles as the callow serviceman in several other war time movies including *Millions Like Us* and *San Demetrio London*, both made in 1943. In the same year, his first stage performance was in a play called *George and Margaret* at a theatre in Rutherglen.

A distinguished career on stage followed with appearances in Orson Welle's *Moby Dick* (1955), Banquo to Alec Guiness's *Macbeth* (1966) and

Horatio in *Hamlet* (1969). But he will always be remembered for his superb performances in film classics such as *Whisky Galore* (1948), *The Great Escape* (1963), *The Prime of Miss Jean Brodie* (1969) and *The Shooting Party* (1984).

His most famous television performances were his Emmy Award winning performance as Hudson in *Upstairs Downstairs*, running from 1970 to 1975 and as Bodie and Doyle's MI5 boss in *The Professionals* from 1977 to 1981. A great character actor, he was respected throughout the acting profession for his self-effacing dedication to his work.

Laurel, Stan (1890-1965)

One half of the world's most famous double act started his stage career in the theatres of Glasgow. Stan Laurel was born Arthur Stanley Jefferson in Ulverston, Cumbria, in 1890. His parents were both in the theatre business and as they were often on the road Stan was brought up by his grandmother.

In the early 1900s Stan moved to Glasgow to join his parents as his father was the theatre manager at the famous Metropole. At 16, Stan's desire to perform led to his first comedy appearance at the eccentric A. E. Pickard's Panoptican theatre. His father saw his son's performance by chance and was so impressed he helped him get more work at other theatres in the city.

He later changed his name to Laurel because he was superstitious and Stan Jefferson had 13 letters. In 1910 Stan joined a travelling pantomime troupe where he became the understudy to London-born comedian Charles Spencer Chaplin. Later that year the troupe moved to America but three years later, when the troupe returned to Britain after Chaplin left, Stan decided to remain in America also.

He formed a couple of comedy trio acts and from 1917 started to appear in films. In 1920 he appeared in *Lucky Dog*. Oliver Hardy also had a part in the film but it wasn't until 1926 that they starred together. The rest of Stan's career is history.

Mackay, Fulton (1922-1987)

One of Scotland's best loved actors started off life as a quantity surveyor.

Fulton Mackay was born in Paisley and served in the Black Watch regiment during WWII. However after the war ended he decided to become an actor and trained at the Royal Academy of Dramatic Arts, making his stage debut in *Angel* in 1947. He was a member of the Citizen's Theatre in Glasgow from 1949 to 1951 and again from 1953 to 1958.

His stage career took him all round the country including a year at the 'Old Vic' in London in 1962. Fulton also directed for the stage, most notably for the Scottish Actors production of *The Wild Duck* in 1969. He also wrote many plays under the pseudonym Aeneas MacBride.

Although he worked for many theatre companies playing both classical and contemporary roles he is best remembered for his television and film characters. Numerous television appearances included *Special Branch* (1969-

'73), *Going Gently* (1981) and *The Holy City* (1986). His first big screen appearance was in *I'm a Stranger* in 1952 and he later appeared in box office hits such as *Local Hero* (1983) and *Defence of the Realm* (1985).

But his most memorable role must be the officious prison warder, Mr Mackay with the famous neck twitch, in the hit TV series *Porridge*, which originally ran from 1974 to 1977. Fulton Mackay was a true craftsman of his profession and brought to life the memorable characters he portrayed before his death in 1987.

MacLean, Alistair (1922-1987)
One of the most popular thriller writers of the 20th century was Glasgow author, Alistair MacLean.

Born in 1922, he was educated at Inverness Royal Academy, Hillhead High School and Glasgow University. He served in the Royal Navy from 1941 to 1946 and his experiences during the war were to inspire many of his bestselling books in years to come. But he did not start writing straight after the war.

He lived in Kingspark and taught at Gallowflat School, Rutherglen, for many years, but in 1954 he won a *Glasgow Herald* short story competition. The story drew the attention of publishers William Collins who persuaded him to write a full length novel. The following year he finished his first book, which many regard as his finest, *HMS Ulysses*, telling of the horrific and harrowing life endured on the North Atlantic run during the war.

An immediate bestseller, MacLean followed its success with another block buster, *The Guns of Navarone* in 1957. Quitting teaching, he wrote prolifically, turning out many books that were made into films, including *Ice Station Zebra* and *Where Eagles Dare*.

As well as sea adventures, he wrote biographies (*T. E. Lawrence, Captain Cook*), a Western (*Breakheart Pass*) and two secret service thrillers (*The Dark Crusader, The Satan Bug*) under the name Ian Stuart. His story lines were global but he did not neglect home, writing *When Eight Bells Toll* in 1966 about the Scottish Islands.

Macrae, Duncan (1905-1967)
One of the greatest exponents of Scottish theatre was the lantern-jawed actor Duncan Macrae.

Born in Glasgow in 1905, he was educated at Allan Glen's School and Glasgow University before taking up a career as a teacher.

But his love for acting blossomed, moving him from amateur to professional by 1940. Three years later he started what was to become a long association with the Citizen's Theatre, appearing in its opening production.

He made his London stage debut in 1945, appearing in *The Forrigan Reel* and his versatility allowed him to assume serious roles in many Shakespeare, Shaw and Chekov productions.

He could also turn his acting skills with ease to produce memorable comic and pantomime characters.

Always drawn to Scottish theatre he set up a touring company with the Scottish playwright and critic T. M. Wilson and together they travelled around Scotland from 1952 to 1955. His archetypal dour-faced Scot's demeanour, mixed with his craggy looks along with his famous loose-limbed gait made him an ideal character for many of Scotland's best loved films.

Some of his most memorable roles were in *Whisky Galore* (1948), *The Kidnappers* (1953) and *Casino Royale* (1967). He was also a familiar face on television with guest performances on the hit show *Para Handy – Master Mariner* in 1959. Probably his best loved and most hilarious 'party piece' was his rendition of 'Wee Cock Sparra'.

A huge contributor to his craft, he became Chairman of Scottish Equity in 1967, the year of his death.

McFlannels, The

Long before people became engrossed with TV soaps, radio dominated and the first and best loved Scottish Soap was about the Glasgow family, *The McFlannels*.

A Saturday evening institution, the live half-hour broadcast, originally called *The McFlannels Rub Along* in 1939, focused on a respectable working class family living up a close.

Written by Helen W. Pryde, all the characters were named after materials such as McFlannel, McCotton, McCorduroy, McVelvet, McTweed. Many of the actors became household names and included John Morton (Willic), Meg Buchanan (Sarah), Arthur Shaw (Peter), Arthur Whiteman (Uncle Donald) and Willie Joss (Uncle Mattha). Uncle Mattha was a very special character whose catch phrase 'You never died a winter yet' always appeared, often as the punch-line.

Some lesser-known actors, later to become famous on radio and television had small parts in the series. They included Mollie Weir, Gordon Jackson and Ricki Fulton as the Church Minister David McCrepe. It was always on Scottish Home Service except during the war when it merged with BBC Home Service.

During the war the series informed listeners how they could help in the war effort such as growing their own food on allotments. After the war it ran every Saturday from 7.30pm but later moved to Mondays with repeats on Tuesdays. It was compulsive listening until television became more accessible and the show was eventually taken off air in 1954. As the show was sent out live there are no recordings but Helen Pryde wrote seven books about the McFlannels.

McMillan, Roddy (1923-1979)

Roddy McMillan was one of Glasgow's best loved actors and playwrights.

As he was growing up he had ambitions to become an aero-engineer when he left school but all that was to change after his first taste on stage when he was only 12. He continued in acting and by 1946 he made it his full-time professional career, joining the Glasgow Unity Theatre. Early appearances included parts in *The Gorbals Story* and *Men Should Weep*.

Later on he became a member of the Citizen's Theatre. Although his greatest love was to perform in front of live audiences he also devoted time to writing his own plays.

In 1954 *All in Good Faith* was performed for the first time and later, another popular play scripted by McMillan, *The Bevellers* in 1973.

But he was also well known for his film work, debuting in the 1950 film *Morning Departure*. Other appearances included *Laxdale Hall* in 1952 and *Ring of Bright Water* in 1969. But it is his television appearances that are best remembered.

His most memorable character was Para Handy, the dour-faced mocking Clyde puffer captain in the hit comedy *The Vital Spark* which ran from 1966-7 and again in 1973-4.

In 1972 he starred in *The View From Daniel Pike* portraying a seedy private detective which won him a TV Personality of the Year Award. After Roddy McMillan died in 1979, his friends commissioned a new variety of rose to be named in his memory.

McInnes, Helen (1907-1985)

One of Scotland's greatest spy novelists was Helen McInnes.

Born in 1907, she attended Hermitage School, Helensburgh, and the Girl's High School in Glasgow before going to Glasgow University in 1925. She studied French and German, graduating with a BA in 1929.

While studying she had worked part-time in the library and decided that she would like to pursue a career with books. After a time with Glasgow University library she worked at Dumbarton County Library.

McInnes then went to the library at University College, London, where she worked while taking a post-graduate course in librarianship. In 1932 she married classical scholar Gilbert Highet and they moved to Oxford when he was offered a post at St. John's College. While there she combined bringing up her son, amateur dramatics and, with the money she made translating books from German, she also travelled extensively in Europe during the summer months. In 1937 her husband got a job at Columbia University and they moved to New York.

It was in America that McInnes started to write her own books but at first she kept her work a secret. However in 1941 her writing career took off dramatically with the publication of *Above Suspicion* which was an instant bestseller. Two years later it was made into a film starring Joan Crawford and Fred MacMurray.

Dubbed 'The Queen of the Spy Writers', many other McInnes novels were made into films including *Assignment in Brittany* (1943) and *Venetian Affair* (1967).

She died in 1985.

McLean, Lex (1907-1975)

Scotland has always been proud of its comedians and their ability to find humour in everyday life. One of the greatest exponents of this art was the legendary Lex McLean.

Born Alexander McLean Cameron in Clydebank in 1907, he started working life as an apprentice at John Brown's shipyard. He first entertained audiences playing the piano in the orchestra pit of his local cinema. Later he joined the Meltonians concert party, playing the straight man to 'Scotland's Queen of Comedy' Doris Droye. But he soon realised he was getting more laughs than she was and decided to go it alone.

His love of performing and natural comic talent made him one of the best loved entertainers in the country. His diverse characterisations ranged from an upper-crust, top hat-wearing, gentleman to the 'bunnet'-wearing 'Daft Jimmy'. But no matter which role he set himself, his mastery of irony and the double entendre made him one of Scotland's most famous adult entertainers during the middle of the 20th century.

He was the country's highest paid performer for many years, becoming a local institution with record-breaking summer seasons at the Pavilion Theatre in the 1950s. Lex maintained his career exclusively in Scotland, not only on stage but was frequently invited to perform on TV variety shows.

Lex died in 1975 but entertainer Billy Jeffrey recently paid a great tribute to his comic genius at the Pavilion Theatre in the highly successful *Lex McLean Story* and *Laugh! Laugh! Laugh! with Lex!*.

Miller, William (1810-1872)

One of the most famous nursery rhymes known throughout the English speaking world was written by a Glasgow wood-turner – William Miller.

William Miller was born in 1810 and in 1842 he contributed a rhyme about Wee Willie Winkie to a book of poems – *Whistle-binkie; Stories for the Fireside*. When it was published his rhyme soon became a great favourite among the children of Glasgow.

Over the years his words have been somewhat changed to a more proper English language format but the original first verse went as follows – 'Wee Willie Winkie rins through the toon, Up stairs an' doon stairs in his nicht-goun, Tirlin' at the window, crying at the lock, Are the weans in their bed, for noo it's ten o'clock.'

Over the years many people have wondered why he chose 10 o'clock as the hour for children to be safely tucked up in bed.

It is quite likely that it was chosen as a witty dig at a curfew that had been imposed on the streets of Glasgow by Calvinists during the 18th century.

Miller died in 1872 and it is often assumed that he was buried at the Necropolis but the stone inscribed 'The Laureate of the Nursery' is only a memorial to him. Funds had been raised by public subscription originally to help nurse the sick and destitute poet back to health but they were too late in coming and he perished. He was buried in an unmarked grave in Tollcross Central churchyard.

Morgan, Tommy (1898-1958)

Tommy Morgan was one of the greatest home-grown comics Glasgow has ever seen.

Born in Bridgeton in 1898, he worked in a local factory when he was 14 but had a great interest in entertaining and avidly read the *Evening Times'* theatre columns. However, any opportunity for a show business career was interrupted by WWI. He lied about his age to the army – he was only 16 – and experienced the horrors of trench warfare.

Ironically the army gave him his first taste of the stage, as a comedian's stooge in concert parties. After the war, Morgan worked in the shipyards but joined an amateur group of entertainers before he and singer Tommy Yorke decided to turn professional. They toured the west of Scotland over the next 10 years, learning their trade before the notoriously hard to please audiences of the day.

Morgan's humour was often rough but never profane.

His real success was that he was a down-to-earth Glaswegian and knew his audience. Eventually Morgan, nicknamed Clairty after his mother's favourite phrase – 'Clare to Goodness' – got his big break as principal comic at the Metropole's panto season in 1931.

During the summer season he performed his own show at the Pavilion, achieving the British record of 19 successive seasons.

His best loved character was his drag act Big Beenie, a classic gallus blonde.

He died in 1958.

Morgan's ashes were scattered over the roof of the Pavilion.

Motherwell, William (1797-1832)

William Motherwell was one of the great Scottish poets and writers of ballads during the early part of the 19th century.

The son of an ironmonger, he was born in 1797 in the High Street where it meets College Street, right in the heart of old Glasgow. Motherwell, when he was only 14 years old, wrote his first and best known ballad, 'Jeannie Morrison', named after a girl at his school.

He was educated at Glasgow University before going to live in Paisley in 1819 where he became the Sheriff-Clerk Depute of Renfrewshire, a post he retained until 1829. As well as his legal obligations, Motherwell also wrote and published some of his greatest work during this period.

They included *The Harp of Renfrewshire* (1819) and *Minstrelsy, Ancient and Modern* (1827) and under the name of Isaac Brown – *Renfrewshire Characters and Scenery* (1824).

He returned to Glasgow in 1830 to become the first editor of the now defunct *Glasgow Courier*, a right-wing newspaper that was published three times a week at that time. As well as editing the paper, he also found time to publish other collected works, including *Poems, Narrative and Lyrical* (1832) which contained 'Jeannie Morrison'. In 1835, while still editor of the

Courier, he published with fellow poet James Hogg *The Works of Robert Burns*. Later in the same year he suffered a stroke brought on by apoplexy and died not long after.

He was buried in the Necropolis and a plaque was mounted at 117 High Street in his honour.

Munro, Neil (1881-1930)

Journalist and novelist Neil Munro is best remembered for the comic adventures of the crew of the Clyde puffer – *The Vital Spark*.

Munro was the illegitimate son of a kitchen maid, born in Inverary, on the west bank of Loch Fyne, in 1863. Educated locally, he started work in the Argyll Sheriff Clerk's office when he was 13, but in 1881 he moved to Glasgow. He trained as a journalist and eventually became editor of the now defunct *Glasgow Evening News*.

His literary career kicked off in 1896 with the publication of a collection of short stories – *The Lost Pibroch* – and was followed in 1898 by one of his finest novels, *John Splendid*.

Several other Munro novels also dealt with the changes that took place in the Highlands during the 18th century including *Doom Castle* (1901) and *The New Road* (1906).

In 1902, Munro retired from full-time journalism but wrote a weekly series of humorous short stories for the newspaper. One of the stories, stemming from his great fondness for the Clyde puffers that plied up and down the west coast of Scotland was turned into his most popular novel, *The Vital Spark*. First published in 1906, it was later immortalised in the hit television comedy series starring Roddy McMillan as the dour-faced puffer captain Para Handy, which ran from 1966-7 and again in 1973-4.

During WWI Munro returned to journalism but wrote little afterwards.

In 1927 he moved to Craigendoran, south-east of Helensburgh, where he died three years later.

Murray, Chic (1919-1985)

Chic Murray, originally Charles Thomas McKinnon Murray, was born in Greenock in 1919. Like many other comedians including Billy Connolly and Lex McLean, he started his working life in Glasgow's shipyards.

He started a marine engineering apprenticeship at Kincaid's yard in 1934 but when not working he devoted his time and musical talents to amateur groups such as the Whinhillbillies and Chic and His Chicks.

He was rejected for military service at the start of WWII but during that time he met his wife to be – Maida Dickson. They married in 1945 and together formed a double act billed as 'The Tall Droll with the Small Doll'.

Their wonderful blend of comedy and music soon delighted audiences in theatres all over the country and they also made frequent TV appearances. Later Chic embarked on a solo career, creating a uniquely funny look at the world.

With his famous tartan bunnet and his unforgettable forbidding expression he painted a hilarious picture of all that was absurd and surreal about every day life to the delight of his fans.

His first film appearance was in the 1967 classic, *Casino Royale.*

In 1980 he starred in *Gregory's Girl* and three years later he appeared in the TV movie *Saigon.* In 1984 he played legendary football manager Bill Shankly in the musical play *You'll Never Walk Alone.*

His life was the subject of a best selling book by Andrew Yule – *The Best Way to Walk* – published in 1989.

Neill, Bud (1911-1970) and Lobey Dosser

Glasgow's best loved cartoon character was Lobey Dosser.

He was created by Bud Neill whose cartoon strip ran in the *Evening Times* from 1949 until 1955.

Lobey was a Glaswegian living in a landscape that was part Partick, part Wild West. This wonderful mixture came in part from Bud Neill's fascination and passion for the American Western films that he grew up with during his childhood in Troon, Ayrshire. And when he combined this story-line with his innate understanding and observation of colourful Glaswegian characters – it produced something quite remarkable. Bud's lead character came from the words lobby and dosser – which combined to mean a tramp sleeping in the tenement close.

Lobey was the sheriff of Calton Creek who was continually battling with arch villain Rank Bajin with help from his faithful two-legged talking steed El Fidelo (Elfie). All Bud's character names made clever use of Glaswegian vernacular – Dunny Dosser (Lobby's brother) and Ima Bajin (Rank's wife). Other characters included Fairy Nuff, Whisk E Glaur, Stark Stairn, the Red Indians Toffy Teeth and Rubber Lugs and the Wifies, who shot at the Red Indians while holding a bairn under their arm.

Lobey became a cult figure spanning all social boundaries in Glasgow. Workmates were branded with character names, Glasgow University founded an appreciation society and Lobey even appeared in a Citizen's Theatre production.

Despite Lobey's popularity, it wasn't until 1992 that a bronze statue depicting him and Bajin astride Elfie galloping down Woodlands Road was erected in his honour.

Petrie, Alexander Wylie (1853-1937)

One of the most eccentric newspaper publishers in Glasgow had to be Alexander Wylie Petrie.

Born in 1853, Petrie wrote, edited and sold on the streets, his own publication, the *Glasgow Clincher.* A hairdresser by trade, his flamboyant style and sharp tongue made him a very popular character in the city. He started selling his newspaper in 1897 and many of the stories he wrote for it directly attacked the Glasgow Establishment and in particular the city council.

His stories proved to be popular with the general public but unfortunately they did not have the same appeal with the city's authorities. He was frequently charged with disorderly conduct and he was arrested when the paper was still in its first year of publication.

He was committed to Woodilee Asylum near Lenzie where it was hoped he would cause no further embarrassment to leading figures in Glasgow society. However, his popularity was such that a public outcry led to an independent doctor certifying to his soundness of mind and he was released.

From the day of his release from the asylum, Petrie declared himself to be the only certifiably sane man in Glasgow.

Pickard, Albert Ernest (1874-1964)

The last of Glasgow's great eccentrics was Yorkshireman, Albert Ernest Pickard Unlimited, as he liked to call himself.

Born in Bradford in 1874, he moved to Glasgow in 1904, buying Fell's Waxworks in the Trongate. He added his own American museum, introducing many weird freak shows to the stage and even had a small zoo on the premises. Buying the old Britannia Music Hall above his waxworks, he renamed it 'The Panoptican' because he said there you could see everything. Many performers at his theatre were amateurs and he always claimed part responsibility for one of the most famous comic duos ever. An unknown comic, Stan Jefferson first performed at the Panoptican, but later the rest of the world would know him as Stan Laurel.

But buying up property made Pickard a millionaire and he eventually owned more buildings than anyone except the council. He claimed after this that Glasgow belonged to him. But when Will Fyffe started singing his famous song 'I belong to Glasgow', he threatened to sue him in court.

Pickard even stood for Parliament as 'The Independent Millionaire Candidate' for Maryhill, feeling he had a good chance as he owned almost every building in the constituency. He failed miserably but continued to make Glasgow a funnier place in his own eccentric way for 60 years. At the age of 90, after an amazingly full life, he died in a fire in his own house in Belhaven Terrace in the West End.

Reid, Alexander (1854-1928)

The only British person ever to have their portrait painted by the world-famous Dutch artist Vincent Van Gogh was the Glaswegian artist and art dealer Alexander Reid. However, it was some years after Reid's death before the art world realised the two portraits were not Van Gogh self-portraits but Reid. Reid was one of the most important influences on a whole generation of Scottish art lovers. He even sold Sir William Burrell some of his most famous French paintings.

Born in Glasgow in 1854, he started his working life in his father's carving and gilding business but in 1887 went to Paris to work for an art dealer. He worked alongside Van Gogh's brother Theodore and over the next two years

Reid became acquainted with many famous artists and their work, including Monet and Gaugin. Many French artists were painting in the Impressionist style, unheard of back in Scotland at that time. So in 1889 Reid returned to Glasgow and set up his La Societe des Beaux-Arts gallery.

He started dealing in Scottish and English artists but in 1892 he put on an exceptional French Impressionists exhibition and his popularity grew. Clients started to buy more French paintings but Reid also pushed local talent, in particular a group of young artists whose own style became known as the Scottish Colourists.

By the outbreak of WWI Reid, was the foremost art dealer in Glasgow and remained so until his death in 1928, after which the local art scene went into decline.

Reith, John (1889-1971)

The most influential shaper of early radio and television broadcasting was John Charles Walsham Reith.

Reith was born in Stonehaven in 1889, educated at Glasgow Academy and later studied engineering at Glasgow Technical College where he met television pioneer, Helensburgh-born John Logie Baird. In early 1914 he worked as an engineer in London but when war was declared he joined the 5th Scottish Rifles and later transferred to the Royal Engineers. Invalided out with a serious head wound, he returned to engineering in London and spent time in America but after the war he worked at the Parkhead Forge in Glasgow.

In 1922 he resigned and was employed by the fledgling commercial British Broadcasting Company. He became managing director and successfully argued broadcasting should be a public service organisation.

In 1927 the company became a public corporation and Reith was made director general and then later knighted.

He repelled political attempts to control the BBC, maintaining a high moral standard, mixing light and factual programming. He refused Baird's invention until 1936 when he inaugurated the world's first regular TV scheduling but two years later he was removed for being inflexible. He headed Imperial Airways, which became the British Overseas Airways Corporation in 1940, the year he became Baron Reith of Stonehaven.

He entered parliament but fell out with Churchill in 1942 when he was Minister of Works and Buildings. Many public appointments followed and he was made Lord Rector of Glasgow University in 1966, five years before his death.

He is remembered in the BBC's annual Reith Lectures.

Tranter, Nigel (1909-2000)

Nigel Tranter was one of the greatest writers of Scotland's historic past, putting a passion and truth into his stories not found in historical texts. Born in Glasgow in 1909, at an early age he went to live in Edinburgh. He attended George Heriot's School but had no great interest in history.

An interest in architecture led him to work for a restoration company but after the death of his father, financial constraints led him to a career in accountancy. However, book-keeping soon moved over for book writing and in 1935 he completed his first piece of non-fiction, *The Fortalicles and Early Mansions of Southern Scotland*.

Two years later, his first novel *Trespass*, a romantic Highland tale, was published.

Even during WWII, when he served as an artillery officer, stationed in East Anglia, he wrote five books. After the war he took up writing full-time and during a prolific career, published more than 130 books, the most famous being the Robert the Bruce trilogy published between 1969 and 1971.

Tranter not only wrote about Scotland but covered other topics including the American West under the pen-name Nye Tredgold.

But his greatest passion was always Scotland. He was inspirational in reclaiming the 'Stone of Destiny' from Westminster Abbey and also campaigned for the construction of the Forth Road Bridge.

Tranter continued writing until his death in January 2000.

Two months earlier, on his 90th birthday, Ray Bradfield's biography *Nigel Tranter: Scotland's Storyteller* was published.

Wilson, Scottie (1888-1972)

Many artists struggle all their working lives to gain some recognition for their work but one Glaswegian found international acclaim almost by accident.

Born in 1888, Scottie Wilson spent the first few decades of his adult working life as a street vendor in Glasgow and also further afield in London and Toronto, Canada. His schooling had been limited and he had never learned to read or write but by the age of 40 he discovered he had an interest in painting and drawing. Using a highly imaginary style he started to produce a whole range of images mostly of fish, birds and trees. His unique and somewhat surreal style began to attract the attention of many influential people in the art world including Picasso who found great favour in Wilson's work.

Wilson went on to exhibit his work not only with other artists but also had many successful individual shows for the remainder of his working life. In 1965, his drawings and paintings had achieved such popular appeal that he was given a very special commission. World famous porcelain manufacturers Royal Worcester invited him to incorporate his distinctive designs into their high quality coffee, tea and dinner ware.

Scottie Wilson died in 1972 and today his works of art are highly sought after by collectors. His work can be seen on display all over the world including the Scottish National Gallery of Modern Art, the Tate Gallery, the Museum of Modern Art, New York, and the National Museum of Canada.

Street Characters
Blind Alick
Blind Alick is probably the most famous of all the Glasgow street characters. His real name was Alexander McDonald.

His father was from Inverness but he was born in Kirkoswald, between Penrith and Carlisle, in 1771. As a child he learned to read and write but he was permanently blinded after contracting smallpox. However, he had a good ear for music and developed a musical gift for playing the flute and fiddle, which would help support him financially throughout his life.

In 1790 he arrived in Glasgow where he settled down and eventually married a capable and caring woman by the name of Mary McPherson. They had three sons, two of whom died at an early age. The third survived through childhood only to be killed while fighting with the 71st regiment of the Glasgow Highland Light Infantry in Spain.

Blind Alick's musical skill was much in demand, plying his trade on the streets by day while in the evenings he was a popular choice for weddings and other social functions.

It was in Glasgow that he was given his nickname.

During the early 1820s he became a friend of the social reformer and founder of the Free Church of Scotland, Dr Thomas Chalmers, who was his patron for a time. But Blind Alick was very fond of the bottle and often took payment for his work in drams.

However, despite his hard life and heavy drinking, he lived to the ripe old age of 59, passing away peacefully in hospital.

Bob Dragon
The most unique of all the street characters in Glasgow was Bob Dragon. Unlike any of the other colourful individuals that became famous on the streets of the city, he was neither beggar, musician nor trader. He was actually one of the richest men in Scotland.

His real name was Robert Dreghorn of Ruchill. He inherited his title from his father, also Robert, and his wealth from his uncle, Alan, the architect who built St Andrew's Church and the old Town Hall, attached to the Tolbooth, during the 1730s.

Alan also built arguably the most lavish mansion in the city, on Clyde Street close to Carrick Quay where modern luxury flats now stand.

This mansion and all the money was left to young Robert by the brothers who had always strived to create a great dynastic family in Glasgow.

Robert was no good at business and had no real interests except to live off his inheritance. He took to swaggering up and down the Plainstanes at Glasgow Cross and thought himself a great ladies' man.

Unfortunately he was remarkably ugly, having a badly-marked face, crooked features and was wall-eyed, which gave rise to his nickname of Bob Dragon. He also had no head for conversation so took to following pretty girls around and leering ingratiatingly at them. His advances were always declined and were often followed by laughter. He eventually became withdrawn and morose due to his lack of success with the fair sex and committed suicide in 1806.

Feea

One of the street characters who was truly a person of the streets of Glasgow was Feea.

He was born in the Stockwell area of the city around the turn of the 19th century. Feea was brought up in a very poor but honest household but when he was still only five years old both his parents died and he was left to fend for himself. From this early age he reverted almost back to nature, sleeping in stairwells and door steps. His diet was mainly worms, insects and any edible rubbish that had been thrown away but he managed to grow up to be a fit and healthy young man. These hardships however, resulted in a regression to idiocy which resulted in him being a simple and passive fellow if unprovoked. And despite his ragged appearance, he was well liked by Glaswegians. A great animal lover, he could always be seen with at least one dog wagging its tail as it followed him through the streets.

Feea scraped together a meagre living by offering to clean the clothes of the well-to-do citizens as they strolled through the dirty roads and lanes. However, he sometimes helped the clothes to get dirty by spitting and throwing mud at them when the wearer was otherwise distracted. Not altogether an honest living, but harmless enough in its way.

Feea eventually disappeared and was never seen or heard of again. It was popularly believed that he had tragically met his end with the Resurrectionists.

Hawkie

Hawkie was one of the best known characters that roamed the streets of the city during the early 19th century.

Born William Cameron in St Ninian's near Stirling in 1790, while still a young boy, his right leg was badly twisted and he spent the rest of his life on crutches. His family was very poor but managed to send him to school and when he left, he was apprenticed to a tailor. But he could not stick to anything for long and wandered around Scotland and northern England undertaking a variety of jobs, including teaching, mending china, making toys and was even a member of a group of travelling actors. He eventually settled in Glasgow in his late 20s where he received his nickname.

Hawkie (later Old Hawkie) earned most of his money by hawking 'chap' literature (a chapman literally means a pedlar) around the streets. As well as selling the chap-book pamphlets containing ballads and stories, he was not averse to speaking his mind on the issues of the day to anyone who would listen. On one occasion he expressed disdain at the number of Irish immigrants in Glasgow, complaining that they were depriving Glaswegians of the use of their own jails.

And after spending many months in the Town's Hospital in Clyde Street, he told the gathered crowd that he had not gone off and died and was now in a lot better shape than most of them.

In 1851, Old Hawkie became ill and died in hospital.

'Hirstling' Kate

One of the most unfortunate of all the well-known street characters in Glasgow during the early years of the 19th century was 'Hirstling' Kate.

In a time when crippling deformity was a common enough site, this poor woman painted a truly tragic picture. Her appearance was extremely coarse, dirty and ragged. She earned her nickname from the manner by which she was forced to propel herself along the dirt-strewn cobbled streets between the merchant city and the River Clyde. Her crippled and deformed legs were almost completely useless. Therefore she 'hirstled' herself along the streets, using her hands in which she held boards with spikes on the underside to provide grip.

As her entire life was spent almost at ground level she was able to see and pick up all manner of objects. She gathered anything from scraps of food to pins and pennies and in this way managed to scrape together a meagre living. And around her neck hung an old shoe on a piece of string which kindly passers-bye would fill with drinking water from the city's water pumps. But despite her pathetic existence she was not a beggar and was a familiar favourite among many people in the city, especially the children.

She had a great store of old ballads and verses which she would sing to the youngsters, who in return, would attach a pin to her dress by way of payment. When 'Hirstling' Kate passed away she was laid to rest in the Cathedral kirkyard.

Jamie Blue

Jamie Blue was one of the great street preachers and vendors on the streets of Glasgow in the early part of the 19th century.

His real name was James McIndoe.

The year of his birth is uncertain. However, he was certainly brought up from an early age in Pollokshaws which at that time was a well known industrial area, specially for its production of patterned cloth, paper and iron. McIndoe started adult life as a soldier with the 71st regiment of the Glasgow Highland Light Infantry but when he was drummed out of the army, he took up street vending to make a living. He became well known for dealing in all kinds of hardware, domestic goods and even leeches.

He derived the popular nickname Jamie Blue from another product that he sold readily on the streets – indigo coloured buttons which stained his hands. He also became a popular street singer between Glasgow and Paisley and the poems that he wrote, especially around election time, earned him another nickname – the Shaws Poet.

One of his biggest rivals in Glasgow was Hawkie (William Cameron) who was born in St Ninian's near Stirling in 1790 but had settled in Glasgow in the 1820s.

For many years McIndoe claimed that Hawkie had stolen his rightful position as Glasgow's unofficial head speech crier. McIndoe died in the old Govan Poorhouse in 1837, which at that time was located in the former Cavalry Barracks in Eglinton Street on the south side of the city.

Old Malabar

One of Glasgow's most popular street entertainers during the 19th century was Old Malabar. His nickname had nothing to do with the south-western tip of India but came from his manner of dress, brightly coloured Oriental style robes.

Patrick Feeny, the son of a poor farmer, was born in Sligo, Ireland, in February 1800. A huge man, well over 6ft, he worked his passage to Liverpool where he learned his trade from a Chinese juggler.

He spent many years travelling the length and breadth of the country, making his first appearance in Glasgow during the Fair of 1822. Unlike most of the street performers in the city at that time, Old Malabar was neither a singer nor played any musical instrument to attract his audience. He also stood out in that he was neither a beggar nor, as was the case with many others, mad or eccentric.

Juggling and sword swallowing were his warm-up acts but what most people paid to see was his finale. As the crowd grew in number, he would announce 'one penny more and up goes the ball'. When the coin had been donated, he would produce a huge lead ball. After making sure his audience was satisfied of its weight, he would toss it in the air and catch it in a large leather cup tied by a leather band to his forehead.

He rarely missed although a large scar and a flattened nose testified to a few failures. Old Malabar died in November 1883.

Penny-a-Yard

The most industrious of all the street vendors in Glasgow during the 19th century was Edward Finlay.

He was born around 1800. Little is known of his early life but by the second half of the century he was selling his wares between the Spoutmouth and the railway bridge in the Gallowgate area of the city. Finlay was a wire-worker and was capable of making lengths of chain at a remarkable speed from a long coil of brass wire he had slung over one shoulder. When the chain was completed he would transfer it to his other shoulder and continue with the next chain.

His favourite call to attract new customers was 'Penny-a-Yard', the price of his work and the nickname he became known by. As well as chains, Penny-a-Yard was also skilled at making puzzles out of the wire that proved very popular with children and adults alike. However, the most remarkable thing about Finlay was that he was a cripple and both his hands were badly deformed.

Still his skill as a craftsman made him one of the most sought-after vendors in the area. He was an amiable and well liked man when sober but whilst under the influence Finlay became very quick-tempered, especially with the police. He managed to accumulate more than 100 charges against him for abusing officers, although it never came to anything more than verbal.

Finlay lived to a great age and is believed to have been in his 80s when he died.

Rab Ha'

A legend in his own lunch time, 'Rab Ha' the Glesca Glutton' was not actually born in Glasgow at all, but in Paisley.

Robert Hall, also known as Rough Rab, was born in Paisley in the early 19th century before moving to the city where his tremendous eating habits made him famous. He would sometimes walk back to Paisley, stopping at a farm on the way to consume porridge served in a bin usually reserved for feeding calves. But his favourite eating haunts were to be found at the Cross and Saltmarket where he was regarded a hero by the youth of the day. It was here where two famous bets were made.

On one occasion, his challenge was to consume four large beefsteak pies, three chickens and seven pounds of potatoes that he washed down with six tankards of strong ale. This was a light snack, however, compared to his most famous act of gluttony.

Some friends challenged him to eat a whole calf at one sitting.

In the form of veal pies, the feast was laid out for his arrival on the night of the bet. As he was about to eat the last one, he turned to his friends to ask where the calf was, thinking the pies only a starter before the bet began.

Not surprisingly, he was found dead in 1843, in a hayloft in Hutchesontown, having eaten himself to death.

Theatres

The first theatre in Glasgow was built in 1764 on the present day site of Central Station. But like many theatres it was burnt down by self-righteous mobs. Acting, especially for women, was considered scandalous and thespians often had to be escorted to and from the venues.

In 1805, the first Theatre Royal, the largest theatre outside London, was built at Exchange Square. It was the first in the country to be lit by gaslight but was later burned down.

In 1845, despite public protest, Britain's largest theatre, the City Theatre, seating 5000, was built on Glasgow Green but its over-ambitious size led to its closure a few months later.

In the 1800s, during the Glasgow Fair, small booths called 'Penny Geggies' staged short plays and launched careers for stars like Will Fyffe.

Many permanent theatres, like the Britannia at 115 Trongate were reached by a stairway. It was bought by the eccentric A.E. Pickard and re-named the Panopticon – it is Glasgow's oldest remaining theatre. Forgotten about for many years, a dedicated group are now hoping to restore it to its former glory. In 1878, Her Majesties Theatre opened in the Gorbals. It became the Royal Princesses Theatre and is now the Citizen's Theatre. Next door was the Palace Music Hall, opened in 1906, with its famed Elephant's Head boxes now displayed at London's theatre museum.

The only theatre in the West End, was the old Empress Theatre at St George's Cross, Glaswegians preferring the city centre and southside venues, unlike Londoners and their favoured West End.

Citizen's
The Citizen's Theatre has always held a special place in Glaswegian hearts because many of its productions reflect the everyday life of the population past and present.

Established in 1943, the Citizen's Company started putting on performances with a Scottish theme at the Old Athenaeum Theatre, Buchanan Street. The brainchild of famous Scottish playwright, James Bridie, their first production was his own *Holy Isle*. He realised early on that their strength lay in tapping into the huge local acting talent in Scotland. Over the years the company has seen great stars including Fulton Mackay, Roddy McMillan and Iain Cuthbertson pass through the company's doors.

In 1945 the Citizen's moved to new premises, taking a 10-year lease at the Royal Princesses Theatre in the Gorbals, built in 1878.

At the end of the lease Glasgow Corporation bought the premises and rented it back to them.

During the 1960s the theatre was losing its appeal but under new direction, the latest Citizen's Company formed in 1970 and has broadened its appeal to encompass a more European flavour.

In 1978 the theatre underwent major renovations changing not only the exterior of the building but the inside as well.

Today it has a main 600-seat theatre and two smaller ones.

The company has performed around 300 productions which include more than 20 world premieres and 30 Christmas shows. The cast are paid the same regardless of their own theatrical standing and over the years they have established a worldwide reputation.

Empire
The Empire Theatre opened in Sauchiehall Street in 1897 on the site of an earlier theatre, the Gaity, which had been demolished the year before.

It was designed by Frank Matcham, the greatest and most prolific Victorian theatre architect, who also built the Kings in Glasgow as well as the Hippodrome and the London Palladium.

It was originally called the Glasgow Empire Palace and could seat more than 1600.

Right from the start it gained a good reputation and quickly drew more and more of the bigger and better variety performers of the day. Its owners,

Moss Empires, closed it in 1930 for enlarging and reopened it as the Empire the following year, at a cost of £250,000, now with a capacity for 2000 people.

Its popularity eventually made it the city's top variety performance venue, attracting major stars not only from England but the US as well. Among these were the great Tony Hancock and Morecambe and Wise. The duo soon found out why the theatre had the reputation of being the English comic's grave. Their first two performances were met with complete silence. It was only during their third that they received sporadic applause from an audience that grudgingly accepted they were getting value for money.

As with most theatres in Glasgow, the Empire's demise came with the increasing popularity of the cinema and television.

It closed its doors in 1963. The following year the magnificent theatre was replaced by a modern concrete office block called Empire House.

Five Past Eight Show
Glasgow audiences have never suffered fools gladly and earned the city the nickname 'the graveyard' after the many would-be comedians and performers who died on stage there. One show that met their whole-hearted approval, however, was the *Five Past Eight Show*, produced by Howard and Wyndham as summer shows prior to the pantomime season.

In 1937 the first *Five Past Eight Show* – named after curtain up time – appeared at the famous Alhambra theatre. From the beginning it was hugely successful and although it spent a few months in Edinburgh, Glasgow was its spiritual home. It was so popular that many groups of people went there to celebrate birthdays, anniversaries and wedding guests would round off the happy day there.

There were glamorous showgirls, singers and variety acts but one act in particular was to become a national institution in its own right.

Francie and Josie was created by Stanley Baxter who originally starred alongside Rikki Fulton but later Jack Milroy took over Baxter's part. The much-loved duo retained a great sense of family humour and fun and their act alone would have filled the house.

In later years the Starlight Room was introduced for the Grand finale.

Featuring magical lighting effects, revolving stages and staircases, it became more and more spectacular until it equalled the London Palladium's splendour. The *Five Past Eight Show* came to an end in the late 60s with the growth in popularity of television.

The King's Theatre
The King's Theatre at the lower end of Bath Street is one of the few major theatre buildings left in Glasgow.

Among the many famous people that have appeared there are Ricki Fulton, Jack Milroy, Harry Lauder, Jack Buchanan, Sarah Bernhardt and Laurence Olivier. However, it is also well known for opening its doors to amateur groups. Every year it allows several companies and societies the unique opportunity to stage their own productions in its magnificent 2000-seat theatre. It was opened for the first time in 1904 having taken more than three years to build.

The King's was designed by Frank Matcham, described as the greatest and most prolific of all the Victorian theatre architects.

Among his many creations were the Hippodrome and the London Palladium. The King's was built for the famous touring company house of Howard and Wyndham.

Today it is the only one of Matcham's Glasgow theatres still being used for its original purpose. His Coliseum on Eglinton Street has long been a bingo hall and the Olympia Theatre in Bridgeton was a cinema, then a bingo hall and is now a carpet warehouse.

When the King's first opened it was the premiere venue for touring companies in the country. But over the years it has become a major stage for a wide variety of theatrical styles. It was the first home of Scottish Opera in 1962 and has also hosted shows ranging from stand-up comedy to musicals and is famous for its lavishly spectacular annual pantomimes.

Metropole

The Metropole Theatre played host to some of the world's greatest stars. The first Metropole opened in Stockwell Street in 1897, taking over the Scotia Music Hall which had been established in 1862.

Sir Harry Lauder, who had made early amateur appearances at the Scotia became a regular patron of the Metropole in recognition of the opportunities it had given him. But the most famous international star to learn his trade on the Metropole stage was Arthur Stanley Jefferson, whose first stage appearance was at the Panoptican in 1906. His father, Arthur, manager of the Metropole, then let him appear on his stage using the stage name Stan Laurel for the first time.

The classic Glaswegian comedian Tommy Morgan spent much of his career at the Metropole becoming its principal comedian from the 20s to the 50s.

From the 1930s the well-known Glasgow theatrical family, the Logans, ran the theatre until it burned down in 1961. The following year the New Metropole was opened by Alex Fruitin, taking over the failed Falcon Theatre arts centre in St George's Road, which had originally been the West End Playhouse in 1913. And in 1964, the theatre was purchased by the most famous member of the Logan family, Jimmy, who sadly died from cancer in 2001. For years he struggled to keep the theatre going but never managed to make a great success of the place. It lay empty for many years before being demolished to make way for modern brick flats in 1989.

Pavilion

The Pavilion Theatre is the last venue in Glasgow to maintain the variety show traditions that made the city so famous during the middle of the 20th century.

It is also one of the few theatres that survives purely on its own merits, receiving no funding from the Scottish Arts Council or other bodies that support more high-brow entertainment. The Pavilion was built in a French Renaissance style between 1902 and 1904 by architect Bertie Crewe but its shiny yellow terracotta exterior has dulled with years of cleaning.

It first opened its doors as the Palace of Varieties in February 1904 and since then it has seen some of the greatest of Scotland's live acts tread its boards. Pantomime was what first made the theatre a huge success, with its long running shows in the 30s starring the likes of Harry Gordon and Dave Willis. The 40s saw a cult following develop for Bridgeton-born Tommy Morgon in his long running summer series and by the 60s and 70s it was the turn of Lex McLean and Jack Milroy to continue the great theatre's traditions.

Not just a variety hall, it attracted established and up-and-coming stars from all walks of show business, including Billy Connolly, Andy Cameron, Lena Zavaroni and Sydney Devine.

During the early 80s the theatre was in serious financial trouble but it pulled through and continues to draw huge crowds through its doors, perpetuating its role as one of the best loved theatres in the country.

Queen's

The famous Queen's Theatre, unlike the majority in Glasgow, prided itself on being in the east end. So much so that well-to-do patrons in dinner jackets were heavily frowned upon, this not being what the management regarded as its true audience.

Established in Watson Street during the 1870s, it was known by many names, including the Star Music Hall, People's Picture Palace of Amusements and Pringle's Picture Palace. And from 1918 it was the Queen's Variety Theatre.

It reached its height, drawing crowds from all over Glasgow, just before, during and after WWI. Its greatest attraction was the pantomimes, which were very funny and often very rude.

The stars were Sam Murray, always a dame called Fanny Cartwright, regardless of the story, and Doris Droy, regarded as the Gracie Fields of Glasgow. Doris' husband, Frank Droy, who also starred, wrote all the productions. However, the police were unhappy with the shows content and insisted the scripts be vetted by the Lord Chamberlain. The problem was that Frank Droy always wrote his scripts in a school jotter, in pencil, caring neither for neatness nor grammar and writing in the broadest Glaswegian vernacular. And no matter what the story was, the principal boy was always called Colin.

Each year the pantomimes got ruder but the Lord Chamberlain continued to pass them, quite possibly because nobody outwith Glasgow could understand them and take offence. Sadly, this great tradition came to an end in 1952 when the building was burned to the ground.

Theatre Royal

The first Theatre Royal in Glasgow opened in Dunlop Street in the late 18th century. After a short lived success, it was sold off and a group of wealthy merchants bought the letter-patent for the name and opened the Theatre Royal, Queen Street, in 1805. It also failed and was destroyed by fire in 1829.

The old Dunlop Street venue bought back its original title and re-opened its doors but had to be rebuilt after a fire in 1840. Nine years later another fire resulted in 65 deaths, Glasgow's worst theatrical disaster. In 1863 another fire almost totally destroyed the building. It was rebuilt the following year only to be bought and consumed within St Enoch's Railway Station in 1869.

To the north of the city the Bayliss's Coliseum Theatre and Opera House had opened at the top of Hope Street two years previously.

It became the Theatre Royal by royal charter in 1869, the patent system having been removed in the 1840s. In 1879, it too was totally destroyed by fire and was rebuilt by architect Charles John Phipps. It reopened the following year but in 1895 was again destroyed by fire. Phipps rebuilt it using the remaining shell and it reopened in the same year. In 1956 it was sold to Scottish Television but the interior was partly burned by fire in 1970.

Two years later the building was sold and in 1975 the magnificent 1555 seat auditorium opened as the new permanent home for Scottish Opera.

Tron Theatre

The site of the Tron Theatre today incorporates the second oldest secular building still standing in Glasgow. Built in 1485, the church fell into disrepair after the Reformation but was rebuilt in 1586.

The square tower was added in 1592 and the steeple by 1631 but the church was burned to the ground in 1793, leaving only the steeple intact. A new church of very plain design was constructed in its place soon after and further additions were made to it in the 19th century.

The church ceased to be a place of worship in 1946 but in 1980, the Glasgow Theatre Club, which was founded in 1978, took over the premises. In 1981 the company, which had changed its name to the Tron Theatre Club, gave its first performance in the Victorian bar with its old fashioned gantry rescued from a disused pub in Govan.

The club's membership grew to more than 5,000 but by the end of the 1980s it started to operate as a public theatre under its present name.

Over the years it strived to become a major theatrical centre for contemporary local writers and actors to present their work.

The Tron Theatre has played host to many home grown stars during their formative years including Siobhan Redmond, Robbie Coltrane and Liz Lochhead, to name just a few. Today it has become one of the most respected venues in the country for Scottish and international productions, providing exciting new works not catered for in other venues.

Choirs
Orpheus Choir

Glasgow is the home of one of the best known choirs in the country, the Phoenix Choir, created after the world famous Orpheus Choir decided to call it a day.

The Orpheus originated from a working-men's choral group, the Toynbee Musical Association, in 1901 which took on a young undertaker to be their conductor. His name was Hugh Roberton.

Born in Glasgow in 1874, Roberton was self taught but was to become one of the greatest composers and conductors of hymn tunes in the world.

In 1906, the choral group changed their name to the Orpheus and by the end of its career, spanning nearly half a century, they had achieved international recognition.

Much of the credit must go to Roberton who expanded the group's repertoire away from the traditional favourites, writing and arranging many of their new songs. His skilful technique of organising the singers and bringing a special mix to the tunes they sang was the envy of all other choral groups.

Many tried to achieve the Orpheus style but none could master Roberton's conducting and the unique arrangements created for his choir. They made many recordings, their most famous being 'All in the April Evening' which became a bestseller all over the world and is still requested today. In 1931, Roberton was knighted in recognition of his contribution to music.

The Orpheus disbanded in 1951, one year before Roberton's death but many members of the choir continued, setting up the Phoenix Choir which continues to this day.

Phoenix Choir

The Glasgow Phoenix choir almost literally rose from the ashes of the city's internationally renowned choir of the early 20th century – The Orpheus Choir.

The Orpheus had been formed in 1906 from the working-men's Toynbee Musical Association by its conductor Glasgow-born Hugh Roberton. Roberton brought a unique style to choral music which many other conductors and composers tried to emulate with little success. However, the Orpheus decided to disband after 45 years but 83 of its members decided they wanted to continue as a choral group. With the consent of Roberton, who became their honorary president, they founded the Phoenix Choir with the aim of continuing the excellent traditions of its predecessor.

Since its formation it has remained at the forefront of choral music in Scotland and has established its own international reputation.

Not only does it perform old and new Scottish songs throughout Britain, Europe and North America but it has extended its repertoire over the years with musical styles ranging from Opera to folk and chamber to highly popular musical scores.

Apart from live performances, the choir has produced more than 26 recordings and has appeared regularly on radio and television.

It promotes and encourages young people to take an interest in choral music and has established a scholarship programme for students at the Royal Scottish Academy of Music and Drama in Glasgow.

A charity organisation with a membership in excess of 100, it has raised more than £1million for worthy charities since its creation half a century ago.

Other Entertainment Venues
Cinemas

Glaswegians have always been mad about the cinema, so much so that in 1939 the city boasted the highest number of seats per capita anywhere in the world.

Glasgow's moving picture fascination started in 1896 at the Ice Skating Palace on Sauchiehall Street. Within a year music halls like the Coliseum, the Alhambra and Pickard's Panoptican were incorporating 'films' into their weekly entertainment.

Glasgow's first purpose-built cinema was Sauchiehall Street's Electric Theatre which opened its doors in 1910. By the start of WWII the Associated British Cinemas, ABC, had established more than 400 cinemas in Scotland alone.

Cinemas were big business and no matter where you lived, there were at least two cinemas within a 10-minute walk. Glaswegians also went to the cinema more, exceeding 50 times a year compared to the Scottish average of about 30.

Going to the cinema then was very different from today. Shows ran continuously throughout the afternoon and evening and had a Saturday morning children's matinee. As well as a main feature there were also trailers, cartoons, a news reel and a 'B' movie.

But as society changed after the war, with TV becoming more accessible and popular and film-makers making less films for children and families, the huge cinema culture declined.

Of the 114 Glasgow cinemas, less than 40 remain today, with only a handful still showing films, the rest now mostly Bingo halls.

However cinemas have made a comeback with the new multiplexes enticing a new generation 'going to the pictures'.

Dance Halls

Glasgow has always been dancing mad and there was once more dance halls per person than in any other UK city. And for many years they were famous for the best dancing standards.

People came from all over Scotland to the city's ballrooms and for many it was where they met their life-long partners as it was one of the few places both sexes could meet. Big venues could hold more than 1000 people and attracted the top Big Bands. Famous names included the Locarno, Barrowlands, Albert, Dennistoun Palais, Green's Playhouse, the universities and also many smaller halls all over Glasgow.

Or if you had a car, there was always The Moorings at Largs. The south side's Plaza was famous for its fountain and many 21st birthday parties and other functions were held there. No alcohol was available and with little late night transport dancing started early.

Even on Saturdays they shut before midnight because of the Sabbath.

Men dressed in shirts and ties and women put on their best dresses.

As the ability to dance was very important, standards were high.

There were several dancing schools in the city, the most famous being Roger and Alice McEwan's and Warrens.

Gentlemen escorted their partners on and off the floor although the usual opening line 'Where do you live' was to find out how far men would have to travel after they had taken their 'lumber' home.

The beginning of the end for ballrooms began in the 60s with the coming of rock and roll.

Kelvin Hall

Today, the Kelvin Hall hosts many of Scotland's major indoor athletics events, but the hall has been transformed many times since it was first built.

In the west end of Glasgow, in 1918, a hall was constructed to form part of the Board of Trade's annual British Industries Fair. Built of wood, metal being restricted during the war, it was sited next to a munitions's factory opposite the Art Galleries. After the war, the city corporation merged factory and hall to house larger exhibitions but it burnt down in July 1925. Two years later, King George V re-opened the beautifully rebuilt red sandstone Kelvin Hall, resurrecting it from the ashes.

It continued as a trade, sport and exhibition hall until WWII, when it was converted into a factory making barrage balloons for the nation's defences.

In 1955, evangalist, Billy Graham preached his 'All Scotland Crusade' to audiences of 14,000 in its hall.

The Kelvin Hall also became the home of the magical Christmas Carnival and Circus, an annual treat enjoyed by thousands of families for many years.

But in 1971, the huge arena was transformed and refurbished into a conference and entertainment centre, at a cost of £500,000.

However by 1988, the Scottish Exhibition and Conference Centre had taken over as the main entertainment venue for Glasgow.

The Kelvin Hall was revamped into the present day sports arena and also houses the vast Transport Museum collection, that for many years had been crammed into a much smaller hall in Pollokshields.

Scottish Exhibition and Conference Centre

The largest exhibition centre in Scotland is the SECC in Glasgow.

It is also the third largest in Britain after the NEC and Earl's Court.

Just a mile outside the city centre, the SECC is also the biggest visitor atraction in Scotland, with more than 1.5 million people passing through its doors every year.

Covering 64 acres on the northern bank of the River Clyde, it was built to replace the Kelvin Hall as the city's major venue.

Plans started for the construction of the centre in 1983 after it was decided to use the in-fill land on the site of the old Queen's Dock, which had been constructed in the 1870s but closed in 1969.

It cost £36million to build and was opened in 1985 although it would be another two years before the entire complex was completed.

Such was the success of the venue in its first year that it was voted the best in the world by readers of the magazine *Conferences and Exhibitions International*.

Over the years the five halls have hosted every conceivable type of show, ranging from pop stars, opera, the European Summer Special Olympic Games (1990) and the famous indoor Christmas Carnival, Europe's largest.

In 1991 Bryan Adams performed in Hall 4, Britain's largest all-standing concert venue, to a packed audience of 12,000. And six years later, the SECC was complemented by the strangest piece of architecture in Glasgow – the 3000-seat Clyde Auditorium, affectionately known as the Armadillo.

St Andrew's Halls

For almost a century, St Andrew's Halls in Glasgow's West End was home to most of Scotland's classical music companies.

It was built between 1873 and 1877 by James Sellars and took up an entire city block. The Halls' main entrance was on Granville Street with its imposing series of four magnificent sculpture groups created by John Mossman. Funded by a private company, the building cost more than £100,000 and contained three major and several minor halls as well as a ballroom. The Grand Hall was by far the largest and could accommodate more than 4,000 people.

The other two main halls were the Berkeley and Kent, named after the streets adjacent to them.

However, by 1890 the owners were financially strapped and were forced to sell to Glasgow Corporation for just under £40,000.

The Halls played host to such companies as the Scottish National Orchestra, Scottish Opera, Scottish Ballet and the BBC Scottish Symphony. But in 1962 the Halls were gutted by fire with only the front exterior facade surviving.

After interior remodelling it is now the entrance to the Mitchell Theatre and James Moir Hall. The rest of the building had to be largely reconstructed. Today it is mainly occupied by the Mitchell Library extension, extending back from the original library, built adjacent to the eastern end of the halls between 1906 and 1911.

For nearly three decades after the fire Glasgow had no large venue for major classical concerts until the Royal Concert Hall opened in 1990.

Clubs and Societies
Boys' Brigade
The Boys' Brigade was founded in Glasgow by a Sunday School teacher in 1883.

William Alexander Smith, an officer in the 1st Lanarkshire Rifle Volunteers, had no trouble controlling the hundred men in his charge but could not control his Sunday School boys. He realised they needed some disciple and structure to their lives and activities.

On October 4, 1883, at the North Woodside Mission Hall, Smith asked the boys if they would join his Boys' Brigade.

Fifty nine of them volunteered but 24 dropped out as soon as they realised just what the discipline entailed. Therefore, with only 35, Smith formed the 1st Glasgow Company. Establishing discipline and order, the brigade ran camps and other recreational activities.

With strong Christian principles, the brigade's popularity expanded throughout the country by the end of the century and eventually spread worldwide.

Along similar lines, the Boy Scouts was founded in 1908, by Robert Baden-Powell.

In the same year, Allison Cargill formed Glasgow's first Girl Scouts, but within a year, the troop was taken under the wing of the 1st Glasgow Boy Scout Troop. Baden-Powell's plans, like Smith's had never intended girls to join the Scouts. However, by 1909, more than 6,000 girls had enrolled, using initials instead of first names to hide their sex, and he was forced to set up the Girl Guides with his sister.

For many years to follow, Girl Guide activities were reduced to domestic activities, preparing them for motherhood, in keeping with Edwardian values of the day.

Glasgow School
The Glasgow School – more famously known as The Glasgow Boys – was a group of about 20 artists who exhibited together in the 1880s and '90s. They were not all Scottish but they were all connected through Glasgow School of Art.

Their landscape and portrait painting was influenced by some of the great European artists but they had no desire to make any revolutionary statement.

They merely wanted to break from the conventional style of the day.

Only a handful of the 20 artists became individually well known.

Greenock-born James Guthrie achieved international recognition for his landscape realism but later became a highly successful society portrait painter.

As president of the Royal Scottish Academy he helped improve the conditions and facilities in Scotland's national galleries. He and Edward Arthur Walton, formed the nucleus of the Glasgow Boys and they persuaded Glasgow Art Gallery to purchase the famous Whistler portrait of Scottish Historian Thomas Carlyle

George Henry, born in Irvine, painted *A Galloway Landscape* and working with Australian-born Edward Hornel, *The Druids Bringing Home the Mistletoe*. They travelled to Japan in 1893, influencing their subsequent oriental decorative style.

John Lavery from Belfast, became a great portraitist like Guthrie.

Studying for a time in Europe, he met famous artist, Bastien-Lepage whose work influenced much of the Glasgow Boys style. Lavery was commissioned to paint Queen Victoria's visit to Glasgow's International Exhibition in 1888.

At its height, more than 600 Glasgow Boys paintings were on display around the world.

Hellfire Club

One of Glasgow's most historically notorious societies was the Hellfire Club. It was one of many such clubs that had sprung up throughout Britain since the founder society was established in the ruins of Medmenham Abbey in Buckinghamshire in 1745.

The Hellfire clubs mocked organized religion and were supposedly involved in debauchery and carrying out blasphemous black masses.

Many clubs later adhered to the radical ideas of the revolutionary philosopher Thomas Paine, who had fled to Paris after committing the treasonable act of supporting the French Revolution (1789).

Whether the Glasgow branch bothered with such practices is questionable but its members, mostly well-to-do young gentlemen, enjoyed getting up to mischief at society's expense.

It was their custom to dress themselves and their horses in white robes and charge through Glasgow at night and imprison any night watchman they could find under his own sentry box.

One night in 1793 they sheltered in the session-house of the 1485 collegiate Church of St Mary and St Ann at Glasgow Cross, where the city's night guard always left a fire burning.

They built up the fire as high as they could to test each others' ability to endure heat, preparing themselves for the rigours of the afterlife, no doubt. But the fire soon raged out of control and the young men fled. The session-house and church burned to the ground.

But the square tower (1592) and its steeple (1631), modelled on the Cathedral's, survived and remain today as one of Glasgow's most historic relics.

Western Club

Unlike many clubs in Glasgow over the last couple of hundred years, the Western Club has lasted longer than the life of its founder. The origins of the club date to 1825 when a Major Monteith founded the Badger Club. Its name was later changed to the Western Club and like many others met regularly in Glasgow's pubs and taverns.

However, unlike other clubs, the Western decided to build its own meeting place in which its members could relax and enjoy their wining and dining in peace and comfort.

The club appointed the famous Glasgow architect David Hamilton to design the building at the corner of Buchanan and St Vincent streets. Work started in 1839 and was completed by 1842 in an Italianate design – one of the first of many buildings in this style to be erected in the city centre in the years that followed.

The club which had been meeting on the south-western corner of the crossing moved diagonally across to the north-east corner to their permanent home.

Since then many other clubs have amalgamated with the Western, including the Junior Club, New Club and ladies' Kelvin Club. As well as social functions for its members, the club also provides business and conference facilities today. However, the club eventually sold up and now meets nearby at 32 Royal Exchange Square.

Between 1968 and 1972, the club's elaborately decorated interior was gutted for conversion to offices and its beautiful exterior has been obscured by a thick protective layer.

CHAPTER 4
Food and Drink

Food and Drink
Auchentoshan distillery
The Auchentoshan distillery is the last remaining Lowland distillers on the West Coast of Scotland. Situated in the Kilpatrick Hills to the north of Glasgow, it was founded in 1800 and uses the waters from nearby Loch Cochno for its whisky production.

Auchentoshan also has its own unique distilling process. It is the only distillery in the country that still uses a triple distillation process.

All other manufacturers use a process that only distils the whisky twice. Originally triple distillation was used by all Lowland distillers to mature the whisky faster.

In the mid 1800s almost every Lowland town had its own distillery.

But today only Auchentoshan and the Glenkinchie distillery, just outside Edinburgh, have survived the changes in the whisky industry.

During the 1870s, higher quality, more sophisticated blended whiskies were introduced and started to become very popular.

Lowland Distillers moved their main production away from malt whisky, using their own malts primarily for the manufacture of blended whiskies. They have always been a lighter and dryer spirit than the heavier, more individual tasting Highland varieties, making them ideal for blending.

Auchentoshan was almost entirely re-built after WWII and by 1974 it was re-equipped. Ten years later Stanley P. Morrison & Co [now Morrison Bowmore (Distillers) Ltd] bought it, adding it to their existing Highland and Islay operations.

Today more than 190,000 bottles of Auchentoshan malt (from 10 to 31 years old) and three and a half million bottles of their Rob Roy blended whisky are sold annually.

Babbity Bowster
Babbity Bowster in Blackfriar's Street in the Merchant City is all that remains of the once splendid street designed by Robert and James Adam.

This beautifully unusual building in its present surroundings, was originally built around 1794, on what was then Stirling Street, which had been laid out and planned by John Stirling.

It was originally the location of a Dominican convent which had been built there during the middle of the 13th century – although no trace of it survives today. Of the 18th-century detached five-bay house, very little of the original structure remains today. The impressive tripartite Roman Doric doorway is original but the top storey and pediment are not. They were faithfully reconstructed in the original style by Nicholas Groves-Raines and Tom Laurie Associates between 1984 and 1985. Much of the interior has also been maintained in the style of an earlier age and it is today renowned for its friendly atmosphere and its high standard of bar and restaurant meals.

The peculiar name of the establishment comes from the name of a Scottish dance that dates back to the 18th century. 'Babbity' means to bob at and 'bowster' is another word for a bolster or large pillow.

However, the meaning of the words may also conjure up other images when the history of the building is considered.

During the 18th and 19th century many pubs in the city, especially those with upstairs sleeping accommodation such as Babbity Bowster, doubled up as brothels.

Camp coffee

They say that an army marches on its stomach but in Queen Victoria's day, every soldier also needed a drink. 'Camp' was ideal for anyone wanting a quick cuppa in a hurry. Sold in a distinctive, tall, square shaped bottle, the coffee and chicory essence could be instantly added to water, making a delicious drink without the bother of grinding coffee beans.

The creator was R. Paterson and Son, from Glasgow.

Founder, Robert Paterson started in 1849 in Hutchison Street, making pickles and sauces and in 1868, his son, Campbell, joined the company, introducing cordials and fruit wines. But their most famous product was Camp, produced from 1885.

Patented and Trade marked, even the company's workers were sworn to secrecy over the special manufacturing process. Scotland became the top manufacturer of coffee essence and Camp, with its distinctive flavour took the lion's share. A year after the company took over their famous premises in Charlotte Street they exported it all over the British Empire and its dependencies.

The bottle's label depicted a British officer in a kilt being served by an Indian sepoy, creating the perfect image of colonial Britain at that time. However, the company also made sure of the prominence of the drink's origins, adapting the Glasgow Coat of Arms on the rear label of the bottle. It showed St Mungo with a steaming hot cup of Camp coffee along with the ever present company motto 'Ready aye Ready'.

Today, McCormick Foods in Paisley make the famous drink.

Miss Cranston's Tearooms

Coffee shops are all the rage these days but just over a hundred years ago, Glasgow started a new trend in hot drink appreciation, opening the world's first tea-rooms in 1874.

Cranston's Tearooms became a hugely popular institution in the days of alcoholic temperance, and the genteel enterprise of providing Glasgow patrons with afternoon tea continues at the Willow Tearooms on Sauchiehall Street to this day.

Kate Cranston was famously eccentric for wearing crinoline dresses years after they had gone out of fashion. Her sense of style, however was never doubted. Her patronage of the Glasgow Art School designers, Charles Rennie Mackintosh and George Walton, gave the tea-rooms their innovative and iconic interior style. She has always been given sole credit for the tea-room's success, but her acclaim should be shared with her brother.

Stuart Cranston, a connoisseur of quality teas, set up the first shop in the Argyle Arcade in 1874. At the start, tea tasting was free, helping customers to decide which teas to buy. He soon realised that many customers used his shop to meet friends and talk, as much as they did to buy tea. He set out tables and chairs and started to charge for cups of tea and snacks. It was so successful that he eventually went on to own the whole Arcade.

Cranston expanded the brand further, opening a branch on Renfield Street before finally launching the Sauchiehall Street Willow Tea-rooms in 1905.

He died in 1921 and Kate in 1934 but Stuart's right-hand man Robert Cairns continued running the business until after the war, when formica-tabled coffee and snack bars became more dominantly popular.

The original Tearooms in the Argyle Arcade closed in 1954.

Horseshoe Bar

The Horseshoe Bar in Glasgow is one of the oldest in the city and boasts the longest continuous bar in the UK, measuring 104ft 3ins. The building was originally a coach house and stables until its conversion to a public house in 1884. The name of the first proprietor, John W. White, can still be seen etched in the bar's stained glass windows.

The Union Jack panes came from his Whyte's Union Cafe when it was closed in the 1920s. The first manager was horse-mad John Scouler who was responsible for the shape of the bar, the mirrored walls, horse brasses and old photographs still seen today.

The Horseshoe has resisted any refurbishments in its long history, unlike many other pubs that are continually re-invented to attract new customers. Tucked away in Drury Street, it has become a Glasgow institution, where friends meet for a couple of pints before heading home after work. It has also been frequented by many celebrities, from Billy Joel to the late Oliver Reed.

Neil Primrose, drummer of Travis, worked there and practiced with the band on the second floor before they became famous. A permanent display case in the bar includes framed gold and double platinum albums donated by the band on their frequent visits to the Horseshoe.

Its upstairs lounge has attracted some of Glasgow's best Karaoke artistes, including Garry Mullen, who went on to win the Stars In Their Eyes competition as Freddie Mercury in 2000.

Irn Bru

'Your other national drink' and 'Made in Scotland from Girders', the famous catch phrases for Barr's Irn Bru were first introduced in the 1970s. But the professed hangover cure has been around for almost a hundred years.

Robert F. Barr launched the soft drink, manufactured at Parkhead, in 1901, originally labelled 'Iron Brew'. During WWII, as part of the war effort, it was not manufactured because it was not included on the government list allowing production of only six types of soft drinks.

After the war, its future was again challenged with the introduction of new legislation, stating products had to live up to their literal name.

Although Iron Brew contains iron, it is not brewed, so the name was changed in 1946 to IRN-BRU to get around the law.

Advertising has always played a big part in the drink's success, with famous sportsmen like Celtic's Willie Lyon and boxer Benny Lynch promoting its alleged strength, health, and fitness properties.

Ba-Bru and Sandy, the turbaned Indian and kilted Scots boys' adventures, ran in newspaper columns from the '30s into the '70s.

The famous Ba-Bru neon sign above Central Station remained for many years afterwards, until it rusted away and was eventually removed.

Irn Bru's secret ingredient has always been held by two members of the Barr family, rather like the manufacturers of Coca-Cola.

While Coke and Pepsi battle each other for supremacy, Scotland continues to be the only country in the world that favours its own national drink over all others.

Loch Katrine

Loch Katrine became the source for Glasgow's water supply in 1859. Until the early 19th century its citizens used the Clyde and other running water sources for their daily needs.

But as the population swelled so did the urgent need for clean water, especially after the cholera outbreaks of 1832 and 1848.

Many options were tried and some were successful – if only in the short term. Eventually it was decided to use the waters of Loch Katrine. The project received royal assent in 1855 and work started the following year.

To ensure a suitable water capacity, the loch was raised 17ft and increased to 10 miles long by one mile wide – obliterating the Silver Strand celebrated in Sir Walter Scott's Lady of the Lake.

A huge 8ft-diameter underground aqueduct was constructed to transport the water on the 34-mile trip to the north of Glasgow.

Here the water is stored in Mugdock reservoir prior to being piped around the city. However, not long after the reservoir opened it was found to be insufficient for Glasgow's needs. Therefore, an ambitious project was undertaken to pipe additional water to Loch Katrine from neighbouring Loch Arklet and Glen Finglas Reservoir. This was completed in 1885 and increased the daily output from 40 million gallons to 110 million.

A second storage reservoir at Craigmaddie was constructed by 1896 to hold additional water required for the rapidly expanding population during the industrial revolution. Loch Katrine still provides water for the majority of the Greater Glasgow area today.

Tennent's

Whisky has always been considered the national drink in Scotland but this was only really so from the 19th century. Before then, the most commonly consumed drink was beer. As far back as the 6th century, starting with St Mungo's monks, beer has been brewed in Glasgow, making it one of the city's first industries.

Cottage industry home brewers sold round the houses daily and it became the main breakfast drink with tea and coffee being unknown for hundreds of years to come. Gradually, larger breweries took over, and from these humble beginnings, the beer giant Tennent's emerged, starting in 1556.

As a family concern, H and R Tennent brewed near Glasgow Cross for almost 200 years before moving to Drygate. In 1745 Bonnie Prince Charlie and his army drank there. By 1793, Tennent's added new premises at Well Park, at the site where the monks drew water from their well for the original beer.

In 1876 the famous 'T' was launched as their trademark. However, by 1885, German beers were competing with the company's pale ale so they launched their own brand of lager in 1890 which became an instant success. By 1935 the first canned beers were produced, shaped like the old 'Brasso' tins. Proving an instant success, they were eventually replaced by American 'flat' cans in 1954.

The first 'lager lovelies' went on the cans in 1962 and popular advertising has boosted sales ever since. Although part of Bass Brewers, Tennent's still sell more lager than anyone else.

Willow Tea Rooms

The shop that stands out from the variety of other decorated facades in Sauchiehall Street is the Willow Tea Rooms at No 217.

Although the ground floor of this magnificently decorated establishment is now a jewellers, there is still enough of the original artistry to remind the visitor of its grandeur.

It was the last of the four great tea rooms to be created by siblings Kate and Stuart Cranston, who opened the world's first tea-rooms in 1874. From then, tea drinking among middle-class women became an essential part of city life. Kate Cranston opened the Willow Tea Rooms in 1903 in a disused warehouse that had been reconstructed two years before. The design and decoration of the premises were completed the following year by Charles Rennie Mackintosh and his wife. They undertook the whole project rather than share it with George Walton as had happened before.

Fitted out in Mackintosh's distinctive and elegant style, the ground floor was split into two rooms while the most elaborate, balconied Room de Luxe was on the first with its floor-level windows.

In 1919 the tea rooms were sold to another restaurateur, John Smith, and the name was changed to Kensington. It was again sold in 1927 to Daly's department store which fortunately left much of the interior intact. Much of the original artwork, along with faithfully reproduced copies, can still be seen today in the present building, which reopened the Room de Luxe in 1983.

CHAPTER 5
Law and Crime

Criminals
Bible John
The longest, most extensive manhunt in Scottish criminal history involved the serial killer, Bible John, so-called because he is believed to have quoted the scriptures to his victims.

In the late 1960s he stalked Glasgow women and created fear and hysteria, but his identity remains a mystery despite detailed descriptions of him at the time and the advantages of modern forensic science.

All three of his murder victims were young, attractive women who he picked up at the Barrowland Ballroom in the east end between February 1968 and October 1969. They all wore black dresses and were menstruating on the night they were raped and strangled with their own stockings. One theory suggested Bible John killed them because his sexual advances were declined by the menstruating women.

There was little evidence after the first murder but for the second, more than a year later, there were witnesses who had seen the woman strolling home with a man on the fateful night.

An Identikit picture, Scotland's first, was widely published in the press as with the third murder 10 weeks later. She and her sister had shared a taxi with a man calling himself John who quoted from the scriptures. Her sister and the taxi driver gave a detailed description of him as being a well-spoken, smartly-dressed Glaswegian bachelor in his 20s who said he lived with a relative in the Castlemilk area.

But after his third murder, the killings stopped and even with modern-day DNA fingerprinting techniques to follow up recent leads, Bible John has never been found.

Burke and Hare
Burke and Hare, the notorious duo who murdered at least 16 people in Edinburgh may well have learned their trade in Glasgow.

It is believed the two men worked in Glasgow burial grounds before moving to Edinburgh to take up their criminal activities. They were overseen murdering their 16th known victim and Burke was hanged in 1829.

Hare escaped hanging after turning King's evidence, only to die around 1860, a blind beggar on the streets of London.

Their activities were not uncommon in the 18th and 19th centuries, with body snatching being an easy source of fresh bodies for medical research.

At the Necropolis, Glasgow's first cemetery, it was customary at this time for the dead to be entombed in catacombs to try and protect the bodies from being stolen. But by 1832, three years after Burke was hanged, the Anatomy Act was passed, making it easier for the medical profession to obtain corpses for research. This effectively ended the practice of body snatching and with a new belief at this time of burying the dead in sunshine rather than darkened catacombs, places like the Necropolis began to take shape.

The end of body snatching enabled Glasgow's most celebrated citizens to have their last resting places laid out in style, with beautifully sculpted memorials visible to anyone who visits the famous cemetery overlooking the city.

Laurie, John Watson

The person who spent the longest time in a Scottish prison was John Watson Laurie.

Born in Coatbridge in 1864, he became a pattern-maker for one of Glasgow's locomotive engineering works. In 1889, Laurie was jilted by his fiancé after a scandal over money stolen from his workplace. But he was never charged as his family repaid the cash.

He went in search of the woman at the favourite Glaswegian holiday town of Rothesay, on the Island of Bute. Failing, and short on funds, he met up with an Englishman, Edwin Robert Rose, and they decided to take a trip over to Arran. While there, they climbed up Goat Fell.

But Laurie returned alone and was later seen wearing his companion's distinctive hat. Listed missing by relatives, Rose's body was eventually found in a gully below Goat Fell and after an exhaustive search Laurie was found and tried for his murder.

Witnesses claimed to have seen Rose at different times on the fateful day, discrediting Laurie's defense and he was convicted and sentenced to death. However, Laurie's sanity was very much in question resulting in the sentence being commuted to life.

Rather than being sent to a state hospital for the criminally insane he was to spend much of the rest of his life in one of Scotland's toughest prisons at Peterhead. He was eventually transferred to Perth Prison where he died in 1930, having served 40 years and 11 months, the longest anyone has ever been incarcerated in Scotland.

Manuel, Peter

Peter Manuel was one of the most callous murderers Glasgow has ever seen. At the time he was Britain's most prolific killer and could certainly be described as one of the first serial killers.

Born in 1931, he started on a sickening spate of killings from September 1956, resulting in at least eight murders before his arrest in January 1958. He strangled a woman in Mount Vernon, battered another to death in East Kilbride and on two other occasions, he broke into houses and shot everyone inside; three people died at an address in Rutherglen and three more in Uddingston.

As well as a calculating murderer, he also regarded himself to be capable enough to take on the courts single-handedly, having defended himself successfully once before.

He dismissed his own counsel in the third week of his murder trial, electing to defend himself, confident in his abilities to outsmart the legal system again.

He tried to incriminate William Watt, who had not been present at the killing of the three people in the Rutherglen house. His confidence was eventually shaken and he lost his case, and the subsequent appeal. The jury found him guilty of seven of the murders and he was hanged on July 11, 1958. The murder of a Newcastle taxi driver was later attributed to him at an inquest jury.

McLachlan, Jessie

One of Glasgow's most brutal murders of the 19th century has never been solved, despite a woman being found guilty and sentenced to death.

Born in 1834, Jessie McLachlan was accused in July 1862 of using a cleaver to hack 40 times into her friend, Jessie McPherson's body. McPherson was a servant in the West End house of wealthy accountant John Fleming. In July 1862, she was hacked to death with a cleaver, in what appeared to be a frenzied attack.

Fleming's father James who was in the house at the time of the murder was also suspected but subsequently became a chief prosecution witness during the very complicated trial.

Apart from a female's shoe print in the victim's blood, there was little evidence to suggest McLachlan's involvement.

James Fleming, who had been trying to force McPherson to marry him, made statements that were contradicted by other witnesses.

And McLachlan, a compulsive liar, made five contradictory statements before and after the trial.

She was convicted and sentenced to death but a 50,000 signature petition supporting her innocence urged a government inquiry.

A conditional Royal Pardon reduced her sentence to life after she made her fifth statement confessing her guilt, which again contradicted her previous statements.

After 15 years she escaped from Perth prison, using a 'ticket of leave' to see her 18-year-old son and boarded a ship at Greenock for America. She died there from a heart attack in 1899.

James Fleming, however, spent the rest of his life under suspicion for the murder. The real truth behind the murder has never been established.

Ramensky, Johnny

One of Scotland's most famous criminals was the decorated hero, 'Gentle Johnny' Ramensky.

Born into a Lithuanian immigrant family in Glenboig in 1905, Johnny followed his long-dead father's footsteps down the mines at 14, where he first became acquainted with explosives. During the depression, he moved to the Gorbals with his mother and two sisters.

With few legitimate jobs around, he drifted into the criminal career he would make his life. At 18, he went to borstal and then to Barlinnie but in 1942, while serving time in Peterhead, his safe-breaking skills attracted the War Office's attention. He agreed to join the armed forces and on his release undertook special military training and was instructed in sophisticated explosive techniques.

With a crack commando unit, often behind enemy lines, he stole important documents and when the Allies took Rome, he blew 14 foreign embassy safes in a single day. He also blew Goering's safes. When the war ended he went back into civilian life with the Military Medal.

He returned to crime after the war but because of his war heroics and his gentle, non-violent nature, he was often given lenient sentences. He escaped from Peterhead and Barlinnie several times but was always recaptured. In 1972, he collapsed and died in Perth Prison and hundreds of mourners, including many criminals, attended his funeral in the Gorbals.

His war exploits formed the basis of the 1958 film, *The Safecracker*. The labour MP Norman Buchan wrote *The Ballad of Johnny Ramensky* in his memory.

Slater, Oscar

One of the worst miscarriages of justice in Scottish legal history was the wrongful murder conviction of Oscar Slater. Slater, a German Jew, was found guilty of murdering wealthy 83-year-old spinster, Marion Gilchrist in her Glasgow flat in 1908.

Three eye-witnesses, Gilchrist's servant Helen Lambie, short-sighted neighbour Mr Adams and 14-year old Mary Barrowman gave descriptions of a man seen leaving the flat. None of them resembled Slater.

However, being already known to the police, Slater was the prime suspect after he tried to sell a pawn ticket for a brooch similar to one stolen from Gilchrist's flat. Slater was arrested in New York after the two women identified him. He was convicted in 1909 in the High Court in Edinburgh but his sentence was commuted to life imprisonment two day's before he was due to hang.

He remained in Peterhead prison until 1928 when his conviction was over-turned, in part due to Arthur Conan Doyle, who funded most of his appeal. Among the evidence revealed to dispel Slater's guilt was that the witnesses had been bribed and shown pictures of Slater before they identified him.

Evidence was suppressed during the trial and the pawn ticket was for another brooch, pawned five weeks before the murder. Gilchrist's nephew Dr Charteris and epileptic relative Austin Birrel, were both suspected but investigations into their involvement had been dropped. Oscar Slater received £6000 compensation and moved to Ayr where he died in 1948, aged 76. The real killer was never discovered.

Smith, Madeleine Hamilton
Madeleine Hamilton Smith, the attractive 22-year-old daughter of a wealthy Glasgow architect, was accused of killing a former lover in the most sensational murder trial of the 19th century.

She was tried at the High Court in Edinburgh in March 1857 for poisoning Pierre Emile L'Angelier with arsenic. She was saved by advocate John Inglis's brilliant defence, which left the jury no choice but to return the uniquely Scottish verdict of 'not proven'.

Public opinion that she was a tease who had led L'Angelier on grew after their intimate love letters, published during the trial, revealed she had lost her virginity to him.

Everyone thought she had poisoned him because he was threatening to tell her family of the affair. It was true she bought arsenic from two chemist's shops before the poisoning but it was white arsenic that was found in L'Angelier's stomach, whereas the arsenic sold to her was pre-dyed, as the law required.

L'Angelier had frequently taken small doses of arsenic to treat his depression and assist his attempts at social climbing. He had ambitions to marry into a wealthy family and had so far failed. After Madeleine Smith rejected him, he started telling friends she was slowly poisoning him. He even started a diary to that effect. On the fateful day, a pre-arranged meeting with a friend was supposed to save him. The friend would then accuse Smith, removing suspicion from L'Angelier himself. The friend was delayed and L'Angelier died.

Although Madeleine Smith may not have been guilty she was spurned by her family after the trial and moved to London to marry under the name Lena Wardle. She later separated, followed her son to New York and re-married, becoming Lena Sheehy. She died and was buried in New York in 1928.

Winters, Larry
The acclaimed hit Scottish film *Silent Scream* was based on the true story of the Glasgow-born murderer Larry Winters.

Winters was born in Townhead in 1943 but spent much of his early years living outwith the city. From an early age he started getting into trouble with the police, resulting in him spending most of his adolescence in approved schools and borstals. He had a drug habit which played a major part in his violent behaviour, and while in London in 1964 he was charged with the murder of a Soho barman. He was found guilty and on conviction given a life sentence.

Sent back to Scotland to serve his sentence, he continued to get himself into trouble with the authorities, attempting to murder two prison officers in

1968. Fifteen years were added to his sentence and five years later a further six were added for his part in the Inverness Prison riot.

Eventually, his behaviour and refusal to accomodate prison regulations led to him being transferred to Barlinnie's Special Unit. There he settled down and took up writing poetry and reading philosophy. His death in 1977, from an overdose of Tuinal, led to a public outcry over the availability of drugs in what was perceived to be a liberal regime in the Special Unit.

In the 1990 film directed by David Hayman, Larry Winters was played by Iain Glen, who won the Best Actor Award at the Berlin Film Festival.

Law
Barlinnie
The only prison left in Glasgow is Barlinnie, the famous Bar-L.

In the 19th century there were eight prisons in the city but by 1840 only two remained. 'North' Prison at Duke Street – known as 'Bridgewall' (closed in 1955) and the 'South' Prison at Glasgow Green – known as 'Burgh' (closed in 1862).

Executions took place at Duke Street until 1928 when they were transferred to Barlinnie. In 1960 Anthony Miller, aged 19, became the last and youngest person to be executed in the city.

Barlinnie was built to alleviate overcrowding in other Scottish prisons. Its construction started in 1880 on land owned by Barlinnie farm in the east end. It was designed to accommodate 1000 prisoners in five, four-storey prison blocks, each 230ft long, 50ft across and 60ft high, linked by corridors. The first block of cells was opened in 1852 and the prison was fully completed in 1884.

Today, Barlinnie has physically changed little, retaining its grim Victorian appearance. It regularly holds more than 1000 prisoners and is the largest prison in Scotland. Barlinnie takes male prisoners from the west of Scotland on remand, serving less than four years or those waiting to go to a different category prison.

In 1973 the controversial Special Unit was opened as an experimental rehabilitation centre to see if a more relaxed regime for long-term prisoners would be beneficial. One of its first and most famous in-mates was convicted murderer Jimmy 'Babyface' Boyle who was released in 1982 and is now a prominent reformed criminal in the public eye. The Special Unit closed in 1993 and has been turned into a drugs reduction unit.

Dalrymple, James, Viscount Stair
The father of Scots Law was James Dalrymple, Viscount Stair.

Born in Ayrshire in 1619, he studied Arts at Glasgow University, graduating with an MA in 1637.

He went to Edinburgh to take up a legal career but became entangled in the civil war, commanding the Covenanting army's Glencairn regiment. Returning to Glasgow University in 1641, he became Regent and taught philosophy and Jurisprudence despite there being no formal legal teaching at the university.

In 1647 he returned to legal work, joining the Faculty of Advocates and by 1671 he was made Lord President of the Court of Session. During this time he produced his most famous work, *Institutes of the Law of Scotland*, published in 1681. It was the first and most comprehensive organization of legal principles, regarded as the Old Testament of Scots Law and is still occasionally cited. However, in 1681 he fled to Holland after refusing to swear an oath to the repressive government's Test Act.

He became an advisor to William of Orange and returned with him in 1688 and was reinstated Lord President. Towards the end of his life he was accused of complicity in the Glencoe massacre which was in fact more down to his eldest son John. Never really trusted he was nevertheless a highly regarded jurist.

And he was certainly an astute politician considering he was raised to the Bench by Cromwell, created a baronet by King Charles II and made a Viscount by William of Orange.

Lord Stair died in 1695.

Dowdall, Laurence

During the 1950s and 1960s 'Get me Dowdall' was a familiar plaintive cry of the accused in Glasgow's police cells. It referred to the greatest criminal lawyer to approach the bench in Scotland during the 20th century.

Laurence Dowdall was born in Glasgow in 1905 and was educated at St Mungo's Academy before studying law at Glasgow University.

After graduating with distinction, he practiced in Glasgow before being called up to serve as an ordinary seaman with the navy in the Far East during WWII. He rose to the rank of gunnery officer before returning to the legal profession in Glasgow in peace time where he decided he was best suited to criminal law. With his quick wit and humour, he loved the parry and thrust of the court room, dealing with real people rather than cases.

Although famous as a defence lawyer, Dowdall is probably best remembered for his prosecution stance in the infamous murder trial of serial killer Peter Manuel. He turned detective and was instrumental in the release of William Watt, accused of murdering three of Manuel's victims. Dowdall's devotion to seeking the truth ensured Manuel was hanged in 1958.

A man of great humanity and humility, he continued to astound and impress the Scottish courts well into his 80s. When he retired, he retained an interest and advisory status in the firm of Hughes Dowdall that he had established with Joseph Hughes in Glasgow and Kirkintilloch after the war.

He died in 1996.

Muir, Thomas

One of the great revolutionaries and libertarians of the 18th century was the Glasgow-born lawyer Thomas Muir of Huntershill.

Born in the High Street in 1765, Muir was originally destined for the church but soon realised the law was a far stronger tool for political reform. He passed his MA at Glasgow University in 1782 but the following year was expelled for agitation and mimicking his tutors.

Muir continued his studies in Edinburgh and became an advocate in 1787. He quickly established a reputation as a champion of the oppressed, inspired by the French Revolution of 1789. Muir established the Society Of The Friends Of Scottish People in 1792 which sought an independent republic free from English influence.

However, his actions angered the Lord Advocate, Robert Dundas, and Scotland's 'hanging judge' Lord Braxfield, who contrived a charge of sedition on him while he was in France. On his return in 1793, Muir was sentenced to 14-years' transportation to Botany Bay which succeeded in making him a martyr to the populace. He escaped from Australia in 1796 on a ship bound for America, sent by George Washington. It was way-laid by the Spanish who charged him with spying.

On the trip back to Spain the vessel was attacked by the British and Muir was badly maimed. But his facial disfigurement aided his escape and he eventually found sanctuary in France in 1798 where he was hailed a revolutionary hero. He continued his fight for a free Scotland until his sudden death in 1799.

Pinkerton, Allan

The most famous private detective in the world was originally a Glasgow barrel-maker. Born in 1819, the son of a police sergeant, Allan Pinkerton founded the Pinkerton detective agency in Chicago in 1852, the first of its kind in the USA. His agency solved a series of train robberies and in 1861, he foiled a plot to assassinate President-elect Abraham Lincoln in Baltimore on his way to Washington. During the American Civil War he became the head of the American Secret Service.

He returned to his agency where their biggest success was, ironically considering his past, breaking the working class movement, the Molly Maguires, who had terrorised Pennsylvanian coalfields for more than 20 years. The reason why Pinkerton went to America in the first place was because he had got himself in trouble with the law back home. As a member of the Chartist movement, defending worker's rights he played an active role in starting the Glasgow spinner's strike and was also involved in trying to break a chartist leader out of Monmouth Castle, Newport, in 1839. By 1842 he was forced to leave Scotland to avoid arrest.

After his death in 1884 the agency continued under the leadership of his two sons, Robert and William.

Police

The first professional police force in Britain was created in Glasgow almost 30 years before Sir Robert Peel started the Metropolitan Police Force in London in 1829.

Two previous attempts to create preventative policing in Glasgow started in 1779 and 1788 but failed through lack of funding, forcing the city to continue with civilian watchmen. But eventually the city fathers managed to get their Police Bill through Parliament.

In June 1800, the Glasgow Police Act received its Royal Assent and in November nine police officers gathered for the first time in the Session House of the Laigh Kirk at the Trongate.

Three sections of one sergeant and two constables each, rotated 12 hour duties between manning the Police Office and patrolling the streets with a 24 hour off-duty period. Their duties covered normal policing similar to todays.

In 1819 the first detective was introduced and two years later, with an assistant, the first detective department was created.

Police officers originally wore top hats and later several forms of helmet were worn before being replaced by peaked hats. In the 1870s badges displaying the Glasgow coat-of-arms were introduced and were not replaced until the Scottish Crest was introduced in 1932.

As the city grew, four police divisions were created in 1846 and by 1858 there were 615 uniformed officers and 21 detectives.

In 1862 the advent of photography helped with the murder investigation of Jessie McPherson, the first case exclusively carried out by the police, investigations previously being undertaken by the Procurator Fiscal.

Royal Faculty of Procurators Hall

The Royal Faculty of Procurators Hall is the smallest but finest example of Venetian Renaissance architecture to survive in Glasgow. It was built by one of the most famous and prolific of the city's Victorian architects, Charles Wilson.

Wilson created the design for the building in record time after the original London-based architect pulled out of the project. The building is situated in Nelson Mandela Place at the north-western corner of the square, where West George Street meets West Nile Street.

Construction started in 1854 and was completed two years later and still houses the procurators' society, the principal lawyer's organisation in the city.

The society was established in 1668 although the work of the procurators in Glasgow dates back more than 500 years to the medieval church's rule and its commissary courts.

The exterior of the building displays 14 sculptured heads in the window arches at ground floor level, often believed, incorrectly, to be that of the Scottish law lords. Among them are representations of some of the finest minds in Scottish legal history over the last three centuries, including the Earl of Mansfield, the Crown's Chief Justice in the 18th century and the Whig judge Lord Cockburn, a rarity in the 19th century when Tories predominated within the judiciary system.

The interior of the building is one of the most impressive in Glasgow, encompassing the elaborate Reading Room with its pedestal mounted busts of the law lords and the Orr Library, created between 1938 and 1939.

Sheriff Court

Glasgow's new Sheriff Court building is the first to be situated on the south side of the River Clyde. Work started on this monumental structure on Gorbals Street in 1980.

Officially called the Sheriff Court of Glasgow and Strathkelvin, this building was designed by the architects Keppie, Henderson & Partners to a style similar to the 1960s Boston City Hall in the USA. The overall shape is that of a simple but imposing rectangle, faced with Danish marble and pale yellow sandstone.

No expense was spared on the interior decoration either, which projects an open and light environment typical of the 1960s, with glass and steel staircases and balconies added more recently.

At the entrance of this austere building, an impressive relief of Saint Mungo, Glasgow's Patron Saint, mounted above the main information desk, is the first thing to strike the eye.

The building houses a total of 21 court rooms. Six of these are double height criminal jury courts, situated on the ground floor, minimally decorated to reflect the gravity of their business. The new court replaces the former County Buildings and Court Houses on Wilson Street, just across the river in the Merchant City. Built by Clarke and Bell during the 1840s, this Greek-style building, with its immense south-facing portico, takes up a whole city block.

Wheatley, John

John Wheatley was one of Scotland's most prominent law lords.

Born in Shettleston in 1908, into a socialist family, his youth was influenced by his uncle John Wheatley, a 'Red Clydesider' and Labour MP.

Wheatley strongly believed in the reduction of poverty and squalor from society. While studying law at Glasgow University he manned pickets during the General Strike while many of his fellow class-mates were driving trams as strike-breakers. Called to the bar in 1932, he embarked on a most remarkable legal career, broken only briefly by WWII when he served with the Royal Field Artillery.

At the end of the war he became an Advocate Depute and by 1947 he had worked his way up to QC, Solicitor General, Lord Advocate and was also the MP for East Kilbride.

Raised to the bench in 1954, he became Lord Justice Clerk in 1972, a position he held until 1985. During his 31 years as a judge he made many radical and sometimes ironic decisions. A devout Catholic and abolitionist, he presided over the notorious Argyll divorce case and pronounced the last death sentence in Scotland.

He was honoured with a life peerage in 1970.

He chaired many committees most notably the Royal Commission on the Reform of Local Government from 1966-1969 which created the two-tier system of local government introduced in 1973.

His autobiography 'One Man's Judgement' was published in 1987.

He died two years later and in the same year the John Wheatley College was established in Shettleston.

Protests
Bread Riot

The largest riot in Glasgow took place in 1848. It was known as the Bread Riot as a great many people, many of them displaced Highlanders and Irish, were starving and there was high unemployment.

There had been great unrest throughout Britain since the Reform Act of 1832 and in 1836 the working class Chartist movement had formed to fight social injustice. In March, spurred on by revolution in France earlier that year, the chartists held a meeting in Glasgow Green. More than 3000 gathered and after the speeches, some rioters, searching for weapons, tore up the iron railings in Monteath Row. Marching into the city, many shops were looted for food and jewellery but some chose to break into a gunsmith's shop in Royal Exchange Square and liberate some guns. In Buchanan Street they fired into the air but were quickly relieved of the weapons by a doctor – guns were all very well in the Gallowgate but not in this well-to-do neighbourhood.

The police and Town Guard were useless against such numbers but they did fire into the crowd and some people were killed. Thousands of sworn-in special constables forced the rioters back into the Gallowgate. Wholesale destruction continued until the following day when the army finally dispersed them. More than 30 arrests were made and several were later sentenced to transportation to Australia. This was the last major riot by the chartists.

Suffrage
Crawford, Helen

Helen Crawford was one of the leaders of the Scottish suffrage movement in the early 20th century.

Born in 1877 into a middle-class family from the Gorbals, she joined women's interest groups as early as 1900, three years before Emmeline Pankhurst started the Women's Social and Political Union.

In 1912 the Glasgow group took on a more militant role in the Women's Suffrage Movement. Crawford, along with a group of other Glasgow women, travelled to London to take part in a window-smashing demonstration. She was among the first to be arrested and was imprisoned for a month.

After her release she returned to Scotland where she became a leading speaker in the fight for the women's right to vote. She joined the Independent Labour Party (ILP) in 1914 and with the outbreak of WWII her pacifism caused her to leave the suffragette movement. A year later she was one of the leaders in the Glasgow rent strikes campaigning against poinding and evictions.

Through her persistent action the Government was forced to pass the Rent Restriction Act of 1915.

Crawford established the Women's Peace Crusade in 1916, which held a mass anti-war demonstration in Glasgow Green.

She continued her work with the ILP and in 1920 joined the Communist Party of Great Britain after attending a conference in Russia.

Crawford stood for Parliament several times during her political career but failed to win a seat. She died in 1954.

Lyness, Elizabeth Dorothea

One of the first female students of medicine in Glasgow is probably best remembered for her part in the Scottish suffragette movement. Born in 1872, she enrolled in Queen Margaret College in 1890 and graduated four years later.

She practised medicine in Glasgow for five years until she met and married the Reverend William Chalmers Smith of Calton Parish Church. A radical supporter of votes for women, Mrs Smith embarked on a series of militant campaigns, the most famous being the 'Park Mansion Affair' in 1914. She and another woman, Ethel Moorhead, were caught in the act of setting fire to an empty house and were arrested and taken to Duke Street Prison. While imprisoned they went on hunger strike. Both were released pending trial but failed to attend their court dates and were subsequently hunted as fugitives. They were rearrested and brought back to Glasgow. At their trial, supporters of the two women showered the judge with apples. They were both sentenced to eight months in prison. During the ensuing social scandal the Rev Smith sought a divorce.

Rev Smith took custody of the couple's sons and Elizabeth their daughters. After her release from prison she returned to medicine to support them and worked for the Glasgow Public Health Department and Glasgow Royal Samaritan's Hospital for Women.

In 1930 she set up a practice in Dennistoun where she worked until her death in 1944.

Suffrage Oak

The Suffrage Oak in Kelvingrove Park was planted in 1918 on the southern side of Kelvin Way near the University Avenue end of the tree-lined road.

A plaque erected beside the oak in 1995 states 'This Oak was planted by the Women's Suffrage organisation in Glasgow on 20 April 1918 to commemorate the granting of votes to women'.

The planting of the tree near Glasgow's oldest seat of learning, marks the first major victory in the long struggle that took place across Britain by women from all walks of life. Although Emmeline Pankhurst is now regarded as the figurehead of the Suffrage movement, many women from

Glasgow instigated major protests in the fight for equality. Among the most famous of the Glasgow women were Elizabeth Dorothea Lyness and Helen Crawford.

Lyness instigated the 'Park Mansion Affair' in 1914, where she was caught in the act of setting fire to an empty house and went on hunger strike in the Duke Street prison. A year later, Gorbals-born Crawford led rent strikes in the city against poinding and evictions which forced the government to pass the Rent Restriction Act of 1915.

Other suffragette acts in the city involved the planting of bombs in the City Chambers, the Kibble Palace and Belmont Church.

In 1918 the government relented, the Representation of the People Act giving women over the age of 30 the right to vote. It took another decade before this limit was lowered to 21 bringing the age in line with men.

Punishment

Hanging

The last person to be publicly executed in Glasgow was Dr Edward Pritchard, hanged on Glasgow Green in 1865, after being found guilty of killing his wife and mother-in-law. He had been slowly poisoning his wife, perhaps because of financial problems or his affair with a former servant. His mother-in-law died two weeks after she started looking after her sick daughter. Her death was not considered suspicious until after her daughter died, when an anonymous letter was sent to the Fiscal. Pritchard was arrested and found guilty and more than 80,000 people turned up for the execution.

Public hangings became common in the second half of the 18th century when the government realised how expensive it was becoming to transport felons to the colonies. There were more than 200 crimes carrying the death penalty, mostly for theft and they were carried out in public as a warning to others. Hanging was the most common form of execution, beheading being reserved for the aristocracy.

Between 1788 and 1813, 22 people were hanged at Glasgow Cross but from 1814 hangings were carried out at Jail Square at Glasgow Green, with 67 men and four women killed, facing Nelson's monument.

After Pritchard, hangings were carried out in private at Duke Street prison until 1928 when the venue was changed to Barlinnie prison.

The last person hanged there was the youngest person executed in Glasgow in the 20th century, Anthony Miller, on 22 December 1960, aged 19.

Whipping

The last public whipping through the streets of Glasgow was in 1823. Richard Campbell, an ex-policeman turned weaver was sentenced to 80 lashes for leading a riot against George Provand, a dye merchant who lived in the now demolished Dreghorn Mansion on Clyde Street. In 1822 someone thought he saw blood and two young children's corpses in Provand's basement. In fact, it was spilled red dye but this was the time when the notorious Resurrectionists were plying their trade, stealing corpses from the graveyards. The body-snatching story spread quickly and an angry crowd soon marched on Provand's house where they looted and destroyed its contents.

The police, unable to control the mob, called on the magistrates who brought in the army from the Gallowgate and from across the river in Laurieston. All was soon under control and nobody was badly injured.

The following day, the Lord Provost offered a handsome reward for information leading to the arrest of the ringleaders and shortly afterwards, five men were arrested. They were found guilty and four were sentenced to transportation.

Campbell, judged to be the leader, was jailed in the Trongate until the following May. He was tied to a cart and wheeled outside where the city's hangman gave him his first 20 lashes with the cat o' nine tails. He received 40 more, 20 at the bottom and 20 at the top of Stockwell Street before ending up at Glasgow Cross for the final 20, after which he was then transported for life.

CHAPTER 6
Medicine

Doctors and Scientists
Black, Joseph

The work carried out by Joseph Black at Glasgow University laid the foundations for much of modern chemistry and physics. He recognised the presence of 'fixed air' (now called carbon dioxide) in the atmosphere and also discovered oxygen, nitrogen and hydrogen.

Black was the son of a wine merchant. Born in Bordeaux in 1728, he moved to Glasgow in 1746 where he attended the university. He studied chemistry under the famous physician William Cullen from Hamilton. Black studied at Edinburgh University for a time, qualifying as a doctor before returning to Glasgow in 1756 to take over from Cullen as Professor of Medicine and Lecturer in Chemistry.

He lectured in English rather than Latin and his reputation as an entertaining and highly informative lecturer soon rose, so much so that it was fashionable to attend his classes. It was at these lectures that he used to demonstrate the ability of 'fixed air' to extinguish fire.

But he is probably best known for his investigations between 1759 and 1763 into the heat properties of materials.

Examining the difference between heat and temperature, he discovered latent heat – the amount of heat required to turn a solid into a liquid or vapour without a change of temperature.

This enabled his friend James Watt to make use of the theory in his work with condensers which ultimately led to the increased efficiency of his steam engines. Black returned to Edinburgh in 1766 to become Professor of Physics and Chemistry. He died there in 1799.

Hunter, William

Scotland's first public museum was opened in 1807 thanks to the generosity of one man, William Hunter.

Hunter was born in 1718 in Long Calderwood, East Kilbride. After studying divinity at Glasgow University for five years he went on to study medicine in 1737 under William Cullen the great physician and chemist. He also studied at Edinburgh University and in 1741 he moved to St George's Hospital, London, where he studied anatomy.

Turning his medical skills to midwifery in 1748 he became physician to members of the Royal Family. Hunter was made the first Professor of Anatomy to the Royal Academy in 1768.

But he is most remembered for his part in setting up the Hunterian Museum. In 1770 he built a house where he gave lectures and taught dissection. But he set aside space to display his famous collection of medals, coins, art, books, manuscripts and ethnographic artefacts that he had been collecting since the 1750s.

Hunter died in 1783 bequeathing his collection to Glasgow University along with £8000 for a museum building to house them.

Constructed at the old university site on the High Street, Scotland's first public museum was opened in 1807.

Glasgow University moved to Gilmorehill in 1870 and the Hunterian Museum was established in the main building. Over the years the collection has grown enormously and parts of his original collection have been moved to other university teaching departments. In 1980, the Hunterian Art Gallery opened nearby, housing his and other university art collections.

Laing, Ronald David

Modern treatment of mentally ill patients owes a lot to one man who was born and educated in Glasgow.

Ronald David Laing was born into a working class family in 1927.

While studying medicine at Glasgow University he tried to change psychiatric practises by bringing together medical and humanitarian studies, forming The Socratic Society in 1948. After graduating in 1951, he practised psychiatry in Glasgow. But in 1957 he moved to London to work at the world-famous Tavistock Clinic. Continually challenging contemporary attitudes towards mental illness, he published a series of books, the first being *The Divided Self* in 1960. He always believed that mentally ill people should be treated with respect and their 'mad behaviour' should be understood rather than just lock them away or treat them with drugs. He told his patients they should regard their illnesses not as a problem but as an enriching process. Laing also believed that mental problems developed as a result of family and social conditions.

In later years he retracted many of these original theories but during 'The Swinging Sixties' he was revered as a popular guru. As well as psychiatric books he also wrote poetry and philosophy and some of his other books included *Sanity, Madness and the Family* (1964) and *The Politics of Experience* (1967). Although many of his more radical theories have now been discredited, his basic principles of sympathy and understanding towards mental patients remains a valued part of modern treatments.

Ronald Laing died in 1989.

Lister, Joseph

Surgery made a huge leap forward in the middle of the 19th century because of pioneering work carried out in Glasgow's Royal Infirmary.

In those days one third of patients died after even the simplest of operations because of extremely low hygiene standards, most fatalities being associated with blood poisoning and gangrene.

One wing of the Infirmary in particular was very bad for 'hospital diseases' as it had been built on a mass grave for paupers and victims of the 1849 cholera epidemic.

But after the French chemist Louis Pasteur discovered live bacteria was the source of infections, a surgeon realised why so many patients died.

Joseph Lister had become Professor of Surgery at Glasgow in 1859 after studying in London. He experimented with carbolic acid as an antiseptic which proved successful, allowing operations to venture into the body for the first time. Before, only amputations and removing skin tumours were attempted because of the high fatality rate. Also in Glasgow, Lister developed antiseptic sprays for operating rooms and wards, sterile catgut stitches and introduced unheard of practices such as washing your hands before dealing with patients open wounds. He became Surgeon-in-ordinary in Scotland after receiving the royal seal of approval after removing an armpit abscess from his most famous patient, Queen Victoria.

Because of the work carried out in Glasgow, Lister, in 1897, became the first doctor of medicine to be honoured into the House of Lords.

He was given the Freedom of Glasgow in 1908 where he said he spent the happiest days of his life. He died in 1912, leaving behind a more sterile medical world.

MacEwen, Sir William

The pioneer of brain surgery was Sir William MacEwen.

Born in Glasgow in 1848, he spent the rest of his working life in the city. His interest in surgery was stimulated by the work of Joseph Lister, Glasgow University's Regius Professor of Surgery.

MacEwen adopted Lister's revolutionary concept of antiseptic working conditions in hospitals.

He was able to carry out more invasive surgical techniques which before the advent of hygiene would have certainly resulted in the death of his patients. In 1879, he carried out the world's first successful removal of a brain tumour. His modern medical techniques enabled him to operate on 18 other patients over the next four years with only one fatality at a time when other brain surgeons were losing 100 per cent of their patients.

MacEwen's techniques were unsurpassed until the discovery of penicillin by Ayrshire-born Sir Alexander Fleming in 1928.

His work was greeted with international acclaim. But he declined an offer to become the head of surgery at the newly established and now world-famous Johns Hopkins Medical School in the United States. He was not given the guarantee that he would have complete control of training and supervising the medical staff and so he remained in Glasgow.

MacEwen also pioneered methods of bone transplantation, inserting small grafts to repair damaged limbs. In 1892, he was appointed to the post at Glasgow University his mentor Lister had held at the start of MacEwen's own brilliant career.

He died in 1924.

McIlroy, Dame Anne Louise

One of the great medical pioneers of the 20th century was Dame Anne Louise McIlroy who did much to promote new treatments during pregnancy. She insisted anaesthetics be provided for women during childbirth and was one of the first to work on resuscitation techniques for new-born babies.

Born in 1878 she was one of the first female undergraduates at Glasgow University and by the age of 20 she became one of its most distinguished graduates. She decided to specialise in gynaecology and obstetrics and by 1906 she was a surgeon at the Victoria Infirmary, a post she held for the next four years.

With the outbreak of WWI she worked in France and Greece for three years, commanding a Scottish Women's Hospital unit, before joining the Royal Army Medical Corps.

She worked as a surgeon based in Constantinople (now Istanbul in Turkey) and was responsible for setting up the only orthopaedic centre for the Eastern Army. During the war she received many honours for her heroic work and humanitarian aid and she later wrote a book on her experiences – *From a Balcony on the Bosphorus*. Two years after the war she became the first female Professor of Obstetrics and Gynaecology at London University.

In 1929 she was created D.B.E and became a Founder Fellow of the Royal College of Obstetrics and Gynaecology.

She practised in Harley Street for many years and in 1937 became a Fellow of the Royal College of Physicians.

Dame Anne McIlroy died in 1968.

Pattison, Granville Sharp

One of America's most eminent medical minds during the 19th century was the disgraced Glasgow anatomist Granville Sharp Pattison.

Pattison was born in the city in 1791 and was educated at Glasgow University. A gifted and hard-working student, by the time he was 18 he had become assistant to the professor of anatomy, physiology and surgery. Over the next few years he was held in high regard by his fellow professionals but his reputation and standing with the public was blown in 1813. Around this time the resurrectionists were as busy body-snatching in Glasgow as in Edinburgh where Burke and Hare made the practice so notorious. In Glasgow, as elsewhere, it was not just the professional 'sack-'em up boys' that carried out the gruesome task but also students and doctors.

In December 1813, the body of Mrs McAlister, wife of a well-known haberdasher in Hutcheson Street, was stolen from the Ramshorn kirk graveyard. Such was the public outcry that the authorities were forced into immediate action and on searching Pattison's home in College Street, found many body parts hidden under the floorboards.

The following June, Pattison and three students were tried at the High Court in Edinburgh but were set free after it was proved the body parts were not of Mrs McAlister. Public anger however, forced Pattison's move to

America for his own safety. There he founded anatomy departments at Jefferson College, Philadelphia, and New York University and was a vigorous medical ethics campaigner.

He died in 1851.

Hospitals
Belvidere
Belvidere Hospital was the first permanent hospital to operate in Scotland.

Glasgow Town Council set up the hospital in the east end of the city with the aim that it would specialise in the treatment of infectious diseases.

Temporary wooden huts, with a bed capacity of around 250, on the Belvidere estate on London Road were used to treat fever patients when the council acquired the land in 1870.

Four years later a three-year construction project began to build five red and white striped brick buildings to house smallpox units.

By 1887 a further 14 buildings had been added to the site along with a mortuary, washhouse, kitchen and storage buildings.

Belvidere treated patients with a variety of diseases including typhus, diptheria and smallpox.

But the majority of its work was involved in the treatment of children suffering from the common ailments of the day – whooping cough, scarlet fever and measles.

The hospital site continued to expand and rebuild into the early part of the 20th century and remained primarily an infectious disease hospital up until the creation of the National Health Service in 1948.

During the 1950s it carried out pioneering work on the treatment of polio which led to the creation of Intensive Care Units.

And over the next half century the hospital branched into other specialization's including respiratory medicine, a maternity unit, radiotherapy and orthopaedic units.

Towards the end of the millennium it became a general geriatric hospital before it was eventually closed in 1998.

Rottenrow
The first hospital in Glasgow to care for expectant mothers started in 1792 but was closed by magistrates soon after. But in 1834 a group of Glasgow's influential citizens pressurized the Lord Provost to re-establish a maternity hospital. The Glasgow Lying-In Hospital and Dispensary was set up in the old Grammar School building in Greyfriars Wynd. But the building proved unsuitable and new premises were sought in St Andrews Square off the Saltmarket in 1841.

Unlike any other hospital at the time, it had an open-door policy, treating the poor, the homeless and even unmarried women, a situation that nearby residents found undesirable.

The hospital was forced to move again in 1860, this time to an old house at the corner of Portland Street and Rottenrow. And 'The Rottenrow' name stuck.

From 1880 to 1881, new buildings were erected on the site providing much needed space. Due to the squalor and poor diet of the city's poor, a skeletal deformity known as 'Glasgow Pelvis' was very common. But a doctor, Murdoch Cameron, brought fame to the hospital, perfecting the Caesarean section, an operation that became routine at Rottenrow.

In 1908 an extension was built providing more than 100 extra beds, a lecture room and operating theatre. In 1914 it became the Glasgow Royal Maternity and Women's Hospital.

Like all voluntary hospitals it was short of funds but it managed to survive until July 1948 when, like all other medical services, it was taken over by the NHS until it finally closed in 2001.

Royal Infirmary
Glasgow's first infirmary was built more than 200 years ago to the west of the Cathedral. The first stone was laid in 1792 on the site of the centuries-old Bishop's Castle which was demolished after the land had been purchased from the Crown. The new building, Glasgow's first Royal Infirmary, was designed by world famous architects James and Robert Adam.

As Glasgow's population grew, additions were made but unfortunately some were built on top of mass graves for cholera victims, resulting in the death of many patients. It wasn't until the 1860s after surgeon Joseph Lister first recognised the need for sterile conditions in hospitals that this unhygienic practice stopped.

By the end of the 19th century it was felt the infirmary would have to be rebuilt as it was no longer practical to continue adding onto the original structure.

The new design was much criticised because not only would it dwarf the Cathedral but many felt it wrong to pull down the original Adam building and the Lister wing. Nevertheless, construction started in 1907. Completed seven years later, the new Glasgow Royal Infirmary, considered the largest public building in the UK, was opened to the public.

After WWII, with new road layouts in the city planned nearby, it proved necessary for any further expansion of the hospital to take place to the north. Work started in the 1970s and by 1981 the last major extension to the infirmary was completed at a cost of more than £40million.

Ruchill
The second infectious disease hospital to open in Glasgow was built in the rather grand and elevated Ruchill Park to the north-west of the city. At the impressive twin gatehouse lodges, a plaque read 'City of Glasgow Hospital for Infectious Diseases opened 1900. Foundation stone laid 1895'.

In 1892 Glasgow Corporation acquired the land which had surrounded Ruchill House since its construction as far back as the 17th century. In the same year the park was opened to the public and Bilsland Drive was built along the western edge of the grounds to provide access to the entrance.

City engineers designed the hospital at the top of the steep slope in a Flemish Renaissance style and at the highest point an ornamental bell-shaped water tower was constructed.

When it opened the hospital had a 440-bed capacity. But because of the large number of tuberculosis sufferers more than 270 beds had to be added by 1915. The wards were laid out in strict regimental rows totalling 16 pavilions, beautifully designed in red brick and finished in red sandstone and terracotta, with bay windows and shaped gables.

By the time Ruchill was absorbed into the NHS in 1948, it comprised 1000 beds. But by the 1960s, infectious diseases were becoming much rarer due to vaccination programmes and the hospital began to specialize in chronically sick children, geriatric and psychiatric patients.

In the early 1990s the hospital beds had been reduced to less than 300 and Ruchill eventually closed in 1998.

Southern General
One of Glasgow's major teaching hospitals was originally the hospital of the Govan Poorhouse.

In 1867 building work was started and by 1872 the Govan Combination Poorhouse, consisting of a 240-bed general hospital and 180-bed lunatic asylum, was built at what is now the site of the Southern General Hospital.

The original hospital building was designed in the French Renaissance style with a central bell tower. In 1883, a northern wing was added which was again extended in 1897. However, major expansion work was started in 1902 with the construction of a new extension that could accommodate up to 700 more patients. Three years later it opened for business, the same year a nurse's home was also completed.

In 1912 the Govan Parish was absorbed into Glasgow Parish and later Glasgow Corporation which took over the running of the hospital. In 1923, it became officially known as the Southern General Hospital and in 1926 psychiatric wards were added to the original asylum building. During the 1930s a mortuary, later attached to the pathology department, a kitchen, laundry and boilerhouse were added to the hospital complex that was spreading in a southerly direction from the Govan Road. The hospital was absorbed into the NHS in 1948.

In the 1950s the hospital began a general expansion programme which ended with the opening of the Maternity Unit in 1970 and the Institute of Neurological Sciences building in 1972. The Southern General is now run by the Southern Glasgow University Hospitals NHS Trust.

Stobhill

Stobhill Hospital was originally built as a Poor Law hospital to supplement the inadequate 700 beds provided by the City Poor House and Barony Poorhouse at Barnhill.

In 1899 Glasgow Parish Council decided to build a general hospital at the Stobhill estate which would accommodate almost 2000 patients. Construction work started the following year and when it opened in 1904, there was space for nearly 900 beds. But with the completion of the 28 red-brick, two-storey wards, a total of 1867 beds were available, of which 200 were for psychiatric patients.

However, a great stigma was attached to the hospital for many years because admission required patients to be destitute paupers. So much so that children born there had their place of birth on their birth certificates marked down as Balornock Road with no reference to the hospital.

During WWI it became a military establishment for treating servicemen and was known as the 3rd and 4th Scottish General Hospitals. It was eventually returned to civilian use in 1920. A few years later the hospital appointed the physician Dr Osborne Henry Maver – who later formed the Citizen's Theatre under the pseudonym of James Bridie. In 1930 Stobhill ceased to be a Poor Law hospital after being taken over by Glasgow Corporation. Stobhill became a teaching hospital in 1937 and was absorbed into the NHS in 1948.

Although the bed numbers have dropped drastically over the years, falling below 1000 by 1965, the hospital has continued to undergo expansion and change.

Western Infirmary

When Glasgow University uprooted from the High Street and moved across the city to Gilmorehill in 1870, it no longer had the use of the Royal Infirmary for its medical school. The university therefore initiated plans for a new hospital to be built to meet its teaching needs as well as provide medical care for the growing population spreading west from the city centre.

Plans for the new 350-bed hospital had been drawn up in 1869 but because of lack of funds the design had to be drastically altered.

In 1874 the Western Infirmary opened its doors to the public with only a 150-bed capacity. However seven years later, with the help from a substantial donation from the Glasgow merchant John Freeland, the original design was completed.

In 1902, the Western Infirmary played a part in one of the most tragic events in Scottish football. On April 5 after the wooden stand collapsed at Ibrox Park, more than 200 injured people were brought to the hospital of which 14 sadly died.

Like every other hospital, the Western was taken over by the NHS in 1948. It continued its pioneering role as a first class medical laboratory service and radiology unit but by the late 1950s it became apparent that the hospital's original buildings were no longer adequate for the job. By 1970 work started on a reconstruction programme to build a 256-bed unit. It was completed and opened to the public in 1974 but further planned work was indefinitely postponed.

CHAPTER 7
Religion

Churches

Barony Church

It may seem strange that the Barony Church on Castle Street was built so close to the Cathedral but this was in part due to an overcrowding problem.

During the 16th century there were two separate churches within the Cathedral. Members of the High Kirk worshipped at ground level while the second had been ensconced in the crypt since 1595. This congregation, made up from worshippers living in areas surrounding the city, were known as the Barony.

By the end of the 18th century, after the Cathedral had been divided again, the Barony decided to build a new place of worship nearby. They moved into their new church in 1798, south of the Cathedral. After they moved out, the crypt was filled in with earth and used as a burying ground, a practice that continued until 1844.

The Barony congregation's new premises was built in a Gothic style by James Adam and John Robertson and for many it was a remarkably ugly building. However, the congregation moved again in 1890 after the new Barony Church had been completed on the other side of High Street, to the west of the Cathedral.

Built by J. J. Burnet and J. A. Campbell who had won the architectural competition, the church was constructed at a cost of £20,000. Built in red sandstone, the south facing entrance was modeled on Dunblane Cathedral. The Barony was acquired by Strathclyde University in 1984 and is now used for graduation ceremonies and other important events.

Bridge of Sighs

The Bridge of Sighs was built to provide easy access to the Necropolis from the Cathedral. It was designed by architect James Hamilton, the son of the renowned grandfather of Glasgow architecture David Hamilton.

Work on the bridge was started in 1833 and was completed the following year. The original reason for the bridge's construction however, quite literally disappeared underground in 1877. Until this time the Molendinar Burn, the famous stream where St Mungo founded his ecclesiastical settlement, ran between the two hills on which the Cathedral and Necropolis stand. But the stream was channeled through a culvert on top of which now runs Wishart Street just over 40 years after this beautiful, dramatically designed bridge was built to span it.

The name of the bridge comes from the world famous Bridge of Sighs in Venice. Unlike the bridge in Glasgow, which takes people from a place of worship to a place of burial, the one in Italy has for many years been associated with death – but not by natural causes. It runs from a prison to the inquisitor's rooms in the Doge's palace on St Mark's Square.

The explanation for the bridge's name was popularised in the 19th century by Lord Byron. He promoted the idea that the name was inspired by the sighs of condemned prisoners going to the executioner. However, the Inquisition was over before the bridge was built so prisoners would more likely have been sighing at the beautiful view of Venice's lagoon.

Caledonia Road Church

One of the saddest pieces of architecture in the whole of Britain is the Caledonia Road Church in the Gorbals. It was the first ecclesiastical work of the famous Glasgow architect Alexander 'Greek' Thomson and was regarded by many as his finest.

Built between 1856 and 1857, its most striking feature is its originally styled, very tall, square tower. The rest of the building was also of spectacular design, incorporating the first floor Ionic portico and other Greek styles that would later make Thomson famous. And its asymmetrical layout lends very much to the idea that this was a very important building in its own right. While in use, the church had a very brightly lit interior, very seldom found in a place of worship during the Victorian era. It was created by the continuously glazed open colonnade, a simpler style of lighting than Thomson later incorporated into his St Vincent Street Church.

Caledonia Road Church eventually ceased to be used for religious purposes in 1962 and three years later it was completely gutted by fire. Much of the stone-work survived and was made safe.

But over the years vandalism and decay have added to the extremely sorry state of this listed building, considered to be of national and even international importance. Many ideas to preserve or rebuild it over the years have so far failed to achieve any lasting result. Conservation groups, however, are now continuing their efforts to save this architectural monument before time eventually runs out.

Carmunnock parish church

The parish church of Carmunnock has been a sight of religious significance since the 6th century. Situated six miles south of the city, this simply laid out church was built in 1767, on land which is thought to have been first used as a religious settlement by St Cadoc in 528.

In 1819 a vestry was added, transforming the rectangular building into that of the more common T-plan church which today can accommodate 470 parishioners. At the churchyard gate stands a watch-house which was erected in 1828 as the villagers were worried about the resurrectionists exhuming their relatives for use in Glasgow's anatomy schools.

Although major repair work was undertaken on the church in the 1830s and much of the original interior was altered in the 1870s, the church still retains an ancient feel. The present stained-glass windows were installed in 1922 and are some of the finest examples of Glasgow artist Norman M Macdougall's work.

The church is surrounded by a much older churchyard and cemetery which has seen several ecclesiastical structures constructed on it since the 12th century. The land was originally owned by the Hamilton family but by 1700 it had passed to the Lairds of Castlemilk, the Stewarts, several of whom are buried in the church vault.

Many buildings around the churchyard in the middle of this conservation village date from the 18th and early 19th century, adding to the village atmosphere which has been retained despite Carmunnock being part of the City of Glasgow since 1938.

Cathedral

In the oldest part of Glasgow stands the Cathedral, occupying a site of religious significance since the 4th century AD.

A Christian site was founded there by St Ninian and again two centuries later by St Mungo, Glasgow's patron saint, who built a wooden church next to the Molendinar Burn. For the next 600 years little history has been recorded of the site but in 1136 the first stone of the original Cathedral was laid by Bishop John Achaius. It stood for about 50 years until it was destroyed by fire but a new, larger Cathedral was started in 1197 during the reign of William the Lion.

Its first foundation stone was laid by Bishop Jocelyn who started the Glasgow Fair around that time. A small part of this structure remains today.

The Cathedral took more than 300 years to build and during the Reformation was protected by the city's trade guilds who regarded it as their church. Glasgow and Kirkwall Cathedral are the only two in Scotland to have survived in this way.

The Cathedral became two churches from the 16th century when the crypt, known as the Barony, was used for worship until around 1800 when its congregation moved to a new church. A thick layer of soil was put into the crypt where members of the congregation were buried, alongside Saint Mungo's tomb.

Many changes have occurred during the Cathedral's long history but the blackened stone walls cannot be cleaned for fear of causing irreparable damage.

Elgin Place Congregational Church

Another building that retains the blackened grime of the city's industrial era is the former Elgin Place Congregational Church.

Situated at the corner of Bath Street and Pitt Street to the west of the city centre, this magnificent temple-like structure was built between 1855 and

1856. Its architect was John Burnet senior, who was also responsible for many other famous structures in the city including the Cenotaph in George Square and the former Stock Exchange House on Buchanan Street.

Burnet's design was a relatively simple one, loosely based on the Erechtheion temple's famous porch of the Caryatids that was constructed on the historic Acropolis hill in Athens about 420BC.

The most spectacular aspect of the whole building is the six massive Greek Ionic columns which are based well above street level. The main part of the building was deliberately raised to this level to provide much more room for the basement halls constructed below the church.

Just as Burnet's reconstruction work at No191 Ingram Street has since been transformed into the lavishly restored Corinthian bar and night club, so too has his church changed from its original use.

Between 1979 and 1983, the entire interior of the church was converted by Holmes and Partners for use as a nightclub venue - a highly popular function the building still serves today.

Garnethill Synagogue

The oldest purpose-built synagogue in Scotland opened in the Garnethill area of Glasgow in 1879. Also one of the oldest places of Jewish worship in Britain, it was built to accommodate the ever-growing population of Jews escaping persecution, mainly from eastern Europe.

Glasgow architect John McLeod designed the L-shaped building for Glasgow's Hebrew congregation which at that time numbered around 700. It is constructed in a Byzantine and Roman style with some Moorish touches that give it a similar appearance to Joseph's Bayswater synagogue, built in London around the same time.

The Garnet Hill (as it was then spelt) Synagogue was regarded by many Orthodox Jews as being reformist, its congregation mainly coming from professional and academic classes.

The opening ceremony was conducted by Dr Herman Adler.

Dr Adler later followed in his father's footsteps to become Chief Rabbi of Britain and the Commonwealth.

Prior to the synagogue opening, the city's Jewish community had made use of several temporary sites, the first being a rented room in the High Street in 1823. As the community grew, a larger flat at the corner of George Street and John Street in the city centre was converted for use in 1857. Around the turn of the 20th century, Glasgow's Jewish population was growing rapidly, especially in the Gorbals area where several synagogues had been established.

Sites in Govanhill and Queen's Park were later established and although the major Jewish centre is now centred around Newton Mearns, Garnethill still remains popular.

Greek Orthodox Cathedral

The Greek Orthodox Cathedral of St Luke is the only orthodox cathedral in Scotland. Situated in Dowanhill in the West End, it was originally built for the Presbyterian church. Belhaven Church was designed by one of its own congregation, the famous Glasgow architect James Sellars.

Sellars must have been persuasive, because he was allowed to proceed with his preferred Normandy Gothic design which was a distinctly Episcopalian choice at that time. The two turrets and many other features of the church were inspired by Dunblane Cathedral. Work was started on the church in 1876, the same year that Hillhead Parish Church, another of Sellars' designs, was completed. Belhaven Church took a year to construct and was finished around the same time as the architect's most famous creation, St Andrew's Halls.

Although the outside of the building was Episcopalian, the interior was very much in the keeping of a Presbyterian church. Today many of the original features have been retained alongside Cretan and Byzantine work added by its present occupants.

Sadly the church was one of the last of Sellar's great works.

The contracts he undertook during the 1870s brought him such notoriety that during the 1880s he was in such demand that his versatility and talent suffered as a consequence.

The Greek Orthodox Church took over the building in 1960 and 10 years later it was elevated to the status of Cathedral and today is a meeting place for all denominations of the orthodox church.

Hillhead Parish Church

Hillhead Parish Church was modelled on the Sainte Chapelle in Paris, quite unusual for a Presbyterian church during the Victorian era. The competition to design it was won by James Sellars who, two years earlier in 1873, had started building Glasgow's famous St Andrew's Halls. Sellar's design showed a great amount of influence from William Leiper, the man responsible for the intricate exterior of the old Templeton carpet factory in Glasgow Green.

Work on the church started in 1875 and was completed the following year. The west side of the building also resembled that of St Finbar's Cathedral in Cork which was still under construction at that time. Nevertheless the overall style of the church with its two solid turrets topped by octagonal spires is striking. Great attention to detail was paid to the interior of the building which is illuminated by some stunning stained glass added in later years. Three of the windows were designed by the internationally renowned Cottier and Co, that designed and fitted the glass between 1893 and 1903.

The windows were not, however, the work of the founder of the company, Glasgow-born Daniel Cottier, who had died two years before the work was started.

The church was called Hillhead Parish Church until the 1950s when its congregation was joined by Belmont and became known as Belmont Hillhead Parish Church.

But in 1978 it was joined yet again by Kelvinside Botanic Gardens' congregation to become Kelvinside Hillhead Church after the Kelvinside church became the Glasgow Bible College.

Islamic Centre and Mosque

One of Glasgow's most modern landmarks is the Islamic Centre and Mosque in the Gorbals. Commanding a view of the River Clyde from the south side of the city, it is surrounded by three other equally contrasting buildings in one of the oldest parts of Glasgow – the new Sheriff Court, the Adelphi Centre and the Citizen's Theatre.

The building itself was completed in 1985 by the Coleman Ballantine Partnership. Much of it is of simple brick construction but it is the magnificent multi-faceted, green-glazed golden dome and the tall, slender concrete minaret that immediately draws the eye. The prayer hall within the mosque itself is merely a large empty space oriented in a south easterly direction to allow worshippers to face Islam's holiest city of Mecca in Saudi Arabia. It was the first purpose-built mosque in Scotland and its ability to accommodate more than 2,000 worshippers makes it one of the biggest in Europe.

The mosque replaced an older temporary mosque in Gorbals Street in 1940 which had been set up to accommodate the growing number of Muslims living in the city. In the 1920s there had been only a few dozen Asians, mostly men, but the numbers grew and by 1937 the Indian Association had been set up in the city. By the start of WWII almost every Asian person in Scotland, about 400, had taken up residence in Glasgow. Most of the population lived on the south side of the Clyde which had been the Jewish community.

Kirkhaven

One of the most grandiose buildings in the East End of Glasgow is Kirkhaven on Duke Street. It was built in 1857 by Peddie and Kinnear for the Presbyterian Church who insisted on a classically austere Grecian style rather than Gothic, which was more in vogue at the time. Opened the following year as Sydney Place United Presbyterian Church, the church's stance was quite unique in that it encouraged the congregations' children to get an education.

This was carried out at the adjacent Wellpark School, opened in 1867, 16 years before compulsory basic education was introduced.

In 1926 the church joined with East Campbell Street United Free Church and in 1949 after a merger with Wellpark Free Church it was called Trinity Duke Street Church.

By 1975 the church was no longer used for worship and its interior was converted for its new purpose as a day care centre and hostel for homeless men.

Called the Church of Scotland Kirkhaven Day Centre and lodging house, the old church building continued to provide this service until 1996 when a fire forced it to be closed. Two years later the former church was acquired by the Glasgow Building Preservation Trust.

It has now become a major part of the extension programme for the Wellpark Enterprise Centre based in the old Wellpark school, providing new units for business women in the east end as well as providing conference and training facilities.

Langside Hill Church

The former Langside Hill Church was built in a Greek/Roman style not surprisingly because it was the work of 'Greek' Thomson's former chief draughtsman.

Alexander Skirving designed the building but sadly failed to capture the real strength of line and imagination of his old master.

It was built for the Free Church between 1894 and 1896. One part of the design that was never completed was the statue that should have been mounted on the pediment. Had the figures of the famous reformer John Knox remonstrating Mary Queen of Scots been set in place the building may well have had a more dominant presence.

This was Skirving's third architectural piece of work in the immediate area. Just across from the church stands the Battlefield monument which was completed by 1888 at the top of which is a lion with its paw on a cannon ball, facing down the hill towards Victoria Hospital.

The monument commemorates the defeat of Mary at the Battle of Langside in 1568 by Regent Moray which resulted in her fleeing to England.

Skirving's first building in the area was the contrastingly Gothic design of Langside Old Parish Church which was built between 1882 and 1885. It stood beside Victoria Royal Infirmary but it burned down in recent years.

Langside Hill Church ceased to be a place of worship in 1979 after a major fire. However, in 1993 it was bought for £1 and was restored to become a bar.

Lansdowne Parish Church

Of all the many magnificent spires that protrude into the Glasgow skyline, the one attached to Lansdowne Parish Church is the most slender.

It stands to the west of another magnificent ecclesiastical architectural masterpiece, St Mary's Episcopal Cathedral.

Together, the spires of each church helps punctuate the otherwise unbroken view out from the centre of Glasgow, created by Great Western Road, the city's longest and straightest thoroughfare.

But of the two spires, Lansdowne's is certainly the most spectacular, having a height of almost 220ft.

Work was started on the church in 1862 and was completed the following year, resulting in probably the most attractive Victorian Gothic church ever built in the city.

It was constructed for the United Presbyterians by architect John Honeyman who, early in his career, had established himself as one of the foremost designers in the Gothic style.

The spire is certainly the masterpiece, incorporating an early French Gothic elegance rather than the more popular English style.

Fine carvings detailing the stonework around the spire is the work of the most prolific master-mason in Glasgow at that time, John Mossman.

The interior of the church was also designed on a grand scale.

The ground-level outer aisles were laid out as enclosed corridors along which individual doors opened to each row of pews that were divided down the centre.

This allowed the better off members of the congregation to enter without having to use the central aisle.

Poorer members of the church were seated in the upstairs galleries.

Queen's Cross Church

Queen's Cross Church was the first ecclesiastical building ever designed by Glasgow's internationally famous architect Charles Rennie Mackintosh.

Situated on Garscube Road, Maryhill, to the north of the city, it is also the only church Mackintosh designed that was ever built.

Mackintosh had been employed by the renowned firm of Honeyman and Keppie, specialists in ecclesiastical design, for four years when he was entrusted with the task.

It was built for the Free Church between 1896 and 1899.

Although it has the basic ingredients found in most churches it is certainly interestingly unique, not surprising considering its architect.

The site of the building was considerably cramped at that time being surrounded by tall tenement blocks and a warehouse.

Nevertheless Mackintosh managed to create the idea of size and space which is especially noticeable inside with the large main hall and its magnificent stained glass.

Most of the surviving fixtures within the building were the work of Mackintosh.

As with most of the architect's creations, the style of the design is sometimes described as Art Nouveau Gothic.

But the most prominent part of the church, the tower, was inspired by a medieval church that Mackintosh had seen while visiting Merriot in Somerset in 1895.

In 1977, the building became the headquarters of the Charles Rennie Mackintosh Society, founded four years before to keep alive Mackintosh's contributions to Glasgow's architectural heritage.

Open every day, it is in continuous use for exhibitions and lectures with the shop's profits helping to fund the society's activities.

Ramshorn Church

St David's (Ramshorn) Church was built on the site of another church that was torn down because it was ugly and the space was needed to widen Ingram Street.

The original church, built in 1719, was pulled down in 1824 and in the same year work started on Ramshorn Kirk, designed by Thomas Rickman.

Rickman, the first architect to classify medieval church architecture into styles, chose to build in Scottish Gothic Revival but his original designs were altered by James Cleland.

Cleland was Glasgow's superintendent of public works and he insisted on a crypt being included which resulted in it standing higher above street level than was originally intended.

Within the crypt are the bones of many of Glasgow's most famous people, including David Dale and John Glassford.

They were originally buried in the cemetery surrounding the old church which had once been an orchard and the kitchen garden of Hutcheson's Hospital.

Also interred in the old cemetery but now outwith the kirk yard are the graves of the Foulis brothers, publishers of the *Glasgow Courant*, Glasgow's first newspaper.

A cross and the initials RF and AF near the church entrance on the pavement marks where they were buried.

Within the boundaries of the cemetery, Pierre Emile L'Angelier, who was allegedly poisoned by Madeleine Smith, was buried in an unmarked grave in 1858.

The origin of 'Ramshorn' is unclear but it may have derived from a monastery that once stood on the site.

The church is now owned by the University of Strathclyde.

Ruchill Parish Church

One of the most interesting aspects of Ruchill Parish Church is that its halls predate it.

Situated to the north west of the city, the halls were designed by Charles Rennie Mackintosh. He was given the work while he was working for architect John Honeyman, who had built Westbourne Free Church two decades before.

The white sandstone, two-storey, Art Nouveau halls, in a very plain style for Mackintosh, were originally built as mission halls for the Westbourne Church between 1898 and 1900.

However, perhaps because of its modern lines and intricate sculpturing around the small windows, Mackintosh was not given the contract to build the church three years later.

The church was built using red Locharbriggs sandstone by architect Neil C Duff, providing a wonderful contrast to Mackintosh's white halls.

Its construction was started in 1903 and was commissioned by the United Presbyterian Church.

After it was completed two years later, the church took over the running of the halls which were now standing behind the new building.

A large and imposing square tower is attached to the west of the church while a well-proportioned Gothic porch was built onto the south of the tower which acts as the main entrance to the church.

The arch also provides access to the courtyard which stands between the main church building and the halls.

A caretaker's house with turret stair closes the courtyard.

Mackintosh's halls are still very popular with church organisations and numerous local community groups.

St Andrew's Parish Church

St Andrew's Parish Church is the second oldest church still in use in Glasgow after the Cathedral and is the only building left that still displays the style and elegance of the Tobacco Lords.

In 1734 the town council decided to build their own Kirk and held an architect's competition.

It was won by Glasgow architect Allan Dreghorn who produced a design that, had any of the town council visited London, exhibited a remarkable similarity to St Martin-in-the-Fields in Trafalgar Square.

However St Andrew's would have a tall, slender steeple.

The town council decided it should be built behind the Saltmarket.

The Molendinar Burn, where St Mungo established his settlement in 543 AD, ran through the area and was moated around the church upon its completion.

But it was five years after Dreghorn and master mason Mungo Naismith won the competition that the first stones arrived on site, dug from a quarry which is now occupied by Queen Street Station.

In 1745, while building work was still going on, Bonnie Prince Charlie and his Highland Army camped in and around the kirk grounds.

When the church was eventually completed in 1756, its giant portico alarmed the residents of Glasgow so much that Naismith spent the first night sleeping beneath it, after its centring was removed, to prove his faith in its strength and stability.

The church stood alone for more than 30 years until building work started on the surrounding square.

The church has been described as the finest of its generation in Scotland.

St Andrews-by-the-Green

The oldest surviving Episcopalian church building in Scotland is St Andrews-by-the-Green.

It is also the oldest surviving ecclesiastical building in Glasgow, after the Cathedral, preceding St Andrew's Parish Church by five years.

The work, paid by public subscription, was started in 1751 by masons William Paull and Andrew Hunter.

Its simple design allowed work to be carried out quickly and it was completed and opened to the public in the same year.

In its early days it was known as the English Chapel because, not surprisingly, the majority of its congregation were English.

The church became known as the 'Whistlin' Kirk' in 1812 after it acquired an organ, built by Donaldson of York in 1795, from the Cathedral.

At the time this was a scandal amongst the predominantly Presbyterian Glaswegians – artificially made music having no place in a church.

Such was the outrage that Hunter soon found himself excommunicated from the Presbyterian church for his part in building it.

In 1848 the church narrowly escaped being burned to the ground when the neighbouring Adelphi theatre burst into flames.

The church roof caught fire but the building escaped relatively unscathed, faring rather better than the theatre which was destroyed.

The church continued as a place of worship until 1975.

Its future was in doubt for many years afterwards as it lay in the path of the proposed east flank of the city's Inner Ring Road.

But nothing came of it and in 1988 the old church was converted for office use.

St Columba's

Squeezed between two glass-fronted modern buildings on St Vincent Street, stands the church of St Columba.

Often referred to as the Gaelic Cathedral, it was built between 1902 and 1904 by Glasgow architects William Tennant and Frederick V. Burke.

It is situated on the north side of the street opposite and slightly to the west of Alexander 'Greek' Thomson's masterpiece, St Vincent Street Church.

One of the most notable features of St Columba's is its tall tower with Gothic-style spire that reaches some 200ft and can be seen from the city centre.

Another interesting aspect of the exterior of the church is that it was constructed using very rough faced red stone which gives it a much older and more rustic appeal.

The funding for the construction of this church came from a generous compensation deal arranged with the Caledonian Railway Company.

The railway company had decided to build Central Station after it had been refused the use of St Enoch Station for its locomotives by the Glasgow and South Western Railway.

However, part of the land the company purchased during the 1870s was home to the Gaelic community's old church on Hope Street.

It was also called St Columba, after the 6th century Irish Abbot and missionary who once visited Glasgow's patron saint St Mungo after hearing of his good works.

This church, built in 1851, had replaced Glasgow's first Gaelic church in Ingram Street, built around 1770 which had been sold in 1837.

St George's Tron

St George's Tron church forms an island at Nelson Mandela (formerly St George's) Place in Glasgow's city centre.

Built between 1807 and 1809, it was the first of the great buildings to be erected on Buchanan Street which at that time was lined with villas and farms.

St George's church was originally built to replace the old Wynd Church in Trongate.

It was also necessary to accommodate new worshipers as Glasgow expanded west from the Merchant City around the turn of the 18th century.

The name of the church was given to the newly developing parish in the surrounding area.

It was designed by architect William Stark, who had already won critical acclaim for building the Jail on Glasgow Green.

Much of the building, especially the upper works, show a distinct influence of the style of the famous English architect Sir Christopher Wren.

However, Stark's elegant Baroque tower, which seems to complement other structures built at that time in Glasgow, is more likely to have been inspired from a visit he made to St Petersburg.

The original drawings of the church included magnificent statues that were to be erected at the four corners of the tower.

But financial constraints made this part of the design too expensive and four obelisks were placed there instead.

Sadly the magnificent facade is not matched inside the church which is an unremarkable box in comparison.

St George's parish church joined with Tron St Agnes in 1940 when it became known as St George's Tron.

St Mary's Episcopal Cathedral

The spire of St Mary's Episcopal Cathedral is one of many to decorate the skyline looking west from the city centre.

It was built by John Oldrid Scott, the son of Sir George Gilbert Scott, who built the main part of the university.

The building was originally designed as a parish church to replace the old St Mary's in Renfield Street, built in 1825.

However, during the 1860s, it was decided to sell this church due to the city centre's rapid redevelopment and move to a more congenial site in the West End.

Perhaps because the new building was only a parish church and not a cathedral, Sir George's design has none of the grandeur and individuality of his Glasgow University.

Built just to the east of Lansdowne Church on Great Western Road, it seems to have been erected with little regard for the amount of space available.

Work was started on this simply styled English Gothic building in 1871 and was completed by 1884, six years after the death of Sir George.

The massive square tower seems to be on a different scale altogether from the rest of the cathedral, deriving its style from Lincoln Cathedral.

Nine years after its completion, the spire was finished but although elegant in itself, pales in comparison to neighbouring Lansdowne Church's 220ft spire, the most slender in the city.

In 1908, the church became the Episcopal Cathedral of the Diocese of Glasgow and Galloway and additional offices and halls were added.

St Simon's

The church of St Simon has played host to many minority communities in Glasgow for nearly 150 years.

It was built at Partick Bridge Street in the west end of the city in 1858 by architect Charles O'Neill.

Built for the Roman Catholic Church, it was designed in a very simple Gothic style with a school building added to the southern end of the structure six years later.

Catholic churches were still rare in Glasgow around this time, Catholicism having been severely restricted in the country by laws up until only a few decades before.

When the church first opened it was called St Peter's.

Its first priest was Daniel Gallacher, an Irishman who had come to Scotland while still a child. He was brought up in Blantyre and had become a friend of the famous African missionary and explorer David Livingstone.

The congregation was composed mainly of Irish immigrants and in later years was added to by Italians who started up many of the cafes and chip shops in the Partick area.

However, in 1903, the congregation moved to a new red sandstone church in Hyndland Street and took the name of their church with them.

Since then it has been called St Simon's and is today the church of the Polish community in the city.

In 1979, a copy of St Simon's Black Madonna, that is usually positioned above the Lady alter, was taken on a pilgrimage to Warsaw to be blessed by Polish primate Cardinal Wyszynski.

St Vincent Street Church

St Vincent Street Church is one of the most splendid works of architectural genius in Glasgow and is the last wholly intact ecclesiastical design by Alexander 'Greek' Thomson.

Construction started in 1857 and was completed two years later.

The building perches high on a huge plinth on ground sloping steeply away to the south and west at the upper end of St. Vincent Street where it crosses Pitt Street.

Its style includes a whole range of architectural themes ranging from Egyptian, Greek, Roman and there are even some Indian influences within the design.

In many ways its essential elements are a rearrangement of the design of Thomson's first church – Caledonia Road Church built between 1856 and

1857, which is now a sad burnt-out shell in the Gorbals.

One of the most remarkable facets to the St. Vincent Street structure is the tall tower set asymmetrically to the church itself.

It is as if it was constructed as an afterthought with extra money left over after the main building had been completed.

The clock faces in the tower were inserted in 1884 and are surrounded by Egyptian, Assyrian and Indian ornamentation which are not found elsewhere in the building.

Inside, the high roof, together with Thomson's eye for detail and use of plate glass to let light pour in, give an altogether grand feel to the place.

Not at all what you would expect in a sanctuary of Presbyterian worship, which was the original purpose of the building.

Trinity College

Surrounded by elegant Victorian architecture near Kelvingrove Park in the west end of Glasgow stands the old towers of Trinity College.

The towers are one of the most endearing and imaginative pieces of architecture which make up the city's skyline, especially when illuminated at night.

The structure was originally built as the Free Church College between 1856 and 1857 by the architect Charles Wilson, a most prolific architect, especially in this area of the city.

Of the three towers, the most dominant is the one at the west of the structure facing along Woodlands Terrace, whose design is rather like that of an ecclesiastical lighthouse.

Its style has been likened, in outline and stature at least, to that of 'Greek' Thomson's contemporary tower incorporated into his Caledonia Road Church in the east end of the city.

The other two towers were part of the original church building which was b urned down in 1903.

However, it was rebuilt for use as the college library with a lavishly styled interior throughout.

Sadly only the galleried hall, the magnificent stair well and a large window in memory of two of the college's professors were left untouched during the mid-1980s.

The rest of the interior's design was destroyed to make way for the building's conversion to flats between 1985 and 1986.

A fourth tower in the area was built in 1858 and was part of Park Parish Church before the building was demolished in 1968 to be replaced by a reinforced-concrete office block.

Tron Steeple

The Tron Steeple is all that remains of the collegiate Church of St Mary and St Ann near Glasgow Cross.

The church was built in 1485 but fell into disrepair after the Reformation and a grass market was established in its burial ground.

In 1586 the church was reconstructed and used as the city kirk.

The square tower was added by 1592 and the steeple, modeled on Glasgow Cathedral, was added by 1631.

It was known as the Tron steeple because the weigh-bridge was housed there for many years after the Bishop of Glasgow was granted the right to set up a public tron in 1491.

The church was burned to the ground in 1793 by a group of wealthy young adults known as the Hellfire Club, supporters of the revolutionary philosopher Thomas Paine.

Returning from a night of revelry, they decided to shelter in the session-house where they knew the city's night guard would have left an unattended fire while on their rounds.

The Hellfire Club decided to built up the fire but it grew out of control and they fled, leaving the church to catch fire.

A new, nondescript church (converted to the Tron Theatre in the 1970s), designed by James Adam, was built in its place, separate from the steeple which had escaped the blaze.

In 1855, to allow pedestrian through-traffic under the steeple, ground arches were built by John Carrick.

Today, these arches are all that remains of the picturesque old piazza system around Glasgow Cross.

Wellington Church

One of the grandest and most imposing churches in the West End is Wellington Church.

It is one of the few surviving Greek revival churches in the city and is unusual in that the huge Corinthian columns at its entrance continue round the sides of the building.

The overall effect is of a Greek Temple and its grandeur is increased as it is built on a huge podium set back from University Avenue in the Hillhead area of the city.

The idea of the elevated site is similar to that of University College, London, and the style of the building is comparable to the Church of the Madeleine in Paris.

Wellington Church was designed by architect Thomas Lennox Watson for the United Presbyterian Church but is now owned by the Church of Scotland.

Work started in 1882 and was completed two years later.

One of the church's most famous ministers was George Morrison who preached there in the early part of the 20th century.

His sermons were so popular that members of the congregation would arrive an hour before the service to be sure of a good seat.

Today the church is used widely by many local community groups and clubs.

It also plays host to many events throughout the year including the West End Festival and BBC Music Live.

During term time, the crypt attracts many students from Glasgow University who like to relax there and take advantage of the snacks and drinks that are on sale.

Religious Figures

Aitken, Rev John

One of Glasgow's most fiery religious speakers during the 19th century was the 'Rev' John Aitken.

He was born and lived his life in the Calton district of the city.

His family earned their living from the weaving industry, the main employer in this area of Glasgow at the time.

Aitken's family managed to ensure that he received a good education and when he grew up he decided to use it to make his own way in life.

He became a street preacher and even went as far as to ordain himself.

The 'Rev' was described as a very lean man and he was known widely to be very fond of strong drink.

He preached from many spots in the east end during the week, including Stockwell Street, Jamaica Street and Barrowfield Toll in Bridgeton.

But on Sundays he set up at the Saltmarket entrance to Glasgow Green.

His preaching style was in the fire and brimstone vein and he drew great crowds who loved to listen to his orations which invariably involved local news and personalities.

He always had a pretty young girl with him, carrying his three-legged stool and holding out his collecting plate after his sermons.

On one occasion, money was stolen from his pewter plate so he ran a rubber tube from the plate to a sealed wooden box into which the coins dropped and were then safe from theft.

When John Aitken died he was buried in the Ramshorn Kirk graveyard in the Merchant City.

Barclay, William (1907-1978)

One of the world's most renowned theologians was William Barclay. He is remembered as a popular religious broadcaster and writer of many books including his own translation of the New Testament.

Born in Wick, Caithness, he was educated in Motherwell before studying at Glasgow and Marburg universities. Ordained into the Church of Scotland in 1933, he was a parish minister in Renfrew for 13 years. Returning to academic work, he lectured at Glasgow's Trinity College, specialising in Hellenistic Greek studies. In 1963 he was appointed Professor of Divinity and Biblical Criticism, a position he held until he retired in 1974.

But he is best loved and remembered for his ability to bring religious teachings to the ordinary person in a lively and imaginative way. Many of his teachings and interpretations of the bible were condemned in ecclesiastical circles but it was bringing a down-to-earth religious relevancy to the public that he enjoyed the most.

A prolific writer, he published more than 60 books including his *New Testament Wordbook* in 1955 and his translation of the *New Testament* in 1968. He was a frequent guest on television and radio programmes with his series of talks for Lent 1965 forming the basis of another of his books, the *New People's Life for Jesus*. His *Daily Study Bible* written for the *New Testament* was acclaimed all round the world and published in many languages and he was actively involved in preparing the *New English Bible*.

Chalmers, Thomas (1770-1847)

A social reformer during the first half of the 19th century, Thomas Chalmers, first made a name for himself with the work he carried out in Glasgow.

Born in Fife, Chalmers was ordained as a minister there in 1803.

His fiery oratory style led, in 1815, to his becoming minister of the highly prestigious Tron Church in Glasgow.

But he felt this parish was not where his ideas for solving the problems of the poor could be put to the test.

In 1819 he was given the newly created St John's, at that time the largest and poorest parish in Glasgow.

A strong advocate of the principles of self-help, with the use of church funds, he managed to achieve a system of poor relief which laid the basis for modern social casework.

In doing so he not only managed to raise the standard of life for many poor people but reduced church expenditure.

In 1823 he was offered the chair of moral philosophy at St Andrew's University, a post he held for five years before moving to Edinburgh University to become Professor of Divinity.

His hatred of civil interference towards the church gained him recognition as a leader of the evangelical group within the Church of Scotland.

In 1843 Chalmers led 470 ministers out of the General Assembly in protest at the lack of spiritual independence offered by the government.

He set up the Free Church of Scotland and was its first moderator.

Currie, James (1921-1987)

One man who became known as the archetypal down-to-earth church minister in Scotland was James Currie or Jimmy Currie as he was known. Although his religious work kept him mainly in Glasgow and Ayrshire, he was well sought after in other parts of the world where his style of preaching met with approval.

Educated at Glasgow University, he was ordained into the Church of Scotland and started his ministerial career at Renton Millburn.

Moving later to Pollok, he stayed there for many successful years before leaving the parishes of Glasgow for a high profile ministry job in Dunlop.

Currie's preaching style and religious views ruffled more than a few feathers within the church on occasion but he was never one to back down from controversy. Although not a popular figure within some religious circles, his outlook on the relevance and meaning of religious affairs met with the approval of many.

His frank way of dealing with religion in everyday life won him a place in the hearts of many an ordinary Scot.

Many other ministers have tried to emulate his characteristic preaching of the gospel but none have succeeded in creating his distinctive manner. Currie was always in great demand for his hilarious, anecdotal speeches and, considered an expert on the nation's Bard, he was never short of invitations to Burns suppers.

Govan Sarcophagus

One of the most fascinating and controversial artefacts ever found in Glasgow is the Govan Sarcophagus.

More than 6ft long and weighing 1,000kg, this piece of hollowed-out sandstone was unearthed accidentally in 1855 at Govan Old Parish Church on the south side of the city.

The discovery, one of the most significant in Scotland after the early Christian settlements at Iona and St Andrews, was part of a find of about 40 objects. As well as the Druid's Sun Stone, there are five elaborately carved Norse hog-backed burial stones at the church. Situated near to where it is believed St Constantine built his church and established a Christian settlement, the historic stone pieces date from the 10th or 11th centuries, Recent theories suggest the sarcophagus may date to the 6th century when the site was a burial ground for Dumbarton Castle, the kingdom of Strathclyde's capital at that time. It was previously thought the sarcophagus was built for St Constantine but some researchers now believe the ornate sculptures are too elaborate for a religious man. Among the many carvings there appears to be a Celtic warrior with the initial 'A' – the legendary King Arthur perhaps?

Certainly, the church was an ancient burial place for Welsh-speaking Strathclyde – Arthur may have come from Wales or Cornwall – and Dumbarton Castle was once called Castello Arturius.

One thing is certain, the mystery of the sarcophagus' last resident which has intrigued historians for 150 years, will continue to do so for some time.

Haining, Jane (1897-1944)

The only Scot to be murdered in a Nazi death camp during WWII was the missionary Jane Haining.

She was born in Dunscore to the north-west of Dumfries and attended Dumfries Academy during WWI. When she left school she worked at a Paisley threadmill for 10 years.

But after hearing of the plight of Jewish children in Hungary, while attending a Church of Scotland meeting in Glasgow, she resolved to become a missionary. After taking a crash course in Hungarian she went to work at a girls' mission home in Budapest.

When the German army occupied Hungary in March 1941, Haining was advised by the Church of Scotland to leave immediately but she refused to leave the children.

In May 1944 she was betrayed and arrested on charges of espionage and assisting Jews. She and the children she hid were imprisoned and later deported to Auschwitz-Birkenau in southern Poland, where she was selected for the gas chambers and put to death on August 16th, 1944.

As she was a British citizen, the Church of Scotland received her death certificate from Auschwitz: 'Miss Haining, who was arrested on account of justified suspicion of espionage against Germany, died in hospital, July 17, of cachexia brought on by intestinal catarrh.'

In 1997 Yad Vashem, the Holocaust Martyrs and Heroes Memorial in Jerusalem, honoured Jane Haining as 'Righteous Among the Nations' for her selfless protection of the persecuted children of Hungary. Jane's medal was presented to her sister, Nan O'Brien by the Israeli Ambassador to Britian at a ceremony in Glasgow. Her selfless actions and bravery are also remembered in the stained-glass windows of Queen's Park Church in Glasgow and at Dunscore kirk.

Knox, John (c1513-1572)

Standing high above the Necropolis, scowling down over Glasgow, is the monument to the Protestant reformer John Knox.

It was erected in 1825 on top of Fir Park Hill, 200 feet above the River Clyde. The 12ft high standing stone statue was designed by William Warren and was carved by Robert Forrest. It stands on top of a huge Greek Doric column designed by Thomas Hamilton.

The monument stood alone for eight years until the city merchants decided to establish the first planned cemetery in Glasgow, the 'City of the Dead' or Necropolis.

John Knox, born in Haddington around 1513, was a Catholic priest during the early 1540s, but was influenced by George Wishart to work for the Lutheran reformation. After Wishart was burned for heresy in St Andrews in 1546, Knox stayed with the reformers defending St Andrew's castle. The French over-ran the castle and he was imprisoned until 1549. Knox served as parish minister in Berwick from 1549-1551, where he earned a reputation as a Puritan. He declined the offer of bishopric of Rochester and at the accession of Mary Tudor, fled to the Continent where, influenced by the French Protestant theologian Calvin, he preached to congregations of English refugees at Dieppe, Geneva, and Frankfurt. In late 1555 and early 1556 he was in Scotland again and encouraged Scots to separate from the Roman Church. He was ordained minister of Edinburgh in July 1559. Knox' preaching is credited with a large influence behind Parliament's passing of an act abolishing Papal jurisdiction and approving the Confession of Faith as a basis for belief in Scotland.

His fierce denunciations of, and interviews with, the Catholic Queen,

Mary Stuart are recorded in his *History of the Reformation of Religion Within the Realm of Scotland*.

Mary Queen of Scots (1542-1587)

Two very important events in the downfall of Mary Queen of Scots took place in Glasgow. The notorious 'Casket Letter' to the Earl of Bothwell, proving her treachery to England was said to have been written from Provand's Lordship, the city's oldest building, and her defeat at the Battle of Langside which resulted in her removal from Scotland for good.

Born Mary Stuart in 1542, she became Queen of Scotland when she was six days old after the death of her father, James V.

She was sent to France when she was six, leaving her mother, Mary of Guise, to oversee Scotland.

Mary was Queen of France from 1559 but reluctantly returned to rule Scotland in 1561 after the death of her first husband Francis II. As a devout Catholic she had an uneasy rule over the increasingly powerful Protestant Lords. In 1566 she married her cousin Lord Darnley, who was murdered the following year by a group which included the Earl of Bothwell, Mary's third husband.

Scotland forced her abdication in favour of her son James VI.

Imprisoned in Loch Leven Castle, she escaped in 1568, only to be defeated by Regent Moray at the Battle of Langside while making for the safety of Dumbarton Castle.

Mary fled to London to the protection of her cousin Elizabeth I, but being implicated in Darnley's murder, based upon the mysterious (possibly even forged) casket letter, she was imprisoned for 19 years before being beheaded.

St Kentigern – St Mungo (d. 613)

Saint Kentigern (which means chief lord), more commonly known as St Mungo ('dear one'), was the founder of the city of Glasgow and is its patron saint. Some legends describe him as the illegitimate son of royalty, perhaps the grandson of Urien. Ruins of a chapel near Culross mark the spot where his mother, Thenew, may have been cast ashore and where she gave birth to him.

Another tradition has Mungo and his mother set adrift in the Forth before landing safely in the Christian community at Fife. He came to the site of Glasgow around 540 and was consecrated Bishop of Strathclyde. Around 543 he founded a monastery at Cathures, today the site of Glasgow or St Mungo's Cathedral, where he had buried St Fergus. According to the legend, he had found St Fergus dying by the roadside, placed him gently in an oxcart and instructed the oxen to take the cart wherever God pleased. The oxen stopped at the place blessed by St Ninian about 150 years before and there, Mungo buried Fergus and built a wooden church.

St Mungo is said to have baptised his converts in the Molendinar burn running past the monastery and it is believed that he died from a cold caught after a mass Epiphany baptism there, in January 613, and died a week later, in his eighties. The date of his death has been kept as the Octave of the Feast of the Epiphany, January 13.

The Molendinar continued to flow past the Cathedral, following the line of the present day Wishart Street, until the early 19th century, when it was re-routed underground by Glasgow Corporation in a bid to drain Glasgow Green, then prone to flooding.

St Ninian (360-432)

Saint Ninian introduced Christianity to Scotland more than 150 years before St Mungo established the religious settlement that eventually became Glasgow.

St Ninian is believed to have been born around 360AD in Northumbria. In 394 he was consecrated Bishop by the Pope and sent as an apostle to Scotland. Around 400AD he founded a church mission at Whithorn on the shores of the Solway Firth and built a stone church which was called Candida Casa, meaning the white house. The Christian missionary travelled widely throughout the west of Scotland and is thought to have founded the most ancient burial ground in Glasgow. In the early part of the 5th century, while St Ninian was returning from Rome he stopped near the village of Cathures where he consecrated a piece of ground which is situated to the south of the Cathedral in Glasgow.

It was in this cemetery that St Mungo, more than a century later, buried a holy man called Fergus, whom he had met after leaving his monastery at Culross.

St Ninian successfully managed to convert the southern Picts to Christianity before his death in 432AD.

It is believed he was buried in his church cemetery at Whithorn although it is also possible he may have died in Ireland.

The feast day of St Ninian is celebrated on September 16.

CHAPTER 8
Shipbuilding

The Clyde

Where has the song of the Clyde gone, the real one, not the words and music?

Not too long ago, day or night, the river was never quiet.

The noise was part of the Clyde's fame.

Apart from 'The Fair' it never slept, there was always something happening but today it is silent. No more do the ships large and small, owned by companies also large and small ply their trade into the busy, thriving docks. Even those same docks are quiet now and some are gone completely, filled in and built upon for housing, working or exhibiting.

The river on which Glasgow, among other townships flourished doesn't hum to the movement of the freighters, ferries (except at Renfrew) or even the once frequent dredgers.

'Cluthas', the little steamers that once ferried millions of passengers up and down the Clyde have disappeared with the trams and succession of bridges built over the river cutting out their need.

And the 'Pride of the Clyde', the shipbuilders, have all but passed into history.

A small vestige remains in Govan and Scotstoun which still echoes to the sound of hammer on steel both manual and pneumatic.

The once world famous yards like John Brown's, Harland and Wolff and Alexander Stevens have gone and all is quiet.

Even without the demise of the yards, the 'song' would have changed with modern technology taking over manpower and methods.

The real song of the Clyde has gone, and is now only a memory.

Companies and People
Anchor Line

The Anchor Line was the dominant transatlantic shipping company during the second half of the 19th and first half of the 20th centuries.

It played a major part in transporting countless thousands of people who left Scotland for a better life in North America and elsewhere around the world.

It wasn't until 1856, four years after opening its New York and Chicago offices, that Anchor Line made its first voyage from Glasgow across the Atlantic.

But as the number of people leaving for the new world increased, the line increased its number of sailings to New York and Quebec. By 1865 it was sailing fortnightly from Glasgow, then weekly, and with the better weather on the Atlantic during the summer, twice weekly. As well as North America, the line also sailed to Portugal, Gibraltar and India via the Suez Canal after its completion in 1869. In 1873 David and William Henderson became managers of the line and by the end of the century many of the fleet's 22 vessels had been built at their Meadowside yard at Partick.

The company became Anchor Line (Henderson Bros) Limited in 1899 but in 1911 became part of the mighty Cunard Line.

However it retained its name for many years, becoming Anchor Line (1935) Limited and the following year just Anchor Line.

All that remains of the company today is its former offices at 12-16 St Vincent Street, built in 1907 and faced with white glazed terracotta blocks by Doulton.

Cunard Line

The Cunard Line is probably the most famous shipping company in the world but it could not have become so without a couple of Scots.

Samuel Cunard was a businessman from Nova Scotia, Canada, who emigrated to Britain in 1838.

In the 1830s a reliable transport and communication service was needed between Britain and North America and Cunard won the contract from Queen Victoria in 1839.

He immediately sought the skills and knowledge of two Scots, Sir George Burns and Robert Napier.

Burns was a ship owner, born in Glasgow in 1795 and with his brother they pioneered steam navigation.

Napier was a shipbuilder and engineer, born in Dumbarton in 1791 who made the Clyde a great shipbuilding centre and built the engines for the first four Cunard ships.

The three men, as well as businessmen, James Donaldson and David MacIver founded the British and North American Royal Mail Steam Packet Company in 1840.

As well as being a mail packet, the company which was later renamed the Cunard Line, pioneered the age of steam.

The company was the first in the world to take passengers on regular scheduled transatlantic trips on the Britannia from 1840.

Most famous of all the Cunard ships were *The Queen Mary* and both *Queen Elizabeth's*.

Built for the line, their construction was at John Brown's yard on the Clyde.

Today the *QE2* is the only liner that still maintains a regular passenger service across the Atlantic as well as cruising.

Colville, David (1813-1898)

David Colville was the original founder of the greatest steel manufacturing business in Scotland.

He was born in Campbeltown in 1813 and his early career was spent as a general provisions merchant.

It wasn't until he was nearly 40 that Colville entered heavy industry.

At a time when Clyde shipbuilding was becoming a world-leader, Colville realised that the use of iron would inevitably be replaced by steel as the material of choice.

With that in mind, he set up in partnership with Thomas Gray and together they started to fabricate steel plates for the shipyards.

But in 1865 Colville decided to go it alone.

He pioneered the use of the highly efficient open-hearth furnace technique, developed by C W Siemens, using scrap and pig-iron to produce his steel.

And with this success Colville set up the Dalzell works near Motherwell in 1871.

During the 1880s, Colville's works was the major suppliers of steel in Scotland, the country itself being responsible for 40 per cent of all the steel produced in Britain.

Colville died in 1898 but his legacy to the Scottish steel industry would continue for another 90 years.

During WWI, Colville's prospered and expanded through military contracts.

And in 1931 it joined up with James Lithgow's highly successful Greenock shipyard to form Colville's Ltd.

Sir Andrew McCance later joined the company and in 1936 the company became the Colville Group which in 1947 established the famous Ravenscraig works which remained in production until it closed in 1988.

Elder, John (1824-1869)

One of the great names in marine engineering who helped make the Clyde the premiere ship building area in the world was John Elder.

Born in Glasgow in 1824, he was the third son of David Elder, manager of the Napiers shipbuilding firm.

Educated at the High School and Glasgow University, he served his apprenticeship with Napiers and after working down south returned in the late 1840s to run the firm's drawing office.

In 1852 he joined with Charles Randolph to form their own shipbuilding company at Govan – Randolph, Elder and Company which later became the renowned Fairfields, before being taken over by Kvaerner.

But Elder really made his mark in the engineering world by introducing the compound steam engine for ships in 1854.

His revolutionary new engine design drastically reduced the amount of fuel consumption.

Economies were huge, savings of up to 40 per cent on the amount of fuel needed to make long ocean voyages.

Elder's breakthrough allowed these trips to be made which were previously impossible because of the refuelling needs during the voyage.

And shipping companies and navies from all over the world adopted Elder's new coal-burning boilers and engines.

Nothing could beat Elder's design until after his death in 1869.

It was eventually superseded by another Scot, Alexander Carnegie Kirk, in the 1880s when he further developed Elder's design, taking advantage of steel rather than iron built boilers.

But Elder's concept has remained even with the advent of steam turbines built in the early 1900s.

Harland and Wolff

One of the largest shipbuilding areas on the Clyde during the 20th century was owned by the Irish company, Harland and Wolff, at Govan.

This Belfast-based group proved to be one of the most successful of all the Clyde yards, weathering the storm of the lean shipbuilding years between the wars.

It established itself on the Clyde in 1912, taking over three shipyards.

One of these was the London and Glasgow Shipbuilding and Engineering Co Ltd while another had been established by Robert Napier, who had ensured Cunard's ocean-going supremacy.

In 1919, Harland And Wolff expanded still further, taking over another yard, this time on the northern bank of the Clyde in the Pointhouse area of the city.

It was owned by A & J Inglis Ltd, which had taken over the site from T B Sneath when his company had moved upriver to Rutherglen.

Under the Belfast company's ownership, the yard built its most famous vessel in 1947, the *Waverley*, the world's last sea-going paddle steamer.

For more than half a century Harland and Wolff played a dominant role in Glasgow's shipbuilding industry, specialising in tankers and cargo vessels.

But it also played another influential role in Glasgow.

A large number of its workforce came from Northern Ireland and they established the large Ulster Protestant supporters' group for the Rangers football club.

During the 1950s Harland and Wolff suffered the same slump in shipbuilding as many other yards on the Clyde.

In 1962 it withdrew to Belfast where it still operates.

Lithgow, Sir James (1883-1952)

One of the greatest names in shipbuilding in the first half of the 20th century was Sir James Lithgow.

But he did much more for Scotland than build ships.

Born in Port Glasgow in 1883, he was educated at Glasgow Academy and spent time studying in Paris before he and his brother Henry entered the family engineering business. They became partners in 1907 and the following year, on their father's death, took over full ownership of the company. Together they produced the greatest commercial firm that Scotland had ever known. Diversifying the company over the next few years, they bought into the coal, iron and steel industries. But they always maintained their marine engineering and shipbuilding interests on the lower Clyde as the mainstay of their business empire.

James, however, was to become more than just a shipbuilder and industrialist.

He took on a more political role within the industry, being a key figure in the rationalisation of Britain's shipbuilding and steel industries during the 1920s and 1930s.

From 1930 to 1932 he was the President of the Federation of British Industries.

And during this time he formed the Scottish National Economic Development Council and was its chairman from its inception in 1931 until 1939.

With a sense of moral and religious duty, he continued to work and motivate others on the national and international scene.

By the time of his death in 1952 he had become not only Scotland's greatest industrialist but also one of its greatest industrial statesmen.

McNaught, William (1813-1881)

One of the great innovators in the development of steam-powered engines was the Scottish mechanical engineer William McNaught.

McNaught was born in Paisley in 1813.

He trained to become a marine engineer under apprenticeship at the 'father of Clyde shipbuilding' John Napier's yard.

While there he also attended evening classes at Anderson's Institute, founded in 1796 by Roseneath-born John Anderson, which allowed working men to continue their education.

After McNaught completed his training with Napier he went to work for his father who made steam-engine components for the booming maritime industry up and down the Clyde.

However, at that time powerful steam engines were relatively inefficient in that a lot of the potential power was lost when the hot steam was expelled.

McNaught set about designing a system that would be able to harness this wasted energy.

In 1845 he succeeded in developing the world's first compound engine, which effectively used the energy from the hot steam twice. By using a second smaller low-pressure cylinder, McNaught collected the spent pressure from the primary high-pressure cylinder. His second cylinder then fed the low-pressure steam back into the engine once more, thus creating a highly efficient recycling system.

McNaught's simple design, for many years referred to as 'McNaughting', was widely used in marine engines until after McNaught's death in 1881. His design was later utilised in the development of more complex triple expansion engines that remained in use until they were superseded by steam turbines at the beginning of the 20th century.

Napiers

The surname of Napier is intrinsically linked with Clyde shipbuilding.

David Napier was an exceptional ship builder and engineer although he was never as internationally famous as his cousin and brother-in-law, Robert Napier.

David Napier was born in 1790 and started out working as a blacksmith at John Napier and Son, his father's works at Camlachie.

David built the boiler for the *Comet*, the world's first sea-going steam ship, launched at Port Glasgow in 1812, and four years later installed his first marine engine in the *Marion*.

He started to develop steam engines for the open ocean, building the engine for *Rob Roy*, built at William Denny's yard in 1818 which sailed between Greenock and Belfast.

And two years later he designed an engine for *Ivanhoe*, built by Scott's of Greenock for the Holyhead to Dublin service.

In 1821, he set up his own yard at Lancefield, Govan, after his cousin Robert, the father of Clyde shipbuilding took over the Camlachie yard.

It was at Lancefield that David started to build his own ships and in 1827 constructed the world's first iron steamship, the *Aglaia*.

He built many vessels during his long, successful career including the steam yacht Menai (1830) and the paddle steamers *Kilmun* (1833) and *Loch Lomond* (1838).

David sold his Lancefield yard to Robert in 1836 and moved to London.

Over the years he was credited with many innovations such as his compact steam engine – the steeple engine – and by feathering paddlewheel blades increased their power.

He died in 1876.

Robert Napier did more than any other to establish the Clyde's world-famous reputation for shipbuilding.

His pioneering efforts and high standard of workmanship shaped the future of the Clyde for more than a century and gave him the title 'father of Clyde shipbuilding'.

He was born in Dumbarton in 1791.

After serving his apprenticeship in the family's engineering firm, he worked for the famous lighthouse engineer Robert Stevenson before going into business for himself in 1815.

In 1821 he leased the Camlachie works in Glasgow from his cousin David and started building land engines.

Within two years he won his first marine contract to build the engine for the steamer *Leven* for Dumbarton shipowner James Lang.

He secured more important contracts including the East India Company's new ocean-going paddle sloop *Berenice* but his most famous work was for Samuel Cunard.

It is unlikely Cunard would have undertaken the high risk contract for the transatlantic mail service if it were not for Napier's totally reliable reputation.

Napier established his own shipbuilding yard at Govan and built many famous vessels including *Leviathan*, *Persia* and *Black Prince*.

But his greatest gift to shipping was the men he trained.

Among them, his cousin William Denny, John Elder, who established Fairfields with Charles Randolph, and James and George Thomson, whose shipyard became John Brown's.

He was honoured by many countries except Britain.

But when he died in 1876, 1,400 of his workforce attended his funeral at the Parish Churchyard in Dumbarton.

Russell, (John) Scott (1808-1882)

The grandfather of modern shipbuilding design was born in Glasgow in 1808.

John Scott Russell studied science at Glasgow University, graduating at the age of 16.

Moving to Edinburgh, he taught mathematics and natural philosophy and began experimenting on steam engines and boilers.

By 1834, he had built several vessels that travelled between Glasgow and Paisley but it was his study of wave motion in relation to hull design that made him famous.

Testing ships of varying shapes and sizes on the Union Canal, he developed his wave-line principle for ship construction, the first person to do so using scientific theory.

Moving to London in 1844, his designs were used by the Royal Mail Company and by 1851 he was appointed Joint Secretary to the Great Exhibition.

He played a leading role in building Brunel's famous *Great Eastern*, launched in 1858.

Two years later, Russell founded the Institution of Naval Architecture, the first of its kind.

His theoretical design approach led to new ways of plating ship's hulls, using a longitudinal system with length-ways girders to maximise the efficiency of movement of large vessels.

This new technique was incorporated into the design of the 90-gun Royal Navy ship, the *Bellerophon* in 1863 that served with the fleet during the Crimean War.

In 1865 he published *The Modern System of Naval Architecture* that was a landmark text book for nautical engineering around the world.

Seath, Thomas Bollen

The famous little passenger ferries, the Cluthas, that plied up and down the River Clyde, were built by Thomas Bollen Seath.

Seath was born in 1820 and from a very early age showed an interest in shipbuilding.

He established his first yard at Pointhouse on the Kelvin in the early 1850s before moving to his famous yard at Rutherglen on the Clyde in 1856.

From here he designed his river steamships which had shallow drafts and were about 70 to 100ft in length.

In 1884 the Clyde Navigation Trust bought the vessels for its new river service.

The Cluthas, the first six being from Seath's yard, at first sailed between Victoria Bridge and Whiteinch but later expanded further down river and became extremely popular.

Over the years Seath continued to build and expand his business and throughout his career more than 300 vessels were built at his yard.

His great strength was recognising new markets and soon realised that his vessels could be used for pleasure as well as just for transportation.

Many of his vessels were used by the public for trips 'doon the watter' and he also sent many vessels to other waterways around the UK, including Loch Lomond and Lake Windemere.

But his most prestigious sales were when he won the contracts to build steam-yachts for the Kings of Siam and Burma.

Ironically, increasing competition by the underground and electric trams forced the last Clutha service to be withdrawn in 1903, the same year Seath died.

Clyde-Built Cunarders
Aquitania

RMS *Aquitania*, like many other of the great Cunard liners built on the Clyde, saw her fair share of war-time duties.

Built at John Brown's shipyard at Clydebank, she was designed to support the ill-fated *Lusitania* and sister ship *Mauritania* on the transatlantic passenger service.

Aquitania was launched in April 1913 in front of a crowd of more than 100,000 people.

She was the largest liner in the world, measuring just over 900ft and weighing 45,000 tonnes.

And the Clyde Navigation Trust had to spend two years dredging to allow her to pass down river.

Just a few weeks before the outbreak of WWI she made her maiden voyage to New York but after two more trips she was seconded to military service as an auxiliary cruiser.

However, she was too big for this role and was converted to a troop ship in 1915, serving at Gallipoli and later as a hospital ship during that conflict.

At the end of the Great War she was refitted to burn oil rather than coal and resumed her New York passenger service in 1919.

From 1932 *Aquitania* also served as a cruise ship in the Mediterranean and Caribbean.

With the outbreak of WWII, she became a troop ship once more, operating in the Atlantic and Pacific.

In 1948, under Cunard, she transported emigrants to Canada.

Two years later, having achieved the longest service record of any Cunarder in the 20th century, she was taken out of service and was scrapped at Faslane.

Lusitania

One of the most tragic events in maritime history was the sinking of the *Lusitania* with the loss of almost 1,200 lives.

Launched from John Brown's shipyard at Clydebank in 1906, she was more than one and a half times larger than any vessel afloat.

She weighed 31,550 tonnes and was 786ft long.

The Cunard shipping line had secured generous loans from the British Government on condition she be used by the Admiralty in times of war.

She proved to be not only the most luxurious vessel afloat but also the fastest, claiming the Blue Riband on her maiden voyage across the Atlantic in 1907.

At the onset of WWI *Lusitania* was requisitioned for war duties but was not suitable as an armed merchant cruiser.

So she continued her regular transatlantic passenger and mail service between Liverpool and New York.

But on May 1, 1915, despite a published warning from Germany and the fact that several British merchant ships had been sunk already, *Lusitania* set sail from New York.

Six days later, off the coast of Ireland a German U-boat fired a single torpedo.

The initial explosion set off a violent secondary blast and she sank in 18 minutes, killing 1,195 people out of a total of 1,959.

Was the second explosion caused by munitions she was not entitled to have on board or was she sunk by the British Navy to hasten America's entry into the war?

The mystery remains unsolved 295ft underwater off the coast of southern Ireland.

Persia

The first Cunard liner to be built from iron rather than wood was the *Persia*.

She was built by Robert Napier, the grandfather of Clyde shipping, who had helped Canadian-born Samuel Cunard establish his famous shipping line in 1840.

When she was launched in 1855 she was the largest vessel afloat, measuring 360ft long, weighing 3,400 tonnes and had a top speed exceeding 13 knots.

Persia still looked similar to other vessels with her three sailing masts, two funnels, two massive paddle wheels and a clipper bow.

She was built to compete with the American owned Collins line which was regarded as the best company on the trans-Atlantic run.

But *Persia* managed to turn this around, picking up the Blue Riband in both directions within three months of her maiden voyage to New York in 1856.

Cunard's success was aided by two Collins' vessels sinking, the *Arctic* in 1854, after hitting a French vessel and three years later the *Pacific*, which disappeared without trace.

Its fate was eventually solved in 1986 when the wreck snagged fishing nets and it was revealed that she had hit ice.

The same month of the *Pacific's* accident, *Persia* also hit an iceberg but survived relatively intact, boosting the reputation of Cunard but destroying Collins'.

Persia dominated the Atlantic until 1863 when her sister ship, the *Scotia*, Cunard's last paddle steamer, took over.

Persia remained in operation for four more years but was sold in 1868, her engines were removed and she was scrapped in 1872.

The Three Queens

On September 26, 1934, the world's greatest ship was launched into the River Clyde from John Brown's shipyard at Clydebank.

Queen Mary launched the £5million Cunard vessel in her name after the owner of an existing Clyde steamer agreed to rename his vessel *Queen Mary II*.

John Brown's was given the contract in 1930 but work had to be suspended due to the Depression.

Almost 4,000 men were laid off until four years later when work resumed with government backing.

She was the largest liner ever built, weighing more than 81,000 tonnes and had a length of just of 1,000ft.

She spent two years at Clydebank being fitted with an interior that heralded her as 'the stateliest liner afloat'.

In May 1936 she left Southampton on her maiden voyage to New York.

She quickly recaptured the Blue Riband from the French Line's *Normandie*, crossing the Atlantic in 3 days, 23 hours and 57 minutes.

When WWII broke out she was commandeered for war service and was refitted to enable her to transport almost 16,000 troops to many battlegrounds including Alamein.

She, with her sister-ship *Queen Elizabeth*, were immortalized by Sir Winston Churchill who said their actions had shortened the war's duration by more than a year.

She resumed her passenger service in 1947 and continued her transatlantic run for the next twenty years until air transport rendered ocean travel uneconomic.

In 1967, after 1,001 Atlantic crossings she was retired and made her last voyage to Long Beach, California where she is now a hotel.

The *Queen Elizabeth*, like her sister ship *Queen Mary*, was built at the world-famous shipyard, John Brown's, at Clydebank.

Work started in 1936 and she was launched two years later by Queen Elizabeth.

During the ceremony, the ship accidentally started moving down the slipway but Her Majesty quickly cut the ribbon allowing the lucky champagne bottle to break on her hull seconds before it passed out of range.

But the fitting of the massive 1,031ft-long, 83,673 tonne vessel was delayed as Britain prepared for WWII.

Two years later she secretly set sail for New York to join her sister *Mary* before steaming to Singapore to be fitted as a troop carrier.

During war service she transported 750,000 men and travelled more than half a million miles.

In 1946 she was converted for luxury passenger service, eight years later than planned for her to join *Queen Mary* on Cunard's proposed weekly transatlantic passenger service.

But her fate was married to that of her sister – cheap air travel.

In 1968 *Queen Elizabeth* was retired and became a floating hotel in Florida.

Two years later she was sold to a Japanese shipping tycoon, renamed Seawise University and was refitted in Hong Kong to be a global traveling learning centre.

But nearing completion in 1972 she was gutted by fire under suspicious circumstances, capsized and lay pathetically on her side for months before she was eventually scrapped.

Like her predecessors the *Queen Mary* and *Queen Elizabeth*, Cunard's next great Queen was built and launched from John Brown's shipyard at Clydebank.

Unlike her sisters, however, she was not designed solely for the trans-Atlantic passenger service – modern commercial necessities demanding she be a cruise liner as well.

She was some 40ft shorter than her older sisters and because aluminium predominated over steel for her superstructure she was 25,000 tonnes lighter, allowing greater fuel efficiency.

Work started in 1965 but by her launch in September 1967 by the Queen, John Brown's was in transition to becoming part of Upper Clyde Shipbuilders.

After engine problems were resolved she made her maiden voyage to New York in May 1969.

She was the first ship ever to be awarded five stars by the RAC – an honour usually reserved for the world's best hotels.

The *QE2* has made the headlines many times.

In 1971 she rescued passengers and crew from the sinking French liner Antilles and the following year was subject to a bomb hoax.

And like the Queens before her, she was seconded to war duties, becoming a troop carrier during the 1982 Falklands War.

Four years later her steam turbines were replaced by diesel engines, making her the fastest liner afloat.

Today she is the only ship still operating a regular trans-Atlantic passenger service but spends four months of the year on her world cruise.

Paddle Steamers
Britannia

The first regular scheduled passenger service across the Atlantic was on board the paddle steamer *Britannia*.

First of four vessels, the others being *Acadia*, *Caledonia* and *Columbia*, Britannia was built by Robert Napier, the father of Clyde shipbuilding.

Napier designed and engineered her but her wooden hull was built at Robert Duncan's shipyard at Greenock.

Britannia was the first vessel ever commissioned for the British and North American Royal Mail Steam Packet Company, the precursor of the world-famous Cunard Line.

Launched in 1840, weighing just over 1,150 tonnes and measuring nearly 230ft long, she made her maiden voyage from Liverpool on July 4.

Averaging 8.5knots, she arrived in Halifax and went on to Boston, completing the trip in 14 days.

Canadian Samuel Cunard, had won the contract for the weekly service because he undertook to sail throughout the winter.

Britannia was by no means a luxury vessel.

In 1842, one of her most famous passengers, Charles Dickens, found the voyage so disgusting and uncomfortable that he refused to return on her.

Nevertheless, *Britannia*, like all Cunard's vessels, was reliable unlike others that sacrificed safety for speed with the consequent loss of life.

No lives were lost aboard any Cunard ship until 1915 when the *Lusitania* was torpedoed by Germany off the Irish coast.

Britannia made 40 return trips across the Atlantic before being sold.

Renamed *Barbarosa*, her engines were removed and she became a Prussian Navy sailing ship before being deliberately sunk as a target ship in 1880.

Caledonia

The first paddle steamer that gave men a real excuse for a drink was the PS *Caledonia*.

Built at the Port Glasgow shipyard of John Reid and Co for the Caledonia Steam Packet Co, she was the first vessel to have open engines.

This provided an ideal opportunity for male passengers to leave their wives on the upper decks while they went down below to 'look at the engines'.

Measuring just over 200ft and with a displacement of more than 240 tonnes, she was launched in 1889 and sailed from just below Central Station down to Rothesay and back.

She was built to compete against privately owned vessels around the turn of the 20th century when railway companies, now legally unrestricted, started to take over the water trade.

Originally PS *Caledonia* was powered by a revolutionary oil-fired boiler but in 1903 she was refitted with a cheaper coal burning one.

However, as competition and faster vessels were built, CSP transferred her to the Holy Loch.

During WWI she saw service along the southern coast of England and also worked up and down the River Seine in France.

After the war she returned to the Holy Loch but at the end of the 1933 season she was scrapped.

A new *Caledonia* for CSP was launched from William Denny's yard at Dumbarton the following year.

It was one of the most unusual looking of all the Clyde paddle steamers.

Her side paddle wheels were concealed behind plating rather than the usual decorated paddle boxes and vents, giving her the appearance of a screw steamer.

However, she was shorter and broader than the turbine vessels and her paddles' shallow draft combined with a fast top speed of 17knots made her ideal for her intended purpose.

The CSP, based at Gourock had been incorporated into the London, Midland and Scottish Railway company's ferry service 11 years before.

Caledonia primarily served as a ferry from Gourock and Wemyss Bay to Dunoon and Rothesay but also undertook short cruises from Largs and Millport.

During WWII she was renamed HMS *Goatfell* and operated as a minesweeper.

Returning to her normal services at the end of the war, she eventually took over the PS *Jeanie Deans* route in 1965, from Craigendoran station to Arrochar and Rothesay.

However, four years later she was sold for scrap but escaped this fate when she was bought by brewers Bass-Charrington.

Renamed *Old Caledonia*, she served as a floating pub on the Embankment in London until she was destroyed by fire in 1980.

Her position on the Thames was filled in 1988 by the TSS *Queen Mary* which had also been built at Denny's yard (1933) but had been decommissioned in 1977.

Comet

The world's first sea-going steam-propelled ship was launched at Port Glasgow in 1812.

Making use of Greenock-born James Watt's steam engine, Helensburgh engineer Henry Bell pursued his dream to power a ship by mechanical means.

Bell worked on his idea from 1790 and in 1811 Port Glasgow shipbuilder James Wood agreed to build a 45ft-long wooden paddle steamer.

In August the following year, PS *Comet*, named after Halley's Comet which had appeared during the vessel's construction, was launched into the Clyde.

Using an engine built by Glasgow engineer John Robertson and a boiler by John Napier, it ran a passenger service between Greenock and Glasgow.

But the twin paddles on each side of the hull proved impractical so they were replaced by a single paddle on either side and the ship was also increased in length by 20ft.

The *Comet* extended its service to Helensburgh but within a few years there were more than twenty competitors building paddle steamers.

Bell changed his route and plied the Crinan Canal to Oban and Inverness.

But commercial success was to elude Bell.

He tried to interest the Admiralty but only Lord Nelson showed any real interest and no funds were made available.

In December 1820, the *Comet* was returning from Inverness when it hit rocks at Craignish, Argyllshire, and sank.

Bell built another *Comet* but with little money it failed and in 1830 he died.

In 1862, the original *Comet* was raised by famous Glasgow engineer Robert Napier and gifted to the Science Museum in London.

Ivanhoe

The paddle steamer *Ivanhoe* was the first tee-total vessel to sail up and down the Firth of Clyde.

Other vessels had become great drinking dens for Gleswegians and there was a market for passengers who wished a less raucous trip 'doon the watter'.

PS *Ivanhoe* was built at the Henderson's yard on the upper Clyde for the Firth of Clyde Steam Packet Company and was launched in 1880.

At a length of just over 225ft and displacing more than 280 tonnes, the Ivanhoe could cater for around 1,200 passengers, accommodating them in a high degree of comfort and luxury.

She cruised between Helensburgh, Greenock, Dunoon, Rothesay and Arran under the management of part-owner Captain James Williamson.

In 1894 she was chartered to the Manchester Ship Canal before returning to upper Firth of Clyde duties in 1897 under the full ownership of the Firth of Clyde Steam Packet Company.

It installed a bar to compete with the other companies for passengers.

In 1911 a new firm bought over the company but retained the name.

Three years later the company was again sold, to Turbine Steamers Limited, who used her on the Lochgoilhead run.

When WWI broke out, Ivanhoe was chartered to the Caledonian Steam

Packet Company for ferry work but after the war she returned to the Turbine Steamer's service.

Ivanhoe continued to cruise until competition with the railway company run services became too great and in 1920 she made her final voyage to Dumbarton to be scrapped.

Jeanie Deans

One of the best known paddle steamers was PS *Jeanie Deans*.

Built for LNER (London and North Eastern Railway) at Fairfield's shipyard at Govan, the *Jeanie Deans* was launched in 1931.

She was the first paddle steamer to be fitted with a three-crank engine and could push her 800 tonnes through the water at more than 18knots.

But her deep draught kept her in the lower reaches of the Clyde.

Based at Craigendoran near Helensburgh, she provided all-day cruises to Arran, Ayr, Girvan and Ailsa Craig.

During WWII she was requisitioned by the government and was stationed on the Thames as a minesweeper.

She later became an anti-aircraft vessel and narrowly missed destruction by a parachute mine dropped during the Blitz.

After the war she returned to her former duties up and down the Clyde estuary and was once more a firm favourite with holidaymakers and day-trippers alike.

Her route was later extended to Arrochar, the Three Lochs cruise and during the 1950s cruised around the island of Bute.

In 1964, no longer able to compete with the multitude of other vessels on the Clyde, she was laid up at Greenock.

However, a paddle steamer enthusiast group bought her and she sailed to the Thames the following year and was renamed *Queen of the South*.

She was employed by the Coastal Steam Packet Company on river cruises until 1967 when technical problems resulted in her being sent to Belgium where she was scrapped.

Lord of the Isles

Two of the most famous paddle steamers were called *Lord of the Isles*.

Both were built at D and W Henderson's yard at Partick and provided speed, luxury and reliability for many years up and down the Forth of Clyde

The first PS *Lord of the Isles* was built in 1877 for the Glasgow and Inverary Steamboat Company.

With a displacement of nearly 430 tonnes and measuring just over 245ft, she could carry more than 1,000 passengers on her regular route between Greenock and Inverary.

She later went south to the Thames where she was renamed *Lady of the Isles* (and scrapped in 1904).

The replacement *Lord of the Isles* was built in 1891 and had a displacement of 450 tonnes and a length of 255ft.

Based at Inverary, her passenger service took her to Greenock via Dunoon, Rothesay and the Kyle's of Bute.

In 1909 she was sold to the Lochgoil and Inverary Steamboat Company who ran her up as far as Lochgoilhead but sold her three years later to the Turbine Steamers company.

Now based at the Broomielaw, she sailed down the River Clyde and up to Tighnabruaich before going round Bute and home again.

During the First World War she returned to the Lochgoilhead route and was again based at Greenock.

But with peace she returned to her service round Bute.

In 1927 she was chartered by Macbrayne's and sailed between Ardrishaig, Lochgoil and Arrochar.

The following year she was condemned and scrapped at Port Glasgow.

Waverley

One of the saddest losses in British maritime history was the demise of the first Clyde-built *Waverley* paddle steamer.

Built at the A & J Inglis shipyard at Pointhouse, Anderston, for the North British Steam Packet company, she was launched in 1899.

At 235ft, with a displacement of nearly 450 tonnes, she was the largest vessel in the fleet and operated long distance cruises from Craigendoran.

But from 1902 she was used for railway transfers to Firth of Clyde resorts, NBSP operations having been taken over by its parent company, the North British Railway.

Seconded to war service in 1915, she was stationed along the south and east coast of England.

Unscathed throughout WWI, she returned to cruising in Scotland and became a very popular vessel out of Arrochar on the Three Lochs tour.

From 1923, *Waverley* was under the control of the London and North Eastern Railway which had amalgamated with NBR and several smaller railway operators.

At the end of the 1938 cruising season, *Waverley* was laid up but returned to Admiralty service after the outbreak of WWII.

She became a minesweeper based at Harwich but while evacuating 800 troops from Dunkirk in 1940, was bombed and sank with the loss of 300 lives.

After the war, LNER built another *Waverley*, its last vessel before nationalisation of the railways.

This, the most famous of the Clyde steamers, was built by Harland and Wolff.

It is the last sea-going paddle steamer in the world and for more than half a century has taken thousands of Glaswegian families on trips 'doon the watter'.

She was launched in 1947 and was built for the London & North Eastern Railway Company to serve on the Clyde.

After nationalisation in 1948 she belonged to the British Transport Commission and by 1951 became the property of the Caledonian Steam Packet Co. Ltd.

Her coal fired boiler was converted to oil in 1957 and by 1972, the paddle steamer was bought by Caledonian MacBrayne.

In 1973 she was taken out of service but the Paddle Steamer Preservation Society bought her for £1, saving her from becoming a museum piece.

Glasgow Corporation and Strathclyde Region grants enabled modernisation and repairs to get her ready for the 1975 summer season.

The preservation society set up the Waverley Steam Navigation Co. to run her and today she is still a popular pleasure craft.

For many it is still great fun to sail slowly along the coast with the huge side paddle wheels thrashing through the waves.

During the summer she travels around the Clyde coast but in September she travels farther afield taking in the Irish Sea and the south coast of England.

With a £3million lottery grant *Waverley* was completely overhauled during her 50th anniversary to keep her going into the 21st century.

Sailing Ships
Britannia – Royal yachts

The Clyde was not only famous for producing the greatest and largest vessels afloat, it was also one of the leading yacht building centres.

One of the most famous yachts ever built on the river was HMY *Britannia*.

She was designed by yacht designers G. L. Watson, which still produces world-class vessels, and was built at Henderson's yard in Partick.

The cutter was commissioned for the Prince of Wales, later Edward VII, who had a passion for sailing.

She was launched in 1893 and was the last of the great royal sailing yachts.

Britannia weighed more than 200 tonnes, had a length of just under 125ft and could carry 10,000 square feet of sail.

For most of her 40-year career, *Britannia* was the world's fastest yacht and managed to win more than 350 first prizes, more than half the number of competitions she entered.

One of the most important and famous victories of her career was winning the America's Cup the year after her launch.

When Edward VII died in 1910 the yacht was passed on to his son, George V, also a keen yachtsman, and *Britannia* continued her illustrious career.

However, his sons did not share his sailing passion so he willed that on his death the yacht should be scuttled.

He died in January 1936 and after her gear had been sold she made her final voyage in the summer to the southern tip of the Isle of Wight.

Explosives were fired into her hull and the famous world-class yacht sank.

The first truly ocean-going royal yacht was built on April 16, 1953.

HMY *Britannia* was launched from John Brown's shipyard at Clydebank.

She was 412ft long, 55ft wide, had a draught of 16ft, weighed more than 5,800 tonnes and could travel at a top speed of 21 knots.

Britannia replaced the *Victoria and Albert III* and became the 83rd royal yacht to be built since the first was commissioned by Charles II in 1660.

She officially went into service in 1954 and over the next 40 years or so she would circulate the globe more than eight times, covering a distance of more than a million miles.

It was a true testament to the engineering excellence of the Clydebank workforce that she remained in service for 44 years, the oldest Royal Naval vessel in commission after HMS *Victory*.

As well as taking members of the royal family on nearly 700 overseas trips to more than 135 countries she also played her part as a vessel of the Royal Navy.

She successfully evacuated more than 1,000 refugees from the beaches of Aden during the civil war in Yemen in 1986.

In December 1997, she was finally decommissioned at Portsmouth Naval Base in the presence of The Queen, other members of the royal family and 2,200 past and present members of her crew.

In April 1998 the historic port of Leith was chosen as her final berth where she is now a tourist attraction and conference centre.

Carrick

For almost half a century the world's oldest 'colonial' clipper ship SV *Carrick* was berthed on the River Clyde below Victoria Bridge.

Originally named *City of Adelaide*, the teak and iron vessel was launched in 1864.

She was the fastest sailing ship in the world and still holds the record of 65 days for the 12,000 mile trip from Adelaide, Australia, to London.

The 176ft-long, 791 ton vessel was built at the Sunderland shipyard of William Pile and was originally used for the passenger and cargo trade between Britain and Australia.

In 1887 she was taken out of service but was bought two years later and converted to a barque for use on the North Atlantic timber trade.

She was again converted in 1893 and used as an isolation hospital until 1923 when she was bought by the Admiralty and renamed HMS *Carrick*.

Moved to Irvine, she became a training ship for the Royal Navy Volunteer Reserve before being commissioned as a Naval Drill Ship at Greenock two years later.

In 1947 the Admiralty gave *Carrick* to the RNVR Club (Scotland) who made it their headquarters and turned her into an exclusive club.

SV *Carrick* sank in 1990 and was sold to the Clyde Ship Trust for £1.

In 1992 she was towed to Irvine, home of the Scottish Maritime Museum.

Sadly this magnificent historical vessel's condition has deteriorated over the years and if the £4.5million required to restore her is not raised she may be demolished.

Cutty Sark

The *Cutty Sark* is the last of the great sailing clippers.

Work started on her in 1869 at the Scott and Linton shipyard in Dumbarton for retired captain, 'Old White Hat' John Willis, to be used for the China tea trade.

The 963 ton, 216ft-long ship was finished by Denny's shipbuilders after Scott and Linton went bust and she was launched in November.

She was undoubtedly the finest and fastest of all the clipper class vessels.

But the opening of the Suez canal in the same year gave the edge to steamers.

Prevailing winds prevented sailing vessels from using it, forcing them to continue braving the long Cape Horn route.

No longer economical on the tea run by 1877, she became a 'tramp' vessel but by the 1880s she gained fame on the wool trade from Australia, beating even the fastest steamers.

In 1895 Willis sold *Cutty Sark* to a Portuguese firm.

Renamed Ferreira, she sailed between Portugal and it's South American colonies and East Africa.

A storm in 1916 forced major repairs and she was re-rigged as a barquentine and four years later she was sold and renamed *Maria do Amparo*.

In the mid 1920s she was sold to a former crew member and retired British sailor, Captain Wilfred Dowman who gave her back her original name and rigging.

Until the Second World War ended the *Cutty Sark* served as a stationary school ship and in 1954 she became a maritime museum exhibit and is permanently docked at Greenwich, London.

Falls of Clyde

The *Falls of Clyde* is the last full-rigged iron sailing ship in the world.

Built by Russell and Co of Port Glasgow, she was launched in 1878, the first of nine vessels built for the Glasgow-based Falls Line.

Her designer was William Todd Lithgow, who eventually took over the yard and, under his own name, built it into one of the world's greatest shipyards.

Falls of Clyde weighed more than 1,800 tons, had a length of 323ft and was 40ft across her beam and although slower than the tea clippers, had a much greater cargo capacity.

In 1879 she sailed from Greenock on her maiden voyage to Karachi and over the next 20 years she travelled between Britain and India and around the Pacific.

In 1898 she came under American ownership and two years later was re-rigged as a barque.

Thereafter, she operated as a Hawaiian transpacific passenger and freight-carrying vessel until 1907 when she was converted into one of the first oil tankers, ironic considering she required no fuel.

She completed her last voyage in 1921 and was used as a floating fuel storage barge in Alaska until 1959 when she was scheduled to be scuttled and used as a breakwater in Vancouver harbour, Canada.

However, a Hawaiian group stepped in and moved her to Honolulu.

She was restored to her original state, partly carried out by Sir William Lithgow, her designer's grandson.

Opened to the public in 1968, she is now on display at the Hawaii Maritime Centre.

Glenlee

The three-mast sailing ship *Glenlee* is one of only a few Clyde-built vessels to begin and end its career on the same river.

Built by Anderson Rodger of Port Glasgow for Sterling & Co Glasgow, the 245ft-long, 1,613 tonne, three-masted steel barque, was launched in 1896.

Her career started towards the end of the great age of sail, competing with the new steel and iron bulk carriers to bring tea, cocoa, cinnamon and other spices from the Far East.

This fact resulted in her being sold only two years later to Robert Ferguson of Dundee who renamed her Islamount.

She worked between Europe and North and South America until 1905 when she was sold to R Thomas & Co Liverpool.

During WWI she proved invaluable as modern ships were seconded into war service.

In 1919 she was bought by the Italian Navigation Society who renamed her *Clarastella* and modernised her, adding two diesel engines.

Three years later she became the property of the Spanish Navy.

Renamed *Galatea*, she was used as a training and teaching vessel until 1969.

She was laid up in Seville Harbour until 1992 when she was bought at auction by the Clyde Maritime Trust for £40,000 and towed back to Greenock.

Once more *Glenlee*, she underwent major renovation work and since 1999 she has been a floating museum and visitor centre at Yorkhill Quay.

Her figurehead is a replica, the original was kept by Spain whose government joked it would be returned when Gibraltar is handed back.

Shenandoah

Of all the Clyde-built ships, the story of the *Shenandoah* is the strangest of all.

She was built by Alexander Stephen & Sons at the Kelvinhaugh Shipyard which was more renowned for building smaller vessels.

The 1,200 tonne vessel, with a length of 220ft, was designed by the famous Scottish naval architect John Rennie.

The clipper, originally named *Sea King*, was built specifically for the China tea run and was launched in 1863 at the height of the American Civil War.

The Federal Government wanted her but the British Government used her instead as a troop carrier for the first Maori War.

From there she went to China but on her return her passenger list mysteriously included a Confederate naval officer.

In 1864 she left Britain again, this time supposedly headed for India but, unknown to the British Government, a deal had been made with the Confederates.

In the Atlantic she was loaded with weapons and was put under the command of James I. Waddell and renamed *Shenandoah*.

Along with other vessels such as the Liverpool-built *Florida* and *Alabama*, she went to war with the Federal merchant navy.

Shenandoah destroyed or captured 38 vessels, although several of these occurred after the Confederate army had been defeated, a fact unknown to Waddell at the time.

Captured by the British she sailed to Liverpool and was handed over to the US Government.

Shenandoah was eventually sold to the Sultan of Zanzibar, having only carried one cargo of tea during her sailing career.

Steam Ships
Athenia
The first ship to be sunk during WWII was the *Athenia*.

She was constructed at the Fairfield shipyard in Govan for the Donaldson Line.

The company had started up in 1855, trading goods between Britain and South America but since 1874 had been involved in passenger transport to Canada.

When the *Athenia* joined the line, it was already established as one of the best known companies involved in the emigration of Scots to Canada.

With a length of just under 540ft and with a displacement of more than 13,500 tonnes, the *Athenia* was capable of travelling at a top speed of 16knots.

She was launched in 1922 and the following year made her first voyage across the Atlantic on the first of many regular runs to Montreal.

On September 1, the same day that Germany invaded Poland, *Athenia* set off from Glasgow.

She made her usual stops at Liverpool and Belfast, collecting more than 1,100 passengers, many of them Americans and Canadians, desperate to escape the now inevitable war.

At 11am on the 3rd, Prime Minister Neville Chamberlain officially declared war on Germany.

Less than 12 hours later *Athenia* was steaming out into the Atlantic but when she was only 250 miles north-west of Ireland she was torpedoed by the German submarine U30 and began to sink.

Most of the 1,400 passengers and crew managed to escape to the life-boats but 112 people were killed – the first official victims of the war.

Bonnie Doon

The passenger steamer *Bonnie Doon* was one of a rare breed of Clyde-built ships in that she developed an unreliable reputation, earning herself the nickname Bonnie Breakdown.

PS *Bonnie Doon* was built at the shipyard of Thomas B. Sneath.

Sneath's yard was highly unusual compared to the other Clyde yards in that it was up-river from Glasgow at Broomloan, Rutherglen.

Due to the navigational restrictions imposed by the weir's down-stream from his yard, his vessels were small, *Bonnie Doon* being only 218ft long with a displacement of just over 270 tonnes.

She was launched in 1874 and was operated by Seath and Steel locally on the Clyde until 1880.

The following year she saw service on the River Mersey before returning to the Clyde in 1882.

Under the ownership of Gillies & Campbell, who had a successful association with the Greenock & Wemyss Bay Railway Company since the 70s, *Bonnie Doon* joined the small fleet of vessels that transported holiday-makers from Wemyss Bay to Rothesay. But it was during this period that she earned her unfortunate nickname.

In 1886 she was chartered for use in the Bristol Channel, providing the first passenger cruiser service in that area of the country.

The following year she was again chartered out, this time to ply the Thames estuary.

However, due to financial problems *Bonnie Doon* was returned to Bristol where she spent the rest of her career undertaking pleasure cruises.

Bonnie Doon was eventually sent to Rotterdam in 1913 where she was scrapped.

Columba

The most luxurious of all the steamers was the RMPS *Columba*.

She was also the longest, at 301ft, and was the first of the steamers to be constructed from steel.

The RM (Royal Mail) in her title distinguished her from other vessels in that she had a small post office on board.

Her link to royalty also came from the fact that for her whole career, with the exception of WWI, she sailed part of the 'Royal Route' between Glasgow and Ardrishaig.

The route derived its title from the trip made by Queen Victoria in 1847 shortly after she made her first official visit to Glasgow since her coronation 10 years before.

It remained a popular route for many years and was commonly used by the gentry travelling to their Highland estates.

Columba was built at J & G Thomson's shipyard at Clydebank.

She was built for MacBrayne's who had been operating a mail service to the Highlands since 1852 and was responsible for establishing many new links and routes in that area.

PS *Columba* was launched in 1878.

With a displacement of just over 602 tonnes and a top speed of 21knots, she was capable of carrying more than 2,000 passengers in a luxury previously not seen on any Clyde service.

In total *Columba* spent 58 summers sailing up and down the Royal Route.

In 1935, MacBrayne's finally removed her from service and she was scrapped at the Dalmuir breaker's yard the same year.

King Edward

The world's first commercial steam turbine ship was the T.S. *King Edward*.

She was one of the few larger vessels to serve most of her life locally.

Built at William Denny's Dumbarton shipyard, she was launched in 1901.

Weighing around 550 tonnes with a length of 250ft, she was built as an experimental vessel for the Turbine Steamer Syndicate.

Her three direct drive turbines proved to be highly efficient, economical and fast, reaching speeds of more than 20knots.

So she was put to work as a passenger and cruise vessel and sailed up and down the west coast, touching in at places such as Campbeltown, Fairlie, Dunoon and eventually even Inveraray.

During WWI she was seconded as a troop ship on the English Channel and also as a hospital vessel in the White Sea in the Russian arctic.

After the war she returned to cruising and by 1927 was travelling between Glasgow and Rothesay on the Island of Bute for Williamson Buchanan Steamers Ltd.

She remained on the Clyde during WWII, undertaking commercial work but by 1946 was returned to passenger cruising, under the ownership of the Caledonian Steam Packet Co Ltd.

Sadly, in 1951, just after celebrating her 50 years service, she was sold for scrap and was broken up at Troon.

Two turbines, however, were saved by the Kelvingrove Art Gallery and in 1987 were transferred to the Scottish Maritime Museum in Irvine.

Livadia

One of the most ludicrously shaped ships ever built on the Clyde was the saucer-shaped *Livadia*.

Named after a Russian town, Admiral Popoff designed it for Tsar Alexander II who was prone to seasickness.

The luxurious vessel weighed 7,700 tonnes, was 190ft-long, 120ft-wide and had an amazingly shallow draught of only six feet.

Interior decorations included a rose garden, illuminated fountains and wine racks to hold 10,000 bottles.

Fairfield's was given the contract and the yard's chief, Sir William Pearce had the un-enviable task of building it with the proviso that it would travel at more than 14knots.

If Pearce failed, the yard would be left with a very expensive vessel that they would be unlikely to sell to anyone else.

Amazingly, test results revealed it could reach 15knots and during construction the world's shipbuilders visited the yard to see the creation.

The Tsar's son, Grand Duke Alexis attended the launch in July 1880, along with 40,000 members of the public.

Impressed, the Grand Duke praised Glasgow as 'the centre of the intelligence of England' and it sailed to London.

With the Duke on board, the maiden voyage was to Sevastopol but they encountered rough weather and the ship's design proved wholly ineffective in preventing sea sickness.

It reached its destination in one peace but sadly, the Tsar was assassinated before he ever saw his royal yacht.

Livadia never sailed again and was stripped, her engines put into coal barges and she was scrapped in 1927.

Lucy Ashton

The PS *Lucy Ashton* was the last passenger steamer built during the Victorian age to sail up and down the Clyde coast.

She was also unique in that she was the only one to remain on the Clyde throughout both world wars.

Built at T B Sneath's Rutherglen shipyard for the North British Steam Packet Company, the 190ft, 270 tonne vessel was launched in 1888 and started her career on the Holy Loch.

Based at Craigendoran, she sailed to Dunoon and up and down the loch, but with the introduction of larger, faster ships, she was relegated to the Gareloch.

The Gareloch in the early 20th century was always laid up with liners and merchantmen.

In 1910, the liner Siberian dragged its anchor in bad weather and the *Lucy Ashton* smashed into her at full speed in the main channel.

But despite severely damaged bows, she made it under her own steam back to port for extensive repairs.

However, the *Lucy Ashton* is probably best remembered as the only steamer left on the Clyde during WWII. She unfailingly kept the Clyde open for six years, a feat made even more remarkable as she had been afloat for more than 50 years.

In 1949, a year after celebrating her Diamond Jubilee, the *Lucy Ashton* was towed to Faslane to be scrapped.

But even then she proved useful – her hull was used by the British Shipbuilders Research Association in many experimental tests including the use of jet propulsion.

Queen Mary

The TSS *Queen Mary* was the largest steam turbine ship ever built for cruising the Clyde coast.

Queen Mary was built at William Denny's shipyard at Dumbarton in 1933 for Williamson Buchanan Steamers Ltd.

Weighing more than 1,000 tonnes and with a length of just over 352ft, she was powered by three direct drive steam turbine engines.

Because of her size and level of comfort, she was a popular vessel at the Bridge Wharf at Glasgow where she picked up passengers for trips down the Clyde and out beyond the estuary.

Two years after her launch she was 'persuaded' to change her name to *Queen Mary II* to allow her original name to be taken by the most famous liner ever built by Cunard.

In 1957, the steamer was converted from steam power to oil burning and her two funnels were replaced by a larger single funnel.

As well as sharing the same name as the world-famous Cunarder, the Clyde steamer was to share a remarkably similar fate at the end of her sailing career.

In 1967 Cunard's *Queen Mary* was retired from service and made her last voyage to Long Beach, California where she became a luxury hotel and restaurant.

In the same year the Clyde steamer returned to her maiden name and continued to ply the Clyde coast for another decade, laterally under the ownership of Caledonian MacBrayne.

After she was decommissioned in 1977, she faced an uncertain future but in 1988, again sporting her twin funnels, she was refurbished as a floating restaurant and moved to London.

Permanently moored on the Thames at Westminster Bridge, she replaced another former Clyde vessel, the *Caledonia* paddle steamer which had been gutted by fire.

Sir Walter Scott

For more than a century SS *Sir Walter Scott* has been taking passengers up and down the waters of Loch Katrine.

SS *Sir Walter Scott* is the last screw-driven steamship still operating a regular passenger service on the inland waters of Scotland.

She was built at the shipyard of William Denny of Dumbarton.

In 1899 the 110ft-long vessel was taken in sections up Loch Lomond by barge and was then hauled over land using horse and cart to her final destination.

She was launched into Loch Katrine in October and the following year took up her pleasure cruising duties, taking visitors up and down the 10-mile-long loch.

Her name is taken from the famous work by Sir Walter Scott – *The Lady of the Lake* – which was written in 1810.

It painted a beautiful picture of the scenery of Loch Katrine and drew the first of many tourists to the area.

Since 1859 the loch has also played another vital role – it is the most important reservoir for supplying the Greater Glasgow area with its water.

Today the tradition continues with the vessel transporting tourists that have travelled from all over the world.

The steam ship is still fitted with her original engines, powered today by smokeless solid fuel – a fitting reminder of the engineering excellence that gave the Clyde it's well deserved international reputation.

In 1989 SS *Sir Walter Scott* was honoured with the Steam Heritage Premier Award for continuing to keep Scotland's national heritage alive.

Ocean Liners
Empress of Ireland
The second worst disaster in maritime history during peace time was the sinking of the *Empress of Ireland* in 1914 with the loss of 1,012 passengers and crew.

Two years earlier the *Titanic* sank with the loss of 1,513 lives.

Titanic's passenger losses numbered eight less than the *Empress of Ireland* but her fate is largely forgotten as it happened just a few months before the outbreak of the Great War.

She was built for the Canadian Pacific Railway Co at Fairfields shipyard in Govan.

Her construction started in January 1905 and she was launched a year later.

In June 1906 she made her maiden voyage from Liverpool to Quebec.

Despite being delayed by fog she managed to achieve a North Atlantic record by covering 460 nautical miles in a single day.

In 1909 she collided with a submerged object in the St Lawrence River but escaped relatively unharmed.

But five years later she was not so lucky.

On May 28, 1914, she set sail from Quebec on her 96th voyage.

The following day close to shore in the Gulf of St Lawrence, disaster struck in the shape of the Norwegian collier *Storstad*.

In heavy fog the fully laden *Storstad*, with her heavily plated bow designed for ice breaking, ploughed into the liner's starboard side, gouging a hole more than 15 feet deep.

The liner sank within 14 minutes in 130 feet of freezing water.

SS *Storstad* survived only to be torpedoed three years later off the coast of Ireland.

Empress of Japan
The most luxurious passenger vessel ever built for the Pacific passenger service was the Clyde-built liner *Empress of Japan*.

She was constructed at Fairfield's in Govan for the Canadian Pacific line who had named all their vessels *Empress* since its founding in the 1880s.

The 27,000 tonne ship was launched in 1929 and the following year made her maiden voyage from Liverpool to Quebec.

She joined the *Empress of Asia, Russia* and *Canada* on the passenger service between the Pacific and western Canada and on her first trip took the speed record for the crossing.

With the outbreak of WWII she became a troop ship.

But despite Japan entering the war in December 1941, it wasn't until October the following year that she was renamed *Empress of Scotland*.

Released from military service in 1948, she underwent a two-year refit before taking on the north Atlantic service, sailing between Liverpool, Quebec and Greenock.

She excelled on this route as well and became one of only a few ships to hold crossing records on both the Atlantic and Pacific oceans.

During the winter she cruised to the Caribbean and South Africa but in 1957 she was removed from service as she was no longer profitable.

Sold the following year to the new Hamburg Atlantic line, she was renamed the Hanseatic and sailed between Europe and New York.

But in 1966, a fire broke out while she was in New York and her owners were forced to scrap her.

War Ships
HMS *Black Prince*
The first ironclad war ship built for the Royal Navy was launched from Robert Napier's Govan shipyard in 1861.

HMS *Black Prince* was constructed in response to France building the worlds first ironclad, Gloire, two years before.

At 9,250 tonnes, *Black Prince* was a much larger armoured battleship than *Gloire* and her sister ship *Couronne*, whose displacements were only 5,600 tonnes.

Black Prince was the most important warship Robert Napier ever built but it also nearly destroyed his career.

Napier had seriously underestimated the cost of her construction in winning the navy contract and as a result he put his yard in dire financial straits for several years to come.

But in February 1861, the 420ft *Black Prince*, the largest Clyde-built vessel at that time, slid into the specially dredged river in front of a huge Glasgow crowd.

She was the first navy vessel, along with her sister ship *Warrior* the following year, to bridge the transition between timber and iron vessels.

A true hybrid, her wooden hull was heavily armoured with iron plate.

Her steam engines allowed speeds of 14.5 knots while her three fully rigged masts could achieve 13knots.

Sadly, the *Black Prince* had a very uneventful career.

Her only voyage of any historical note came in 1878 when she became the largest masted battleship to cross the Atlantic.

After this she spent much of the rest of her career with the Fleet Reserve in Plymouth before being scrapped at Dover in 1923.

HMS Hood

When *HMS Hood* was launched in 1918 from John Brown's shipyard at Clydebank she was the biggest warship the world had ever seen.

She was built after the British victory over Germany at the battle of Jutland which saw three battle cruisers, HMS *Invincible*, *Queen Mary* and *Indefatigable* destroyed.

Construction of the ship started on September 1, 1916.

More than 1,000 men worked on her at any one time for almost three and a half years.

When completed she was the longest ship the Royal Navy had ever built, measuring 860ft in length.

Her powerful engines allowed her a top speed of 31knots.

On August 22, 1918, *Hood* was launched into the Clyde, christened by Lady Hood, widow of the late Admiral Sir Horace Hood, who had died during the battle of Jutland.

The *Hood* was not specifically named after Sir Horace but the greatest of all the naval Hoods, Lord Samuel, 1st Viscount Hood.

While she was being fitted out on the Clyde, a massive explosion in May 1919 resulted in the death of two men.

During more than 20 years of service she is remembered for a single day, May 24, 1941, when she encountered the German battleship Bismarck in the Denmark Strait.

After only eight minutes of fighting, a shot from Bismarck penetrated Hood's woefully inadequate armour plating, hitting the ammunition store.

The resulting explosion literally ripped Hood in half and she sank in less than two minutes, killing all but three of her 1,400 crew.

HMS Howe

HMS *Howe*, the last of the famous King George V class battleships, was constructed at Fairfields yard in Govan.

The 36,000-tonne, 745ft long *Howe* was launched in April 1940 but it was two years before she eventually entered service with the Home Fleet.

But because of her late arrival into WWII she was equipped with better radar and greater defensive fire power gained from the experiences of her sister ships in earlier conflicts.

Her first job was to escort the notorious Russian convoys, horrifically and accurately detailed in Alistair MacLean's 1955 best-selling first novel, *HMS Ulysses*.

She survived the Murmansk run and in 1943 was part of the invasion of Sicily which culminated in the surrender of Italy.

She remained in Italy for a refit and did not resume service until the summer of 1944 when she set sail for South East Asia where she operated out of Ceylon.

And the following year, as part of the Pacific Fleet, she took part in the bombardment of Japan.

With the surrender of Japan in September she sailed to South Africa for a refit and the following year served as a training ship.

However, in 1958, after only 16 year's service with the Royal Navy she was taken to Inverkeithing in Fife and was scrapped.

Her bell was saved and is on display at St Giles Cathedral in Edinburgh.

HMS *Vanguard*

The last and greatest battleship ever built for the Royal Navy was launched on the Clyde in 1944.

She was the HMS *Vanguard*, a name that had been proudly borne by naval vessels since the 16th century and of course Lord Nelson's famous flagship during the Napoleonic Wars.

Launched from John Brown's yard at Clydebank, she was more than 800ft long, almost 110ft wide, had a displacement of more than 51,000 tonnes and could travel at 30 knots.

She cost £9million and was named and launched by the future Queen, Princess Elizabeth, the Clyde having been specially dredged to accommodate Vanguard's massive bulk.

However, she was not fully fitted out until a year after the war in Europe was over, despite rushing to get her ready by taking the formidable 15" guns from vessels that were being refitted for other duties.

Sadly *Vanguard* was not destined to have an outstanding service and would not fire a single shot in anger throughout her entire career.

She was stationed in the Mediterranean for the first few years of her service and was the Home Fleet's flagship during the early 1950s.

A few years later it was suggested she be refitted with modern warfare technology but this idea was abandoned because of the expense.

Instead the decision was taken to scrap the great warship that never really was.

HMS *Vanguard* returned to Scotland in 1960 and was broken up at Faslane naval dockyard, having served her country for less than 15 years.

CHAPTER 9
Sport

Lynch, Benny (1913-1946)
The first Scottish international boxing legend was the flyweight, Benny Lynch, who was born in the Gorbals in 1913. Lynch won the National Boxing Union/International Boxing Union version of the world flyweight title in 1935 and after his famous victory he was cheered by 20,000 fans in George Square.

Boxing in Scotland was at its height during Lynch's career, almost equaling the popularity of football, with crowds of up to 40,000 attending fights at Shawfield Park. He was the undisputed world champion in 1937 but the following year, because of a lax training regime, he forfeited his title because he failed to get under the legal weight limit in a title bout against the American Jacky Jurich. Still, he brought fame to Scotland as its first international boxing legend and out of an impressive career of 110 fights, he won 82 of them.

Like many boxers in Scotland at that time, his first trainer was his parish priest. Young boys were trained in local church halls by their priests or ministers before being moved on to bigger clubs when they were older.

Today, there are very few boxing clubs left in Glasgow. And with little support for the sport, it may mean a final knock out blow for any more home grown champions to follow on from Benny Lynch and latterly, Jim Watt.

McColl, Robert Smyth (1876-1959)
One of the great Scottish footballers around the turn of the century was a real 'sweetie'. Born in Glasgow in 1876, Robert Smyth McColl started playing for amateurs, Queen's Park in 1894 before signing for Newcastle seven years later, where he turned professional. In 1904, he came back to play for Rangers but in 1907, returned to Queen's Park, becoming the only professional to rejoin the amateur side.

Known as the 'King' of the centre-forwards, he won 15 caps for Scotland, scoring a hat-trick against England in 1900. But despite his football glory, Robert's lasting fame started with a sweet shop.

Robert and his brother Tom opened their first shop in 1901 on Albert Drive, specialising in hand made confectioneries. Taking advantage of Robert's fame, they called it R.S. McColl. Business boomed and by 1916, eight years after Robert's last international match, they installed machinery into their North Woodside Road factory to supply their 30 shops.

During WWI Tom ran the business while Robert joined the Royal Army Service Corps, where he rose to the rank of Sergeant Major.

After the war the business continued to prosper and in 1925 they became a limited company.

The shops suffered during the General Strike and the 30's depression and they sold a controlling share to Cadbury in 1933 but retained their positions as Chairman and Managing Directors.

R.S. McColl later expanded into England and started selling ice cream and cigarettes as well.

The brothers retired in 1946 but stayed as board members until 1951. Robert, affectionately known as 'Sweetie Bob' died in 1959.

McGrory, Jimmy (1904-1982)

Football legends don't come much greater than Scotland's Jimmy McGrory, the greatest scorer in the history of the British game.

McGrory was born in Garngad in 1904. His footballing career started with St Rochs but in 1922 he signed for Celtic.

During the 1923-24 season he was on loan to Clydebank but for the rest of his career he wore the famous Hoops jersey. He achieved many goal-scoring records with Celtic, many still unequalled, including netting 472 in 445 appearances, bringing his professional record to an amazing 550. Remarkably, almost half of these were put away by his famously powerful and accurate heading ability.

Another unbeaten record was established in 1928 when McGrory put away eight goals against Dunfermline. During his time with Celtic he picked up two League Championship medals, four Scottish Cup medals and was Europe's top scorer in both 1927 (49 goals) and 1936 (50).

Despite these remarkable achievements his appearances for his country were surprisingly small, collecting a mere seven caps.

He retired from the park in 1937 and took the manager's post at Kilmarnock before returning to Celtic to become its third manager, succeeding Jimmy McStay in 1945.

His remarkable career on the pitch was not to be matched as a manager. In the 20 years he managed the side he still chalked up a Scottish Cup (1951), League and Cup Double (1954) and League Cups in both 1957 and 1958. McGrory was succeeded by Jock Stein in 1965 and died in 1982.

McIntyre, Bob (1928-1962)

One of the great motorcycle racers in the history of the sport was Bob McIntyre.

Born in Scotstoun in Glasgow in 1928, McIntyre became the first man to break the 100mph lap record in the famous TT. McIntyre's first appearance at the famous Isle of Man event was in 1952.

Riding a BSA in the Junior Clubman TT, he came in second and later that year furthered his newly-found reputation with a win in the Junior Manx Grand Prix.

McIntyre's greatest racing season came five years later at the 50th anniversary of the TT. Now riding a 500cc Gilera, he entered the history books in the Golden Jubilee Mountain Course, clocking the ton in four out of the eight laps. It was an achievement equivalent to beating the four minute mile at the time, first with a speed of 101.03mph before securing the final record of 101.12mph.

He went on to win the Golden Jubilee Junior to go with his senior title and two years later picked up his third Tourist Trophy in the Formula 1 500cc on a Norton. Now established as one of the greatest competitors, he signed with Honda in 1961.

He secured many fastest lap times but never picked up any trophies as in every race he was forced to retire with mechanical problems.

In August 1962 he crashed at a meeting at Oulton Park, Cheshire, and died two weeks later - the greatest rider never to have won a world championship.

McPhail, Bob (1905-2000)

Bob McPhail was one of the giants of Scottish football, picking up 36 medals, more than any other player in the 20th century.

He was born in Barrhead in 1905 and started his career in the local Barrhead Ashvale team. When he was just 18 he picked up his first Scottish Cup medal with Airdrieonians, playing alongside legend Hughie Gallacher. He later picked up another six, wearing the light blues of Rangers which he joined in 1927. During his first season, his left wing partnership with Alan Morton helped bring the club's first double in 25 years, the league and the cup.

Over the next decade the inside-left collected five more cup medals and nine Scottish Championship medals. He also scored 230 league goals in 354 appearances, a record that stood for more than half a century until Ally McCoist brought the new record to 250.

McPhail was capped for Scotland 17 times and was in the 1931 side that defeated England, the year the 'Hampden Roar' was born. But he never played at Wembley, as Rangers manager Bill Struth wouldn't risk him being injured in cup final years.

McPhail later managed Rangers' reserve team and even ran the first team for a short period when Struth's health was failing him.

But he declined to take on the job full time, deciding to concentrate on his own electrical business.

He died on August 24 2000, the last of the great Rangers players of the 20s and 30s.

Queen's Park Football Club

Scotland's first officially recognised football team was Queen's Park, formed in 1867 at White's public house on Victoria Road. Soon after, more teams formed and regular games were played all over the country. Pioneering the game, Queen's Park, nicknamed the 'Spiders' because of their passing, weaving game, established the country's early playing style.

England was more organised than Scotland and in 1872, Queen's Park took part in the first FA Cup. The same year, on November 30, the first international was played against 'the Auld Enemy' at the West of Scotland Cricket Club, Partick.

Queen's Park dominated the national squad. Paying a shilling each, 4000 spectators watched the world's first great football fixture, which ended in a goal-less draw.

The Scottish Football Association formed the next year with eight leading teams each paying £1 to buy the Scottish Cup trophy. Sixteen teams started the first competition in 1874 with Queen's Park, wearing their black and white hooped jerseys for the first time, beating Clydesdale 2-0. Victorious three years running they won the cup 10 times in the first 20 years.

Professional teams appeared in England in 1885 and the league in 1888 but Scotland maintained amateur status for another eight years. In 1891, the Scottish league started but Queen's Park refused membership until 1900, fearing professional status and to this day have remained amateur.

Their dominance in Scotland disappeared with the league but in 1903, the world famous stadium, Hampden was built on its present day site.

Stein, Jock (1922-1985)

Although never a great footballer, Jock Stein was certainly one of the greatest managers Scotland has ever known.

Born in Burnbank, near Hamilton, in 1922, he worked in the pits in Lanarkshire and started his footballing career with Albion Rovers.

He moved to non-league teams in Wales for a while before being recalled to Scottish football to play for Celtic. At that time they were going through a bad patch but Stein's centre-half reliability easily steadied the side's game. However, it was his understanding of the strategy of football rather than his own skill on the park that was to make him legendary. Entering management, he started with Dunfermline Athletic, successfully leading them to a Scottish Cup victory before moving on to Hibernian. But in 1965 he was back at Parkhead managing his old side. Under his leadership they won nine league championships, five league cups and several Scottish Cups.

Most famous of all was their Lisbon victory in 1967 when they beat Internazionale Milano to lift the European Cup. Stein left Celtic the following year for a brief spell with Leeds United before returning to manage the national squad after Ally McLeod's Argentinian World Cup fiasco. It was Stein's leadership and knowledge of football that rebuilt the national side, achieving a more creditable performance during the next World Cup in Spain, restoring national pride.

Jock Stein died in Cardiff during a World Cup qualifier against Wales in 1985, suffering a heart attack in the last few minutes of the match.

Waddell, Willie (1921-1992)

One of the great lasting legends of Rangers Football Club played over 500 games for the side, scoring more than 140 goals between 1938 and 1956.

Willie Waddell was born in the little village of Forth in Lanarkshire in 1921. After many years playing outside-right for Rangers he retired from the field in 1956. He became Kilmarnock's manager in 1957, building the side up and leading them to two league cup finals between 1960 and 1963 and the league championship in 1965.

In 1969 he returned to Rangers, but just over a year later he had to face up to one of the worst football disasters this country has ever known.

On January 2, 1971 disaster struck after a game against Celtic, resulting in 66 supporters being crushed to death on stairway 13 leaving the Ibrox stadium. Determined that a disaster like that could never happen again Waddell spent around £10million building a new modern stadium to replace the old one. The following year he led Rangers to Europe resulting in the team winning the European Cup Winners' Cup. In the same year he was made general manager and in 1973 he was promoted to Director. And with the signing of Jock Wallace as team manager in 1982, many great years of football were just around the corner. Willie Waddell died in 1992 at the age of 71, having dedicated 56 years of his life to a club that remembers his achievements by naming the club's member's suite after him.

CHAPTER 10
Trade

Tobacco Lords

Today tobacco is a dirty word but without it the shaping of Glasgow may have been very different.

Even more so than cotton, the tobacco industry was the major import for the city more than 200 years ago.

The Clyde was perfectly situated compared to other parts of the UK because being further north it was so much quicker to get to the Americas and back again.

Several weeks could be saved travelling to Virginia and other important tobacco growing areas.

Savings in time meant reduced wages so Glasgow's 'Tobacco Lords' could get their cargoes home quicker and cheaper than importers further south.

Unloading at Port Glasgow and Greenock, the cargo was brought up river in smaller craft as the upper Clyde was much shallower in those days.

The Tobacco Lords swaggered in their finery up and down the 'plainstanes', the pavement at Glasgow Cross reserved exclusively for the city's quality citizens.

But without their huge wealth the city would not have acquired the banks, warehouses and docks that shaped its prosperity.

Many of their fine mansions remain today in the Merchant City.

However, by 1775, Glasgow as a tobacco importer lost its edge with the competition because of the colonial war with America.

Tobacco, along with sugar and rum, had to be obtained through the Caribbean and after eight years of war the trade never really recovered.

Still, without the Tobacco Lords, Glasgow as we know it today may well have been a very different place indeed.

Merchants, Industrialists and Philanthropists

Beardmore, William

During the 1920s, the world famous engineering firm William Beardmore & Co was the single biggest employer in the west of Scotland, employing more than 45,000 men.

The company started in the east end, at the Parkhead Forge.

The forge was originally founded in 1837 and in 1841 it was bought by the father of Clyde shipbuilding, Robert Napier.

But by 1863, the forge was under the control of William Beardmore, senior.

He had served his apprenticeship there when he was 14 and over the years had worked his way to the top.

The business expanded and in 1887 the company started to make high-quality steel for use in naval shipbuilding and other heavy engineering operations.

In the same year, William Beardmore junior took over at Parkhead, having previously set up in partnership with his uncle eight years before.

The company increased production of heavy steel plate for the Admiralty and by 1900 it took over Napier's shipyard near Dalmuir.

Using its steel manufactured at the Parkhead Forge it became one of the country's main shipbuilders and prospered during WWI.

But it failed to cope with the post-war depression and was forced to close, having built more than 60 ships in 30 years.

However, the Parkhead Forge continued and it prospered once more during the Second World War. At the start of the 1970s the forge also ceased operations, with only 400 employees.

Part of the site is now covered by the shopping complex aptly named The Forge.

Burrell, Sir William (1861-1958)

Of its many benefactors, the city of Glasgow's most well-known must be the philanthropist, shipping magnate and art collector Sir William Burrell.

Born in Glasgow in 1861, he started working for his father's shipping business at the age of 15.

For much of his life he travelled around the globe acquiring one of the world's most eclectic private art collections. Tremendously varied, the collection of more than 8,000 pieces was donated to the city in 1944 and is the most valuable ever given freely to the people of Glasgow.

As well as the modern French paintings it includes many other types of prints and paintings, furniture, ceramics, bronzes, silver, glassware and the famous tapestries.

Burrell also ensured for the provision of a museum building to house and display them for the benefit of all members of the public.

However, his priceless collection was stored away in boxes all over the city for many years until after much debating and argument, a suitable location was agreed upon.

In 1983, the Burrell Collection was eventually opened to the public in a purpose-built contemporary styled museum complementing the parkland of Pollok Country Park.

Using vast areas of plate glass, it takes full advantage of natural light to best display the treasures inside while attempting to cope with the variable Glasgow weather. Burrell never lived to see his legacy comprehensively displayed. He died in 1958 before the museum's completion.

Campbell, Sir Malcolm Brown (1848-1935)

The introduction of the banana into the Scottish diet was the result of the enterprising greengrocer and philanthropist, Sir Malcolm Brown Campbell.

Born in Kilwinning, Ayrshire, in 1848, of humble beginnings, he started at the bottom, working as an errand boy and child labourer for a Glasgow greengrocer.

By 1878 he owned three grocer's shops in the city and through continued hard work he rapidly climbed the business ladder.

Eventually he became chairman and managing director of one of the largest chains of greengrocer shops all bearing his, by now, familiar household name.

Malcolm Campbell's shops earned much of their success through the ability to take advantage of the rising urban population.

Demand for a greater variety of fresh fruit and vegetables was on the increase and he worked to make sure his company was there to provide them.

He brought a much larger selection of exotic produce to his family stores which not only satisfied his customers but provided them with a better diet.

Campbell's growing market also increased with the introduction of small kiosks at many railway stations throughout Scotland and northern England.

This expansion allowed commuters to purchase their fruit and vegetables more conveniently on their way to and from work.

For his services to the greengrocer's trade, particularly in Glasgow, he was knighted in 1922.

Never forgetting where his business started, he gave generously to many institutions in Glasgow including the People's Palace and the Royal Infirmary.

Cochrane, Andrew (1693-1777)

Andrew Cochrane is considered to be one of the greatest and wisest of all the Provosts of Glasgow.

He moved to Glasgow from Ayr in the early 1720s and set himself up in business to become a highly respected and prosperous tobacco merchant and shipowner.

He would certainly have been one of the city's leading businessmen that aided the great political economist Adam Smith in his research for his book *The Wealth Of Nations*.

Cochrane rose through the political ranks to become the city's Provost prior to the Jacobite rebellion of 1745 and strongly opposed Bonnie Prince Charlie's legality to the Scottish throne.

When the Young Pretender demanded Glasgow contribute the sum of £15,000 plus military equipment to aid his cause, Cochrane defied him.

Under his influence, no Glaswegian signed up with the Jacobites or provided any sustenance on the four occasions the Jacobite army passed through Glasgow.

Cochrane stalled for time using political arguments until after the Jacobite victory at Prestonpans, when he grudgingly handed over £5,000 to avoid the threat of armed force.

In 1748, he travelled to London to demand financial compensation in light of Glasgow's support of the government in quashing the Jacobite cause.

After more than six months arguing and waiting for a decision he returned to Glasgow with a most reluctant payment of £10,000 for the city's losses.

Cochrane died in 1777.

Cochrane Street, running along the southern side of the present City Chambers, is named in his honour.

Colquhoun, Patrick (1745-1820)

Patrick Colquhoun was one of the great inspirations of Glasgow's social and mercantile development at the end of the 18th century.

He left his birthplace, Dumbarton, at 15 to travel to Virginia in the United States to learn the skills and knowledge he would need to become a Glasgow merchant. He did just that, returning in 1766 to build up a business that gained him acceptance among the exalted and powerful tobacco lords.

Colquhoun also developed political skills and was Glasgow's Lord Provost between 1782 and 1783, involving himself in various schemes to improve education and poor relief.

He also played a part in early attempts to police the city; groundwork that later evolved into Britain's first professional force.

In 1783 Colquhoun established Glasgow Chamber of Commerce, the second oldest in the world after New York's, and was its first president.

Also in that year Colquhoun employed the renowned architect Robert Adam to build him a magnificent mansion to the west of the city on land that has since become Kelvingrove Park.

The mansion remained an important fixture on Glasgow's map until it was pulled down during the 19th century, but Colquhoun's stay was much shorter.

He was the Chamber of Commerce's London representative for many years but in 1789 he left Glasgow permanently because of the restrictions imposed on his improvement plans.

After three years in London he became a metropolitan police magistrate and wrote several influential pamphlets documenting its crime and public institutions before his death in 1820.

Cottier, Daniel (1838-1891)

One of the best known stained glass designers to come out of Scotland was Daniel Cottier.

Little is known about his childhood and education in Glasgow, but by the 1850s he was apprenticed to David Kier, one of the top stained glass firms in Glasgow.

In 1862 his artistic skills and craftsmanship led to him being taken on as the chief designer for the Leith-based company, Field and Allan.

Two years later he set up on his own company in Edinburgh, and in 1867 he returned to Glasgow and set up a studio in Anderston. There he worked on several collaborative design projects with the renowned architect Alexander 'Greek' Thompson.

Cottier's most notable works to come from this partnership were the painted panelling at the United Presbyterian Church, Queen's Park, and the interior designs of the eastern section of Great Western Terrace.

Influenced by William Morris, he was also a great exponent of the 'Aesthetic Movement' – art for the sake of art.

In 1870, he moved to London and set up in partnership with Bruce Talbert, William Wallace and J. M. Brydon, establishing Cottier and Co.

The company's reputation for fine decorative works grew and within a few years they had opened branches in Australia and America.

Today, examples of his work in Scotland include stained glass in Paisley Abbey, Greenock West Kirk and also Dowanhill Church in Glasgow, which has now been converted and renamed Cottier's Theatre.

Dale, David (1739-1806)

Famous for starting workers' welfare reforms at his New Lanark cotton mills, philanthropist and industrialist David Dale's remarkable lifetime included many other less-known achievements.

A grocer's son, born in 1739 in Stewarton, Ayrshire, much of his working life was spent in the mill industry. As a firm believer in practical Christianity, he was a founding member and the best known lay preacher of the dissident 'Old Scotch Independents' of 1768.

In 1783 he became the Royal Bank of Scotland's first Glasgow agent, having married one of the directors' daughters in 1777.

First-hand knowledge from his industrial background of the ill-health and disease common among the poor eventually led him to become one of Glasgow Royal Infirmary's first directors in 1795.

But it is his pioneering work at the New Lanark mills that he is remembered for. He began as a Paisley weaver's apprentice and in 1763 set up his own business in Glasgow, importing yarn from the continent. In 1784 he started the New Lanark mills and went on to build more factories.

However, by 1791 his concern was to improve the lives of the impoverished people of the highlands and islands. He resolved to provide his employees with decent housing, schooling and medical care – at that time an unprecedented act of consideration.

Finlay, Kirkman (1772-1842)

One of Glasgow's most important merchants not only influenced the prosperity of the city but many trading organizations around the world.

Kirkman Finlay was born in the Gallowgate and worked in the family business, which he inherited in 1790 after the death of his father.

James Finlay and Son was the largest British exporter of cotton materials to Europe, but its whole future came under threat when Napoleon imposed a trade embargo on Britain in 1806. Finlay set up trading ports on islands off the northern coast of Germany and in the Mediterranean, and broke the blockade.

His other great international achievements included the breaking of the stranglehold on trade that the East India Company had established in India (Charter Act of 1813) and China (Charter Act of 1833).

At home, he became the first Glasgow-born MP for the Clyde Burghs in more than 70 years and was also elected Lord Provost of Glasgow in 1812.

He proved popular with the public until he voted for the controversial corn laws in 1815, which resulted in his house in Glasgow being attacked by a mob.

Three years later he bought some land on the Cowal peninsula on the Firth of Clyde and built the magnificent Castle Toward which is now a residential outdoor educational centre.

Before his death in 1842, Finlay played an important part in many of Glasgow's affairs, holding senior positions in the Clyde Navigation Company, Chamber of Commerce and was Lord Rector of Glasgow University.

Glassford, John (1715-1783)

John Glassford of Dougalston was one of the most eminent tobacco merchants in Glasgow during the 18th century. He was one of the first tobacco lords and in consequence exerted a great influence on Glasgow's prosperity for much of his career. At the height of his wealth he had 25 sailing ships transporting tobacco back from North America.

Along with James Cunninghame and Alexander Spiers, Glassford controlled more than half of Glasgow's tobacco trade and was making as much as £500,000 annually.

He was one of the key figures credited with laying the foundations for Glasgow's mercantile success, and along with 30 other merchants, Glassford launched the second of Glasgow's private banks – the Glasgow Arms Bank – shortly after the first, the Ship Bank, opened in 1750.

However, like many merchants in those days, he felt he owed Glasgow a debt for his own fortune and was always prepared to fund worthy projects in the city.

Glassford was one of the main financial contributors who helped set up the city's academy of fine arts.

With his money, printer Robert Foulis's dream came true in 1754, establishing the academy 15 years before the Royal Academy of Arts was established in London.

However, the great profits made from tobacco ceased during the 1770s with the War of American Independence.

Glassford lost his fortune through gambling and unsound speculation and died in 1783, three years before Glassford Street was laid out, appropriately situated in today's Merchant City.

Harley, William (1770-1829)

One of the great philanthropists who shaped Glasgow during the 18th and 19th centuries was William Harley.

Born in Glendevon in the Ochil Hills, he moved to Glasgow in his early 20s and established a successful cloth manufacturing business in the city. He realised that people wanted to move westwards from the crowded city centre, and around the turn of the century he purchased Blythswood Estate. As he developed the land, building new streets for housing construction, Harley's area quickly became known as the New Town.

He realised that as well as better areas to live, the population required a supply of clean drinking water. Using water from the natural springs at what is now Charing Cross, he distributed pure drinking water around the city and was soon making huge profits from the venture.

But when Glasgow opened its first water company in 1807, demand for Harley's spring water diminished. So he decided to build a bath house at his public gardens, located at present-day Blythswood Square. His road to the baths soon became so popular with the public, keen to take advantage of the first hot and cold bathing house in the city, that the street was named Bath Street.

Again, as this business venture lost its initial appeal, Harley moved into the dairy market, producing for the first time an efficient and hygienic milk delivery service.

He died after a short illness, while travelling to Europe to promote his innovative techniques.

Lipton, Sir Thomas Johnstone (1850-1931)

One of the great entrepreneurs and yachtsmen at the turn of the last century was a boy from the Glasgow tenements.

Sir Thomas Johnstone Lipton was born in Glasgow in 1850 and built a business empire spanning the globe; today his teas and other groceries are still a familiar site on the supermarket shelves.

At the age of nine he started work as an errand boy and in 1865 he went to America, where he successfully grafted in the tobacco plantations and rice fields. He worked in a grocer's shop there for a time before returning to Glasgow in 1879 to set up on his own.

His first discount grocer's shop in Finnieston was a success and new shops opened quickly afterwards. Advertising boosted his business, earning him his first million before he was 30.

With the profits, he invested in tea plantations, rubber estates, packing houses and factories around the world, as well as buying farms and factories at home.

He created Lipton Ltd in 1898, the same year he was knighted, but he was also renowned for his generous donations to charity.

Business aside, his great passion, yachting, led him to challenge for the Americas Cup on five occasions between 1899 and 1930, but he failed to skipper a winner. He was created a baronet in 1902, and died in 1931.

McIver, Maggie (-1958)

The famous weekend institution the Barras, in the east end, was created by Maggie McIver, affectionately known as the Barrows Queen.

But Maggie was not born a Glaswegian.

Born Margaret Russell in Galston, Ayrshire, she moved at the age of seven when her policeman father was transferred to the city.

When she was 13, she was asked to look after a Parkhead vendor's barrow and found she was more successful then he was.

Her career was launched within the year, selling fruit and fish from a barrow of her own.

She met and married fellow barrow trader Samuel McIver in 1898.

They soon realised there was money to be made hiring barrows and eventually they bought land, creating a permanent market site.

In 1926, the Barras market was covered over to cope with the Glasgow weather, and in order to expand, they bought some shops along the Gallowgate.

In 1930 Samuel died, leaving Maggie with nine children and a thriving business to look after.

But her famous motto, 'Work hard and keep the heid' kept her going.

The market was completely enclosed by 1931 and in 1939 she built the famous Barrowlands Ballroom above the market.

It quickly attracted great band leaders like Joe Loss, and today is still one of the top venues in the city.

Maggie became a millionaire but continued to work a nine-hour day, seven days a week in her market.

In 1958, the same year the ballroom burnt down, Maggie died.

The Barrowlands Ballroom re-opened again in 1960.

Tennant, Charles (1768-1838)

One of Victorian Britain's greatest industrialists revolutionised the use of bleach, making a chemical works in Glasgow the largest in the world.

Charles Tennant was born in Ochiltree, Ayrshire, in 1768.

He was educated at the local parish school before entering an apprenticeship as a weaver where he studied bleaching, and set up his own business in Paisley in 1799.

Charles Macintosh, the Glasgow-born inventor of the famous waterproof raincoat joined him and they took out a patent for the manufacture of a dry bleaching powder. Made from chlorine and slaked lime, its easy transportability resulted in a great demand from the textile industry. Its success allowed Tennant to build a new factory at the St Rollox site in Glasgow in 1800 and it soon became the world's largest chemical works. The lack of environmental concern and ethical production control inherent throughout the industrial revolution made St Rollox one of the country's most polluted sites.

Charles Tennant died in 1838 but the legacy of industrial achievement continued with his son. John enlarged the business, leaving a mark on the Glasgow landscape with the 'Tennant's Stalk' chimney, and his son, Charles, continued to expand the company around the world. He invested further afield, buying up several mines including a pyrite mine in southern Spain and a gold mine in India, both contributing to industrial expansion in Britain.

The Tennant family industrial empire also formed the Scottish Steel Company, a major contribution to the expansion of Clyde shipbuilding.

Weir, William Douglas (1877-1959)

One of the most prominent figures in Scottish engineering during the first half of the 20th century was William Douglas Weir, born in 1877. He was educated at the High School of Glasgow before serving his apprenticeship in his father's well-established engineering firm of G & J Weir. He rose quickly to the top, becoming a director in 1902 and chairman the following decade.

The company was internationally renowned for its pumps and other machinery for marine engines and supplied most of the world's navies. Weir had the foresight to see the pitfalls of over-specialisation; throughout his career he ensured there was a variety of diverse contracts to keep them going, no matter what the commercial climate.

During WWI he continued to supply marine engines but also moved into aircraft assembly and munitions.

Such was his success in these fields that he was made Controller of Aeronautical Supplies in 1917 and later Secretary of State for Air. He was created Viscount Weir of Eastwood in 1918, and at the end of the war he returned to his company.

Many of his competitors were ruined by the Depression but Weir managed to continue his diversification strategy until WWII brought renewed prosperity.

A special advisor at the Air Ministry from 1935, it was his company that put up the funding to make Sir Frank Whittle's jet engine a reality.

After the war he returned to chair his company until he retired in 1954.

Wolfson, Sir Isaac (1897-1991)

One of the 20th century's greatest philanthropists was born in Hospital Street in the Gorbals in 1897.

He left Queen's Park secondary school at 15 to become a salesman. By 1932, he was a buyer for Great Universal Stores, which owns numerous companies including Argos and Burberry.

Within two years he became a director and was appointed its chairman in 1946.

He greatly expanded the company's interests in many areas of business, retiring as its life-president in 1987.

Although Wolfson was one of the country's leading businessmen, he is best remembered for his benefactory work and huge donations to many charities, especially for education.

In 1955 he established the Wolfson Foundation to fund education and medical research and promote youth development projects in Britain and the Commonwealth.

Devoutly religious, Wolfson was active in many Jewish causes both in Britain and in Israel where a number of institutions were established in his name.

In 1962 he was honoured with a baronetcy. Four years later Wolfson College at Oxford University was established from one of his foundation's many endowment schemes and in 1973, Cambridge University renamed its University College after him because his foundation provided grants to allow the construction of the college's main building.

Throughout the 1970s he donated many hundreds of thousands of pounds to the Sir Isaac and Edith Wolfson Scotland Trust to finance numerous educational and artistic activities.

Young, James (1811-1883)

A Glaswegian was the first man in the world to extract paraffin from mineral oil, providing a vital fuel for much of the world into the second half of the 20th century.

Born in the Drygate, James Young started his working life as an apprentice to his carpenter father, but like many Scots of his time, he had a thirst for learning. He attended evening classes in chemistry at Anderson College where he met a young medical student, David Livingston. In 1832 Young became a lecturer's assistant at the college, and five years later, with his professor, Thomas Graham, one of the founders of physical chemistry, went to University College, London. In 1839 he moved to Lanarkshire, taking up a chemist's post where he proved cast iron could be used to manufacture caustic soda rather than the more expensive silver.

His greatest work came while working at a petroleum spring in Derbyshire some years later, when he discovered how to extract petroleum products from coal and shale.

In 1850 he patented his distillation process and moving up to the Lothian's, he set up his successful factory producing vital fuels for heating and cooking.

His discovery allowed paraffin, petrol, lubricating oils and other fuel liquids to be extracted from thick bituminous substances.

This process known as 'cracking' is still used today in the petro-chemical industry and is vital for the modern industrial world we live in.

James Young died a wealthy man in 1883 and is buried at Inverkip.

Inventors
Baird, John Logie (1888-1946)

Pioneering and shaping the future of television was the work in the 1920s of engineer John Logie Baird.

Born in Helensburgh, Baird's early inventions included an unofficial telephone line to communicate with school friends and a dynamo driven gas engine to supply electric light to his home.

After leaving school, he studied engineering at Glasgow University.

Because of poor health, he worked for the Clyde Valley electrical engineering company during WWI, which ended abruptly after he blew up the local supply attempting to make diamonds by passing a huge current through blocks of carbon.

Moving to London, he invented an undersock but despite being profitable, he joined a friend in Trinidad in 1919 to escape the British winter. They started a jam and chutney business that only succeeded in attracting thousands of insects.

Returning to Britain in the '20s, he embarked on the work that would make him famous. Broadcasting the first 30-line mechanically scanned images in 1926 and the first transatlantic images in 1928, the British Broadcasting Corporation eventually adopted his system in 1929. His 240-line system was used in 1936 but was superseded quickly by Marconi's 405-line system the following year. But Baird's invention formed the basis for television production to this day.

Before his death in 1946, he worked on high definition colour TV that the Japanese only mastered in 1990.

Working on radar during WWII, he developed infra-red TV, stereoscopic colour television, video recording and the multi-gun colour television tube, a forerunner of the type used in most homes today.

Clerk, Sir Dugald (1854-1932)

Sir Dugald Clerk was one of the greatest engineering pioneers Glasgow has ever produced. Born in the city in 1854, he attended the Andersonian College where he studied science. He was fascinated by the practical applications of petroleum oils and how they could be used in the production of power, and towards the end of the 1870s Clerk decided to devote his talents to harnessing gas as a fuel for engines. In 1877 he built a gas-powered engine and over the next few years refined and improved its design, based on the two-stroke principle of internal combustion. In 1881 he patented the first ever two-stroke engine which was used for motorcycles and large gas engines. His two-stroke system of operation proved to be popular and was universally referred to as the Clerk Cycle. Its simple but unreliable design has been much refined over the years, especially in Germany and Japan.

With the potential for a higher output, two-stroke engines may soon make a come-back and be used for the cars of the future, taking over once more from the four-stroke engines found in cars today.

As well as his pioneering work in engine design, Clerk also advocated the use of gas for heating, lighting and other urban energy requirements.

In 1916 Clerk was appointed director of engineering research for the British Admiralty and also became the director of the National Gas Engine Company.

He was knighted for his services to engineering in 1917.

Cullen, William (1867-1948)

Despite making advances in explosives manufacturing, William Cullen was also a great humanitarian and a Red Cross leader.

Born in Shettleston, William Cullen was educated at Hutcheson's Grammar School before attending the Andersonian College where he studied chemistry and metallurgy.

He continued to study chemistry in Saxony under William Ditmar before returning to Scotland in 1890 to work with Swiss scientist Alfred Nobel's Explosives Company in Ayrshire.

Cullen worked hard applying scientific principles to the testing of the explosives in the Ayrshire factories, and in the end his hard work paid off.

After 10 years working for Nobel he went to South Africa to become the manager of the Modderfontein factory.

The factory, which had only been open for about five years, had already become the largest of its kind anywhere in the world.

Cullen continued the work he had been doing in Scotland, developing new techniques for the production of smokeless powders, especially useful for mining operations.

And he also looked at how the volatile and dangerous materials could be handled and stored safely.

Concerned with the working conditions in South African mines, he helped promote health and safety measures for the workforce underground.

Cullen also cared about living conditions and poverty in his new country and became the first chairman of the South African Red Cross Society that had been set up in 1896.

Cullen also became commander of two of the South African Army's cavalry regiments.

Mackintosh, Charles (1766-1843)

With Scotland being famous for its wet climate, it is not surprising that waterproofing was developed here.

Chemist Charles Mackintosh was born into a wealthy Glaswegian manufacturing family. After an education at the Grammar School and also in Yorkshire, he worked as a clerk before joining the family chemical manufacturing works. Mackintosh hit on the idea of using a plentiful supply of ammonia, mixed with lichens to create a variety of colourful clothing dyes. The ammonia he used was distilled from human urine which in those days was literally thrown away, usually out of windows into the street.

But with fashions changing over the years to darker colours, the firm eventually ceased its production.

Mackintosh's chemical knowledge also led to the production of Alum, extracted from shale found in abundance in coal mines.

It was used in many processes including tanning and sugar purification and today is still used in water purification.

He developed a beautiful variety of Prussian Blue dye and in collaboration with Glaswegian, Charles Tennant, manufactured powdered bleach in 1799.

But he became a household name after patenting and developing fabric waterproofing in 1823.

He had taken a great interest in the juice from a certain South American tree, namely rubber. Using naptha, a distilled product from tar, which Edinburgh-born James Syme had used to soften surgical gloves, Mackintosh treated cloth with the liquid rubber. This new treatment to garments kept out the rain and the 'mackintosh' was born.

Neilson, James Beaumont (1792-1865)
One of the greatest changes to heavy industry during the 19th century was the hot blast furnace.

It was a huge step forward in the smelting of iron, pushing down the costs of raw materials for shipbuilding and steam locomotive production. Its inventor was James Beaumont Neilson who was born in Shettleston in 1792. He left school before he was 14 and worked for two years at the Govan colliery before serving his engineering apprenticeship at Oakbank under his elder brother John. Time served, he continued to work under his brother until 1814 when he became engine-wright at a colliery in Irvine.

But in 1817 he returned to Glasgow to take on the post of foreman at the newly built Gasworks. He studied chemical science in the evenings at the Andersonian College and used these theoretical skills to improve gas manufacture. He was the first person to pass gas through charcoal to remove its oily and tarry elements.

His idea for using hot air rather than cold in the production of iron was his greatest achievement. At first the idea was scoffed at but eventually the Clyde Ironworks agreed to let him try out his theories.

His system eventually tripled iron output per ton of coal and in 1828 he patented his invention. Within 10 years it had been adopted throughout Scotland and eventually became absolutely essential for smelting around the world.

Neilson became manager of the Gas Works and continued in this post until his death in 1865.

Watt, James (1736-1819)
The romantic tale about James Watt being inspired about how to build a steam engine after watching a kettle boiling in his kitchen is sadly not true. It seems the idea came to him while walking near Nelson's monument and Glasgow's first golf course in Glasgow Green, one Sunday in 1764. Although not such an inspiring story, a small twist to it was that he should never have been there and could have been sent to prison had he been caught. Walking on the Green on the Sabbath was an illegal act at that time and had he been spotted by zealous Presbyterians he would have been fined or even jailed.

Son of a merchant and town councillor, he was born in Greenock in 1736, and became one of the world's great inventors.

Watt gave his name to the unit of power used for light bulbs and was the first to use the term 'horse power'.

Other inventions included the air pump, steam jacket and smokeless furnace.

His engineering skills are less well known, but he surveyed the routes for the Caledonian and Forth and Clyde canals and was instrumental in dredging the shipping channels in the Clyde and Forth rivers.

But he is best remembered for his work developing the steam engine.

He retired in 1800 and two years before his death in 1819 his son, James, a marine engineer, fitted his father's engine into the Caledonia, the first British steam ship to put to sea.

Politicians and Civic Leaders
Bannerman, Sir Henry Campbell (1836-1908)
Glasgow's only home grown Prime Minister was the Liberal, Sir Henry Campbell Bannerman.

Born Henry Campbell in 1836, he was educated at Glasgow High School and Trinity College, Cambridge.

He worked at his father's drapery firm before being elected to Parliament in 1868, representing Stirling and holding the seat until his death in 1908.

In 1872 he assumed the name Bannerman.

A supporter of Irish Home Rule, Bannerman was appointed Chief Secretary for Ireland in 1886 and held the position of Secretary of State for War from 1892 to 1895.

During the Boer War he stood firmly against the barbarities inflicted by the British, a stance that caused a major split within the Liberal Party. Ultimately this factioning within the party resulted in Sir William Harcourt resigning as leader in 1898 and Bannerman took over. He succeeded Arthur Balfour as Prime Minister on December 5, 1905.

His government granted self-rule to the Transvaal and Orange River Colony in South Africa, helping to ensure the Boers supported the Empire during WWI.

Many of his reforms were continually blocked by the ultra-Conservative House of Lords.

He did manage to get his Trades Disputes Act passed in 1906 – a memorable piece of legislation that gave the unions considerable powers to strike.

Bannerman also influenced the Duke of Cambridge to retire as commander in chief of the army, shaping a new modern army away from the practices of the 18th century.

On April 4, 1908, he resigned as Prime Minister and within the week he was dead.

Cleland, James (1770-1840)
James Cleland was one of the city's most influential men during the early 19th century. He was born the son of a cabinet maker in 1770 and became

an eminent statistician in Glasgow by his mid-30s. He spent much of his time working with and advising the council but never became a councillor.

He was honoured with the title 'Bailie' in 1806 and was appointed Superintendent of Public Works in 1814, a post he held until he retired in 1835.

He wrote two books, *The Annals of Glasgow* and *The Rise and Progress of Glasgow*, as well as conducting the Government census of Glasgow in 1821 and 1831.

However, Cleland was so used to impressing others with his knowledge that he was not always accurate with his facts and many mistakes were re-iterated for many years to come.

During his period in the public works office, he conducted many innovative moves, including having Glasgow Green levelled and grassed extensively. He was also responsible for redirecting underground the Molendinar Burn, on the banks of which St Kintegern had established his monastery in the 6th century.

Among the many other activities Cleland undertook, was the design of St David's (Ramshorn) Kirk in the 1820s.

In his honour, Glasgow erected the Cleland Testimonial building in 1836 which later became the George Hotel (1907) where the Virgin megastore in Buchanan Street now stands.

When Cleland died in 1840 he was entombed in the Ramshorn crypt which he had insisted be included in its design.

Dinwiddie, Robert (1693-1770)

The 'Grandfather of the United States', Robert Dinwiddie, was born into a wealthy merchant's family in Germiston near Glasgow in 1693.

Educated at Glasgow University, he worked in his father's counting-house before becoming a successful merchant in his own right. In 1721 the British government appointed him colonial administrator of Bermuda and after six years service he became collector of customs.

By 1738 he was surveyor-general for the southern colonies of British North America, a position that entitled him to a seat on the Virginia Council, the largest colony.

In 1751 he became lieutenant-general of Virginia and promoted his firm views on British expansion to the west.

During his time in office he tried to prevent the troubles along the frontier that gave rise to the French and Indian wars and pressed for funds to be raised to protect the colonies.

He advocated the use of the regular army rather than the less reliable militias.

Dinwiddie spotted the potential of a young soldier, George Washington, whom he promoted to lieutenant-colonel in 1754, and sent him to resist the French.

Dinwiddie's work generally went down well in the colonies.

But on one occasion he tried to levy a tax on land-holders for the Crown, an action that was a precursor of future arguments that would start the American War of Independence in 1776.

However, poor health resulted in Dinwiddie requesting to be relieved of office in 1758 and he returned to Britain.

Elliot, Walter (1888-1958)

Very few Scottish Conservatives have made their mark at Westminster, but Walter Elliot was one of the exceptions.

Born in Lanark in 1888, he was educated at Glasgow Academy before studying medicine at Glasgow University.

During WWI he served as a doctor with the Scots Greys and won the Military Cross in 1917.

In 1919 he was elected MP for Lanark.

He had no time for Socialism, advocating Free Trade, but he also urged State intervention in certain areas, especially public health.

In 1923 he lost his Lanark seat, but became MP for Kelvingrove the following year, a seat he held until 1945.

As Minister of Agriculture he instigated systems that provided a stable farming economy until Britain entered the Common Market.

And as Secretary of State for Scotland between 1936 and 1938, although a Unionist, he established many administrative devolution policies.

He set up the Scottish Special Housing Association, backed the Scottish National Development Council, created the Scottish Economic Committee in 1936 and promoted the 1938 Empire Exhibition in Glasgow.

From 1938 to 1940 he was Minister of Health and from 1946 until 1949 was MP for Scottish Universities.

Elliot was left out of Churchill's Cabinet in 1951 and never returned to office but continued to pursue Scotland's political interests and became a well regarded and prolific writer and broadcaster.

A life-long supporter of women's admission into the House of Lords, after his death in 1958, his widow was created Scotland's first life peeress, Baroness Katharine Elliot of Harwood.

Henderson, Arthur (1863-1935)

Glasgow-born Labour politician Arthur Henderson was awarded the Nobel Peace Prize for his efforts to promote peace between the two world wars.

Born in 1863, Henderson started life as an iron moulder at the foundry in Newcastle-upon-Tyne where Stevenson's 'Rocket' had been built in 1829.

He became secretary of the foundry's union and was an active member of several municipal councils.

By 1900 he was elected Mayor of Darlington, the same year he joined the Labour Party.

He did much to build up the party and was elected chairman from 1908 to 1910 and again from 1914 to 1917.

He actively supported the need to fight during WWI and from 1915 served in the coalition cabinet under Liberal Lloyd George.

Henderson was sent to Russia in 1917 to hear plans for its international socialist government. But Lloyd George's indecision over the proposals led to Henderson resigning from the cabinet in the same year.

After WWI he started reforming the Labour Party into a confirmed socialist organisation and played an instrumental role in creating the party's first constitution.

He became Home Secretary in 1924 and was Labour's Foreign Secretary from 1929.

But, along with many others refusing to enter Ramsay MacDonald's government, he resigned his position in 1931.

Serving as President of the World Disarmament Conference in 1932, he tried to promote armament limitations with Adolf Hitler in Germany.

Two years later he was awarded the Nobel Prize for Peace but died the following year in 1935.

Kirkwood, David (1872-1951)

Socialist David Kirkwood spent most of his turbulent working life at Beardmore's Parkhead Forge. Kirkwood, born in Glasgow in 1872, is best remembered for his protests for the working man and his strong political beliefs.

After working at the forge for only a short period, he was sacked for inciting strike action and was banned from working there.

Yet he returned as a chief shop steward in 1910, and later joined the Independent Labour party.

The year after the beginning of WWI he became the treasurer of the Clyde Workers' Committee and in 1916 Kirkwood again instigated strike action at Beardmore's. However, on that occasion he lost more than his job – he was deported to Edinburgh. After this order was lifted he returned to Glasgow and took up employment yet again at the forge – this time as foreman.

In 1919 he was elected as councillor for the Mile-end ward and three years later became an MP for Dumbarton.

As a Red Clydesider, he perhaps didn't capture the public imagination as much as Manny Shinwell or James Maxton.

But he was certainly instrumental in their campaigns and was twice suspended from the Houses of Parliament for his behaviour.

When he returned to Parliament in 1935, like many other 'Clydesider' MPs, he calmed down.

After WWII he joined the Labour Party and became a Privy Councillor in 1947.

In 1951 he was created first Baron Kirkwood of Bearsden.

He died four years later.

Law, Andrew Bonar (1858-1922)

Often referred to as the 'unknown prime minister' Andrew Bonar Law made his first break into the political arena when he became a Tory MP for Glasgow Blackfriars in 1900.

Born in Canada in 1858, to an Ulster Presbyterian minister and a Scottish mother, he was sent to live in Scotland when he was 12 after his mother's death.

When he was 16 he started working in his family's Glasgow ironworks and later became a partner in the firm, a move that affected his political career in years to come.

In 1902 he became the Secretary to the Board of Trade in Balfour's government but like many Conservatives lost his seat in the 1906 election.

However, he became MP for Dulwich later that year and on Balfour's resignation in 1911, he became party leader, a position he held until 1921.

At the outbreak of WWI it was claimed his family had been selling iron to Germany for its armaments programme until 1914.

This embarrassment prevented him gaining a senior Cabinet position in Asquith's government.

He became colonial secretary, but the following year Lloyd George became PM and Bonar Law was made Chancellor of the Exchequer.

He became Lord Privy Seal in 1919 but resigned in 1921 due to poor health. He returned as prime minister in October 1922, the first man from a British overseas possession to hold the position.

He remained PM until the following May when ill-health again forced his resignation.

Bonar Law died a few months later.

MacCormick, John MacDonald (1904-1961)

One of Scotland's greatest nationalist politicians was the lawyer John MacDonald MacCormick. He was a founder member of the National Party of Scotland and later established the Scottish National Party.

He studied law at Glasgow and in 1927 formed the Glasgow University Scottish Nationalist Association.

The following year his group formed with the Scots National League and the Scottish National Movement to become the National Party of Scotland.

After the formation of another group – the Scottish Party – in 1932, a meeting in Glasgow decided they should amalgamate.

MacCormick, knowing the National Party was in dire financial straits, argued that both groups should fight together rather than against each other, and in 1934 the Scottish National Party was born.

MacCormick's publicity and propaganda skills created a significant swing among the public in favour of Scottish self-government.

But in 1942 he resigned from the party following controversy over attitudes towards the war, and formed the Scottish Convention, later the Scottish Covenant.

In 1950 MacCormick's fame brought about his election as Lord Rector of Glasgow University, a position he held for three years.

Also in 1950 he was involved in the Stone of Destiny being liberated from Westminster Abbey and returned to Arbroath Abbey, more than 650 years after it was stolen by the English King, Edward I.

MacCormick never managed to get the Self Government debate decided in Parliament, and his early death in 1961 saw his own organisation disintegrate.

MacDonald, John Alexander (1815-1891)

The Scots have played a major role in changing many aspects of global history and Glasgow-born John Alexander MacDonald was no exception.

He was largely responsible for the historical development of an independent Canada, free from a union with the United States of America.

Born in 1815, he emigrated with his parents in 1820 to Kingston, which is now in Ontario.

He studied to become a lawyer and was called to the Bar in 1836 and was later appointed a Queen's Council.

But his ambitions led him down the path of a political career.

MacDonald, like many other Scots in the country at that time, was very loyal to Great Britain.

From 1848 to 1854 he helped ensure the British America League worked in order to unify Canada and maintain ties with Britain.

His political opponents regarded him as a hard-nosed tactician and many thought him devious and unscrupulous.

But he became leader of the Conservatives in 1856 and joint Premier with George-Etienne Cartier for the Province of Canada in the same year.

He continued to strive to strengthen the divided Canadian provinces and succeeded in 1867 with the British North America Act, creating the Dominion of Canada, and so uniting the West and East provinces.

He was elected its first Prime Minister in the same year, holding the post until 1873, and expanded the dominion's territory to include Manitoba, British Columbia and Prince Edward Island.

MacDonald returned to power in 1878, leading his country until his death in Ottawa in 1891.

MacLean, John (1879-1923)

John MacLean, the great labour leader at the turn of the century, was born in Pollokshaws on August 14, 1879.

Second youngest of seven children from a very poor family, his widowed mother made sure he got a good education, sending him to Pollokshields Academy and Queen's Park School.

Becoming a pupil-teacher in 1896, he then joined the Free Church Teacher Training College.

Graduating in 1900, he taught in Govan, was sacked in 1915 and started

Marxist classes for working men, proving very popular with attendances of 1,000 at times.

Pacifist and anti-militarist, he campaigned for peace during the war and afterwards formed the Tramp Trust Unlimited, campaigning for a minimum wage, a six-hour day and full wages for the unemployed.

He was the local Soviet Consul after the Russian Revolution and has a street named after him in St Petersburg.

He refused to join the Communist Party, setting up his own, more nationalistic Scottish Workers' Republican Party.

Inciting sedition and strikes, he was jailed several times, once being sentenced to five years in Peterhead Prison. However, a mass protest gained his release after only six months.

He suffered greatly from poor health, made worse by his times spent in prison, and died on St Andrew's Day 1923, aged only 44.

Many history books fail to mention him but he is immortalised by the folklorist, Hamish Henderson, who wrote two songs about him, 'Freedom Come all Ye' and 'The John MacLean March'.

Maxton, James (1885-1946)

One of the great socialist politicians of the first half of the 20th century was James Maxton.

Born in Glasgow in 1885 to parents who were both teachers, he was educated at Hutcheson's Grammar School and Glasgow University before becoming one himself. But his exposure to Glasgow's poverty was enough to change his outlook from conservatism to socialism.

He joined the Independent Labour Party, becoming a leading figure by 1912, and helped form teachers' unions.

Along with another famous Glasgow socialist, John MacLean, he lectured at the Scottish Labour College.

But during WWI he was imprisoned for a year. A pacifist and strike organiser at munitions factories and shipyards, he also lost his teaching job.

After the war, he continued political campaigning and was elected as Labour MP for Bridgeton in 1922, a seat he retained until his death.

A major critic of Conservatives and moderate Labour, he became one of the great 'Red Clydesiders' and in 1923 was suspended from the House of Commons for calling another MP a murderer.

In 1926 he was active during the General Strike and in the same year was made chairman of the Independent Labour Party, a position he retained until 1940.

He lead the ILP's split from Labour in 1932 and continued to become isolated from mainstream politics, but gained respect for his sincerity and resolve.

He wrote several books including *The Life of Lenin* in 1932 and *If I Were Dictator* in 1935.

McCulloch, James (1819-1893)

Many Scots have played a major part in Australian history.

James McCulloch did much to establish a stable political base in Victoria in the second half of the 19th century.

An enterprising young man, he established himself as a well-respected merchant in the city, and spent many years building up his own company.

In 1853, he left Glasgow and moved to Melbourne, the capital of Victoria, to open a branch office for his mercantile firm.

He quickly managed to set himself up in the independent colony of Victoria, which had been established only two years before.

Within three years of his arrival in the country, McCulloch had been voted into politics as an Assemblyman and became Minister of Trade and Customs and Treasurer in 1859.

From 1863-68 McCulloch served as Prime Minister of Victoria.

His leadership helped make Victoria one of the most stable colonies in the Australian province at that time.

One of his major achievements was in winning the fight for protective trading tariffs against the resistance of the Legislative Council.

He served as Prime Minister again from 1868-1869 and was elected for a third time in 1870, the same year he was honoured for his services to the colony with a knighthood.

He lost the election the following year but was returned to power again in 1875.

But in 1877 he was defeated and decided to return to Britain.

Oswald, James (1779-1853)

The least recognised statue in George Square is perhaps that of James Oswald. Designed by Baron Marochetti in 1856, the bronze statue was originally erected at Charing Cross before being moved to the square in 1875.

For many years it was a source of amusement to youngsters who used to play games, throwing stones and coins into his top hat.

On many occasions it was also used as a nesting site for sparrows.

Oswald, despite being little known today, was a very important man in Glasgow during the early part of the 19th century.

Born in 1779, he became an influential merchant and his staunch liberal political beliefs in reform aided him in becoming one of the first MPs in the reformed parliament of 1832.

As a Whig, he had been heavily involved in ensuring the Reform Act was passed. At a demonstration of more than 70,000 people at Glasgow Green, it was he who was called upon to officiate at the meeting.

The passing of the '32 Act substantially increased the size of the electorate to include the wealthy middle classes as well as the landed gentry.

But it also created a number of new seats which gave Scotland's commercial interests a greater voice at Westminster.

Glasgow gained two seats where before it had only one shared by Rutherglen, Renfrew and Dumbarton.

Oswald was elected to one of them and served from 1832 until 1837 and again from 1839 until 1847.

Shinwell, Manny (1884-1986)

Although born in England, Manny Shinwell was one of the greatest left wing politicians to fight for workers' rights that Glasgow has ever produced.

Emmanuel Shinwell was born in London in 1884 but began his working life as an errand boy in Glasgow at the age of 12.

Expounding street corner socialism, he was elected to the Glasgow Trades Council in 1911.

One of 'the wild men of Clydeside', he was jailed for five months in 1921 for incitement to riot.

Becoming a Labour MP the following year, he was appointed Secretary to the Department of Mines in 1924 and again in 1930.

In one of the bitterest fought election campaigns, he defeated Ramsay MacDonald, who had been the first Labour Prime Minister, at Seaham Harbour, Durham, in 1935.

As Labour Party Committee Chairman from 1942 he helped draft the manifesto 'Let us face the future', which led his party to victory in 1945.

Having nationalised the mines in 1946 as Minister of Fuel, he was quickly made Secretary of State for War, and after the fuel crisis he became Minister of Defence from 1950-51.

Despite his belligerent political style, his considerable skill for defence administration earned him the respect of critics such as Churchill and Montgomery.

In later political life he mellowed into an 'elder statesman' back bencher and became a life peer in 1970.

He completed several autobiographies including *Conflict without Malice* (1955), *I've Lived through it All* (1973) and *Lead with the Left* (1981) before his death in 1986.

Banks

Banking in Scotland had always been based in Edinburgh until 1750 when the first Glasgow bank was founded.

The Glasgow and Ship Bank opened its doors to business where the Ship Bank Tavern stands today at the corner of the Saltmarket and the Bridgegate.

It remained there for 26 years before moving up to the Trongate.

Eventually merging with the Thistle Bank to become the Union Bank of Scotland, it was later taken over by Scotland's oldest existing bank, The Bank of Scotland, founded in 1695.

The Scottish banking system was the most developed in Europe and remained so until England caught up in the 1820s.

By 1836 the Savings Bank was founded and soon after the First Penny

Savings Bank in Britain was formed in Glasgow, setting up its headquarters in Glassford Street.

The City of Glasgow Bank, on the site between Virginia and Glassford Street now occupied by Marks and Spencer, went bust in 1878, causing one of the city's worst financial disasters.

It created repercussions still visible in Glasgow today. Some tenements look as if one end has been demolished but actually they were never completed; many construction companies were bankrupted after the bank collapsed, losing more than £6million through irregularities and fraud. Shareholders committed suicide, three bank directors and the manager were jailed and one investor was seen carrying a loaded gun hoping to spot one of the directors. As a result, legislation was passed allowing banks limited liability status to prevent a disaster of this magnitude occurring again.

The largest bookshop in Scotland – Borders – now occupies what used to be the Glasgow headquarters of the Royal Bank of Scotland.

The Royal Bank was responsible not only for the construction of this building, but also for instigating the development of the elegant surrounding square to the rear.

For 10 years prior to 1827 the bank was based in the old Cunninghame mansion – now the Gallery of Modern Art in the centre of Royal Exchange Square.

The mansion building was subsequently converted into the Royal Exchange after the bank's new building had been completed.

It was built in a pure Greek style and was designed by Archibald Elliot II. At this time the mansion and the new bank were the only structures in the area. However, the bank decided that the rest of the land surrounding the two imposing structures should be used to build other premises and form a commercial centre. Between 1830 and 1839 Elliot's plans for the square were carried out.

Nevertheless, the actual design for the three storey business chambers and shops were not his, but the work of David Hamilton and his son-in-law James Smith.

These terraces are physically linked to the bank by two triumphal arches that allow pedestrian access from Queen Street to Buchanan Street via Royal Bank Place and Exchange Place.

The Royal Bank vacated the premises in 1997 and leased it to Borders UK, which, after extensive interior remodelling, opened its doors in October 1998.

Buildings and Organisations
Chamber of Commerce
The Glasgow Chamber of Commerce was established in 1783 and is the second oldest in the world, the oldest having been established in New York some years before.

With the ever-increasing volume of trade with North America and the

Caribbean, it was felt that a formal organisation should be set up to co-ordinate manufacturing and trade.

The man who most encouraged the move was a tobacco merchant and, at that time, Lord Provost of Glasgow – Patrick Colquhoun.

He was the chamber's first president, which had a membership of more than 200, mostly from Glasgow.

Other businessmen soon joined from nearby towns such as Paisley, Port Glasgow and Greenock.

It was called the Glasgow Chamber of Commerce and Manufacture, and it originally met in the Tontine Tavern near the Tolbooth up until 1822. As membership fluctuated, so did the venue, and for the next half century or so, it met in various parts of the city.

But in 1877 it moved to the Merchant's House at the north-west corner of George Square, where the chamber continues to meet to this day.

For more than 200 years the Chamber of Commerce has been looking after the interests of the city, campaigning and fighting for the promotion of commercial activities.

Up until the end of WWI, membership was restricted to the most important businessmen in the area, who had the power to pressurise and influence local and central government.

However, in 1937 a junior chamber was established for members between the ages of 20 and 40.

City Chambers

Glasgow's City Chambers is one of the most impressive buildings in Scotland.

In fact, it was designedwith that intention in the first place, to bring pride to the city and create a landmark that would show that Glasgow was indeed the 'Second City of the Empire'.

The foundation stone was laid in October 1883 in front of the largest crowd ever to assemble in the city, estimated at more than 600,000 people.

Architect William Young, who was born in Paisley, won the competition for his imaginative combination of primarily Venetian and Roman designs.

The exterior was built in a three-tiered formation with a central tower surrounded by domed cupolas at every conceivable corner.

At the very top of the building there are three statues.

The central figure holding a torch of liberty represents truth, while the figures on either side represent riches and honour.

It took five years to construct the exterior and it was opened by Queen Victoria in 1888.

However, the magnificent splendour of the outer facade almost pales in comparison with the interior, which was started in 1887 and was completed by 1890.

The galleries, marble staircases, art treasures, the grand Banqueting Hall and numerous other rooms certainly let visitors know they are somewhere special.

But the most impressive single element within the building is probably the Venetian-style mosaic ceiling as you first enter.

It is made from more than 1.5 million half-inch marble cubes, all inserted by hand.

Co-operative Wholesale Society building

Standing just to the east and almost under the Kingston Bridge on the South Side of the River Clyde, is the massive and imposing Co-operative Wholesale Society building.

Situated at the intersection of Morrison Street and Paisley Road West, this huge warehouse was built for the Scottish Co-operative Society which was founded in 1868. It cost more than £55,000 and was designed by architects Bruce & Hay.

Constructed between 1886 and 1895, the lower floors comprised the wholesale departments and the upper level housed the Co-operative Hall and the committee rooms.

By far the most impressive part of the exterior of this building is the front, facing Morrison Street and the river beyond.

At the time it was suggested that the plans were recycled from a failed 1880 design put forward for the new City Chambers in George Square.

But this allegation was strongly denied by the architects.

In 1911, just 14 years after it opened, a fire raged through the building.

Fortunately most of the damage was confined to the upper floors which were salvaged and restored.

The Co-op kept its headquarters there until 1973, after which the building was largely left to deteriorate.

In 1995 the famous 11ft-high golden statue of Light and Liberty with its electric torch, standing at the top of the central tower, was destroyed while undergoing essential repair work.

The building is now a commercial and luxury residential development which has breathed new life back into this once great Glasgow landmark.

Customs House

One of the most stunning 19th century buildings in Glasgow is the former Customs House on Clyde Street.

This Greek-Doric style building has been described as one of the most elegant of all the buildings overlooking the Clyde.

Built with well-cut yellow sandstone, it was completed in 1840 to a design by Irish-born Customs official John Taylor.

The two lower wings, with Venetian windows on either side of the original nine-bay structure, are 20th century additions.

Considering the huge importance of trade and commerce, on which Glasgow thrived and prospered during the 19th century, the building is rather small and insignificant by comparison.

It would once have overlooked a throng of vessels putting in at Customs

House Quay to load and unload an amazing variety of goods from which the merchants derived their wealth.

The building itself certainly does not meet with the grandeur and eminence placed upon other custom houses built around the same time in other parts of the UK.

Certainly Taylor's other custom houses in mercantile cities such as Dundee and Liverpool convey a greater sense of importance, and symbolise the significance of their function.

However, its magnificently sculptured coat-of-arms does lend a sense of importance to it, in an area of the city that has long since ceased to be a centre for trade and commerce.

Although the original purpose of the building has changed, it now serves an entirely different but equally important function for the city – it is the Procurator Fiscal's Office.

Delftfield pottery

Delftfield is probably the most famous pottery to come out of Glasgow.

Named after the tin-glazed delftware pottery originating from Holland, it was not only the city's first large-scale manufacturer, but also the first in Scotland. It was established in the late 1740s by the famous Dinwiddie tobacco merchants, Laurence and Robert.

They wanted to exploit clay deposits at their Germiston estate to the north-east of Glasgow but this failed immediately, as the clays proved unsuitable. The brothers were forced to import materials from southern England and Ireland, and knowing nothing of pottery manufacture, also imported skilled craftsmen from England.

Their works were located in a lane near Broomielaw Quay and produced large quantities of pottery in all shapes and sizes, much of it destined for the American colonies.

One of its earliest investors was the famous Greenock-born engineer James Watt, who became a partner and advisor in the 1760s.

When Delftfield Lane was widened almost 100 years later, it was renamed James Watt Street in his honour.

However, Delftfield had moved away from its original site in 1810, amalgamating with the Caledonian Pottery company, which had been trading since 1790.

Delftfield ceased trading in 1824 – a quarter of a century before Glasgow's pottery industry had reached its peak, and more than 100 years before the industry went into serious decline.

The most famous piece of Delftfield pottery still in existence is the four-gallon Saracen Head Inn punch bowl, dating from the 1760s, which is held at the People's Palace.

Distillers' building

One of the most unusual looking buildings in Glasgow is the Distillers' Building.

Tucked away on Waterloo Street, this quirkily styled piece of architecture was built for the distillers company of Wright & Greig.

It was designed by architect James Chalmers who used a marvellous mixture of styles including Renaissance and Tudor, with a little touch of baronial grandeur.

Work on the building was started in 1898 and was completed by 1900.

Constructed in red sandstone, the lower levels of the structure are fairly unremarkable.

Above the entrance stands the statues of two Highlanders.

One of them, not surprisingly, is Rhoderick Dhu, the chieftain who fought against King James V of Scotland, and is one of the principal characters in Sir Walter Scott's *Lady Of The Lake.*

Rhoderick Dhu became the distillery's most famous whisky blend.

Above the oriel window is another Highland figure, that of a woman holding her malting shovel.

But the most spectacular aspect of the building can be seen by looking at the roof: here is a most peculiar tower with a tent-like scalloped roof, supported by columns, sticking out from the main structure.

It was originally intended that statues depicting the four seasons would be installed under the roof at each corner, but this part of the design was never completed.

There are also protruding pieces of carved stone which from a distance give the visual illusion that cannons have been mounted on the upper floor.

It is now owned by United Distillers.

Dixon's Blazes

For many years the night sky of Glasgow was coloured a dark red, but not from the setting sun.

The fiery glow that could be seen all over the city was from Dixon's Blazes at Polmadie, where the foundry fires were kept burning 24 hours a day.

The ironworks was founded by William Dixon who had taken over the Little Govan Colliery, which had been extracting coal from the area since the 17th century.

Dixon took over the management of the colliery in 1774, and while overseeing this venture decided to set up an ironworks there as well.

He chose to build the foundry near where Cathcart Road meets Aikenhead Road, to the south of the Southern Necropolis.

Ever the entrepreneur, Dixon even built his own timber railway to transport his coal and iron to the coal quays on the Clyde, because he felt the Navigation Trust was charging too much.

After Dixon's death in 1822 the Blazes continued to produce iron and steel for more than a century.

During the 1850s, as the area was being developed for housing, it was feared that the foundry would not aid in attracting people to live there.

But, on the contrary, it became a major selling point and was one of the most popular features of the district.

The foundry eventually closed in 1958 and the night sky became a duller place.

But its memory lives on in name at least, as the area is now called Dixon's Blazes Industrial Site.

House of Fraser Department Store

Probably the most dominant figure in Scotland during the middle of the 20th century was the famous department store owner, Hugh Fraser.

Born in 1903 and educated at Glasgow Academy, he joined the family drapery business in Buchanan Street, becoming its Managing Director in 1925.

By 1941 he was chairman of the parent company Fraser, Sons and Co.

It was his remarkable skill in guiding trends in the retail industry that made him a dominant figure in the business world for almost two decades. During the 1950s he started an expansion programme spreading throughout the country, buying up competitors' stores. Intent on monopolising the high street, he undercut competition, filling his stores with fast moving, affordable products.

Post-war prosperity kicked in and he focused his attention on capturing the increasing middle class population of shoppers at a time when other stores were complacent.

His highest profile take-over was the purchase of the world-famous Knightsbridge store Harrods, which he maintained as his flagship.

His diverse business interests included becoming chairman of Scottish Universal Investment Trusts.

Using this position and that of the House of Fraser, he gained control of George Outram and Co's ownership of the *Evening Times* and *Glasgow Herald* in 1964, the same year he became Lord Fraser of Allander.

He also played a major role in promoting the Scottish economy and tourism industries, and was instrumental in setting up Aviemore as a tourist centre.

Lord Fraser died in 1966, leaving his son Sir Hugh in charge of his business empire.

Mercat Cross

Throughout the history of Glasgow there have been several crosses, but the most important was the Mercat Cross.

The Mercat Cross, or crux foralis, was a visible marker representing the legality of holding a market in the burgh.

A replica of the medieval cross standing opposite the Tolbooth Steeple was built by Edith Burnet Hughes in 1929, and consists of an octagonal base and a single-storey column with a heraldic unicorn at the top.

However, there is some doubt as to where the original cross would have stood along the High Street. It would either have been at the top near the Cathedral, where the Drygate and Rottenrow met, or near the bottom where the Gallowgate, Trongate and Saltmarket converge.

It is more likely to have been the latter, as this was the hub of business and commerce in Glasgow, whereas the Cathedral site was always the ecclesiastical centre.

The earliest record of its existence is from 1590 when two boys were charged with damaging it, but for over 100 years it is not written of again.

But during the mid-17th century two reports mention it being removed.

It is most likely that it was removed at some point towards the end of the 18th century, when the council offices moved west from the Tolbooth in keeping with Glasgow's expansion.

During the second half of the 19th century excavations, were made in a few likely places but no trace of it was uncovered.

Merchant City

The Merchant City today is one of the most dynamic and thriving areas of the city with its new shops, bars and restaurants.

It has become a fashionable district to socialise in and for those that can afford it, a splendid place to live, right in the heart of Glasgow.

Indeed this area of the city was Glasgow's original new town more than 200 years ago.

At the end of the 18th century, the city merchants had become very rich with the boom in textiles and tobacco and decided to move north and west away from the Clyde.

Although there were no official plans drawn up the new area quickly developed a grid pattern with streets running north from the Trongate and west from the High Street.

Four-storey shops and warehouses with private accommodation above lined the streets, many ending with magnificent houses and churches looking down them.

But the heyday of the new town was short-lived and by the 1820s the merchants again moved west, leaving behind the ever-increasing immigration of Highlanders and Irish.

But the warehouses, banks and counting houses remained, and the area continued to thrive for the next 150 years until industrial decline left many buildings empty and derelict.

The city decided that something had to be done, and in the 1970s and 1980s a major clean-up campaign was started.

Gleaming red and gold sandstone buildings were unmasked from decades of industrial grime and the old Merchant City was restored to its state of beauty once more.

Merchant's Steeple

One of Glasgow's great city landmarks, the Merchant's Steeple, is all that remains of the 17th century Merchant's Hall.

It rises from the surrounding modernised Briggait Centre, which was built on the site of the old 19th century Fish Market.

The Fish Market, built between 1872 and 1873, replaced tenements that had been built in 1817, replacing the Guildhall and Hospital of the mid-17th century.

The steeple was finished in 1665, six years after the completion of the surrounding Merchant's Hall, which had been started in 1651.

Although dating from this period, the steeple is very much in a Gothic style, with a touch of Renaissance to its upper works.

The steeple's designer was thought to be Sir William Bruce, but the city records that could have verified this have been missing for a long period of time.

However, the first record of Bruce's connection with the building was mentioned in 1816 and seems to cast doubt on his contribution to this architectural work.

Standing 164ft-high, it was used as a lookout for merchants awaiting the first sighting of their returning ships coming up the River Clyde with their cargoes from around the world.

Above the four square towers, which diminish in size as they rise up the elevation of the steeple, is a ship in full sail atop a globe.

This symbol of Glasgow's trading origins was duplicated when the merchants moved to their current premises next to George Square in 1877.

Paddy's Market

One of the most famous markets in Glasgow is Paddy's Market.

Set up by poor Irish immigrants almost 200 years ago, it became a necessary way of life for many of the city's poor to scrape together a living.

Until the end of the 18th century the east end had been the hub of affluent merchant-living, but as the population size increased they moved away. Overcrowding and poor and unsanitary conditions prevailed, and the once fashionable area became a slum-land occupied by the poorest citizens.

During the 1820s some Irish immigrants set up a few shops in the Bridgegate, buying and selling second-hand clothing. Within a decade there were more than 1,500 dealers and hawkers in the area.

The numbers continued to rise due to the potato famine of 1845-1850 bringing thousands more immigrants into Glasgow.

However, public protest forced the authorities to move the market on to new premises just north of the High Court building.

Over the next 100 years the market place moved many times due to new building projects and changing poverty levels, reducing the demand for second-hand goods.

In the 1930s the market was moved again with the building of the new City Mortuary.

Many of the traders opted to lease the arches under the railway viaduct along Shipbank Lane.

Over the years the demand for second-hand clothing has diminished, with cheap domestic products being sold instead.

Today, only the remnants of the once thriving market can still be seen.

Savoy Centre

The Savoy Centre in Glasgow's Sauchiehall Street is today dwarfed in size by the huge shopping malls that have sprung up in the city centre over the last few decades.

However, it has one of the most remarkably intricate frontages of any of the shopping centres.

This beautifully carved facade was created more than a century ago by architects H & D Barclay.

Work started on this very grand warehouse for the furnishing company of Cumming and Smith in 1891.

It was completed four years later with entrances on both Sauchiehall Street and Hope Street, now completely obscured, to the east.

The Sauchiehall Street entrance, in dark red sandstone, is intricately detailed with Ionic columns with large arches and classical figures leaning their heads against the sides.

There are also ships, swords and torches, providing a beautiful contrast to the drab and flat concrete facades of many of its present-day neighbours.

In the early part of the 20th century, the interior of the building was redesigned and in 1910 it reopened as the Glasgow Picture House, one of the first so close to the city centre.

It later changed its name to the Savoy Cinema but like many of the 100 or more cinemas in Glasgow, after WWI it was destined to close with the general industry slump.

The use of the building changed for the third time, after extensive interior remodelling was carried out between 1971 and 1979.

Steamies

Public baths up until the second half of the 20th century were not only a place where people went to bathe but, for many, it was the only place to wash their clothes.

For centuries Glasgow women did their laundry in the Clyde and then hung their washing up on the poles at Glasgow Green.

But with the industrial revolution came pollution.

As the tenements were poorly supplied with water the City Improvement Trust decided to set up public baths with wash houses – known as the steamies.

The first steamie was built on Glasgow Green in 1732 and over the years many more sprung up all over the city.

Women would gather up the family washing every week, load it into tin baths and wheel it down to the wash houses in prams to use the sinks, boilers, wringers and dryers.

Washing clothes by hand was an extremely laborious job but 'the talk of the steamie' – catching up on the local gossip – made it a more bearable experience.

The atmosphere of this way of life was wonderfully captured in Tony Roper's play *The Steamie*, first performed on stage in 1989.

Steamies eventually disappeared with the advent of launderettes and domestic washing machines years later, when they became affordable for most people.

But some women living near Glasgow Green continued to hang their washing on the poles right into the late 1970s.

Glasgow's last steamie survived in Partick up until 1982 when washing machines were eventually introduced.

St Enoch Centre

The St Enoch Centre is the largest glass structure in Europe.

After its recent multimillion pound redevelopment, it is still the largest retail space in Scotland, as befits Glasgow, the second biggest shopping area in Britain after London.

The St Enoch Centre contains more than 80 stores, and houses Scotland's biggest food court.

Construction started in 1981 and it started trading in 1989.

It was officially opened the following year by the Prime Minister at that time, Margaret Thatcher.

Covering an area of more than four acres, the original project cost £65million and required more than 2,500 tons of steel and 300,000 square feet of glass.

It was built on the derelict site of the old St Enoch Hotel and Station which closed in 1966 and was demolished by 1977.

Just as the shopping centre interrupts the Glasgow skyline today, the hotel and station were also invaders of the area when they were built during the 1870s.

The St Enoch area, the name deriving from a corruption of Thenew, the name of St Mungo's mother, had been designated for residential use by Glasgow Corporation as far back as 1768.

However, the need for a central Glasgow railway terminus overcame this provision.

It was constructed by the City of Glasgow Union Railway and opened in 1876.

Three years later it became the first spot in Glasgow to use electricity as an illumination source.

Today, the shopping centre continues that tradition, brightening up the skyline of central Glasgow under its massive glass pyramid.

Stock Exchange House

One of the most interesting frontages on Buchanan Street is the former Stock Exchange House.

Its design is rare as very few secular buildings in the city were ever designed in the Gothic style, in this case early French.

Situated on the corner of Buchanan Street and St George's Place, it complements its neighbour, the former Western Club, built more than 30 years before.

The Stock Exchange was designed by architect John Burnet whose critics quickly commented on the remarkable similarity of his plans to those of the London Law Courts, built nine years before.

Work started in 1875 and two years later when it was completed, Burnet's work revealed he had managed to achieve a less severe appearance than the law court.

As with many buildings of the era, a great deal of attention was paid to exterior carvings.

In particular, the figures above the Buchanan Street entrance, representing the four continents, were the work of the master stone-mason John Mossman.

Between 1904 and 1906, the building was skilfully extended along the southern length of St George's Place by Sir J J Burnet.

The interior of the building was originally on four levels, with the clearing house on the second floor, directly above the exchange.

But it was completely gutted between 1967 and 1971 and recreated on six levels by Baron Bercott and Associates to accommodate shops and offices.

The exchange, like those in other cities elsewhere in Britain, merged with the London Stock Exchange in 1973.

St Rollox Chemical Works
St Rollox Chemical Works was the largest in the world during most of the 19th century.

It was built to the south of Springburn near Townhead in 1799 by the great industrialist, Ayrshire-born Charles Tennant.

Originally a weaver, he studied bleaching techniques and set up a business in Paisley.

He enlisted the help of the Glasgow-born inventor of the waterproof raincoat, Charles Macintosh, and patented the manufacture of dry bleaching powder.

His product was soon in great demand from the textile industry and the St Rollox site expanded over the years to meet production needs.

By 1830 the factory, now covering 50 acres of land, was the world's largest.

But it was also producing a massive amount of pollution, even by Glasgow standards during the Victorian era.

Three years after Tennant's death in 1838, his son John who had taken over the plant, decided to build a large chimney to try to dispose of the toxic gases.

The chimney, known as Tennant's Stalk, was completed by 1842 and, rising more than 455ft from its foundation, was the tallest in the world.

It was eventually demolished in 1922.

St Rollox had been taken over by United Alkali in 1892 and was later bought by ICI before it was eventually shut down in the 1960s, when the M8 was built.

Almost the only indication of the factory's existence today is the existence of the huge landscaped mounds of solid waste that were used as the site for the Sighthill tower blocks.

Templeton carpet factory

Glittering and shining in the sunshine, the old Templeton carpet factory overlooking Glasgow Green is still regarded today as one of the most beautiful buildings in the city.

However, it has a tragic and secret past.

While still being built in September 1888, a 70ft-high gable wall collapsed in high winds, killing 29 women, including a 13-year-old girl.

The new building was being constructed around the existing cotton mill shed that James Templeton had bought from McPhail's when his original King Street factory burnt down in 1856.

Despite the fact that none of the new walls were properly secured, neither the architect nor the builder were officially blamed for the tragedy at the inquest into the disaster.

After the inquest, construction continued on the Moorish-Italian design, inspired by the Doge's Palace in Venice, and it was eventually completed in early 1892.

The Helensburgh architect William Leiper was commissioned to design the beautiful exterior of the new Templeton carpet factory because the council refused to allow the construction of a drab, common factory building which would deface the beauty of Glasgow Green.

Templeton's factory produced some of the best carpets and held international acclaim for quality and design.

The company managed to secure the worldwide patent (except for America) for the famous Axminster carpets, after inventing a new spool manufacturing technique.

The factory is now the Templeton Business Centre, but the lives lost more than 100 years ago remain a secret, masked by the external beauty of one of Glasgow's great architectural masterpieces.

Tobacco Merchant's House

The oldest house in Glasgow's Merchant City is the Tobacco Merchant's House at 42 Miller Street, the rest having been pulled down during the 19th century.

Miller Street was laid out in 1762 on land owned by maltman James Miller of Westerton.

In 1761 he decided to demolish half of his own mansion, built in 1754, and use his surrounding land to build a new street to accommodate more wealthy merchants' villas.

Miller Street opened in 1773 and No 42, designed, built and occupied by the wright John Craig, was completed on the eastern side of the narrow street in 1775.

Although he was not a tobacco merchant, the house has taken the name because it is the only one left to retain the style of the tobacco lords' villas.

Only one other house in Glasgow retains a similar architectural design – No 52 Charlotte Street to the east of the Merchant City on the other side of the Saltmarket.

They are the last of their kind and hark back to the elegance and grandeur of the merchants' villas, epitomised by Campbell's Shawfield Mansion of 1712, which stood at the top of Stockwell Street until it was demolished in 1792.

In 1992 the Tobacco Merchant's House was acquired by the Glasgow Building Preservation Trust.

It carried out a great deal of work to restore it to its former glory and now uses the building as a visitor centre for those wishing to know more about its preservation work in Glasgow.

Tolbooth

The Tolbooth steeple at the Cross is one of Glasgow's most impressive structures.

At the heart of the city's history from the 13th to the 19th century, the area around the Tolbooth had always been at the hub of commercial and civic life.

However, there is no visual evidence of what stood there until 1626 when an impressive set of new buildings, including the steeple, were constructed.

The five-storey building had a broad 65ft frontage along the Trongate with a 126ft square tower looming above.

As the name suggests, the Tolbooth was where local tolls, taxes and custom dues were collected and stored.

The surrounding buildings housed the courts and city jail.

In 1740 the city fathers decided to put their council offices alongside it, for convenience as much as anything else.

In 1777, 'plainstanes' were laid in front of the steeple and its surrounding buildings to allow the wealthy merchants and city dignitaries to stroll without getting their shoes dirty.

Today the remnant of this fine pavement remains to the west of the Tolbooth on the Trongate.

From 1788 until 1813, the front of the steeple was the place to go if you wanted to see a public hanging in Glasgow.

In total, 22 people, including one woman, were hanged there before executions were moved south to Jail Square at Glasgow Green.

Today the Tolbooth stands alone at the junction of the High Street, Trongate, Gallowgate and Saltmarket, while the city traffic bustles around the ancient stone structure.

Trades House

The Trades House is the oldest secular building in Glasgow that is still being used for its original purpose.

It is also the last remaining building in the city designed by the world famous architect Robert Adam.

Building work started in 1791 and it was completed in 1794.

The exterior style of the building has been more or less maintained despite its being totally refaced in the late 1920s.

But once you step inside the Glassford Street entrance in the heart of the Merchant City, there is very little of the interior that has not been redesigned or altered in some way over the years.

All that is left of Adam's original interior is a simple white marble fireplace in the hall with a matching one that was removed and now stands in the saloon.

One thing that has never changed since the building opened, is its function as the meeting place of the 14 incorporated trade guilds in the city.

The guilds of hammermen, masons, gardeners, bakers, skinners, wrights, coopers, tailors, cordiners, maltmen, weavers, fleshers, barbers and dyers have been around for many hundreds of years but they were first officially incorporated together in 1605.

The members of the Trades House were entitled to vote for and be elected to the Town Council and for many years, along with members of the Merchant House, they shared in its running.

Today the Trades House is mainly a charitable institution which raises funds for worthy causes around the city.

Photographers

Annan, Thomas (1829-1887)

One of the most successful and inventive photographers in Glasgow during the 19th century was Thomas Annan.

Annan's pictures captured the images of a city that have been swept away with the modernisation of Glasgow.

He was born in Fife but moved to Glasgow where he trained as a lithographer and copperplate engraver.

A skilled technician, Annan established his own printing business in the west end of the city in 1855 but within two years he had embraced the new medium of photography.

He bought a Hansom cab and converted it to a darkroom to allow him to process his plates while on location.

Over the years Annan became renowned for his landscapes, reproductions of famous art works and architectural work.

He is chiefly remembered for recording images of the streets and slums for the Glasgow Improvement Trust before they were demolished during the 1860s and 1870s.

These images were brought together in the 1871 publication *Photographs of the Old Closes and Streets of Glasgow*.

But Annan was also a skilled and imaginative portrait photographer who avoided many of the stereotyped poses that were in vogue at that time.

One of his most famous subjects was the African explorer and missionary David Livingstone whose portraits he took in 1864.

However, Annan was also a pioneer in the photographic world and developed many new techniques such as the Carbon process and photogravure.

When he died in 1887, his sons continued the business that is still operating in Glasgow today.

Graham, William (1845-1914)

William Graham was born in Springburn and for much of his life was employed by the North British Locomotive Company.

He spent much of his spare time taking photographs of his working environment, a very new format of recording information at that time.

But as his hobby grew he expanded the subject matter to include almost everything, from cathedrals and churches to mansions and slum dwellings.

In 1893 he was suspended from his train driving duties for his part in a strike and decided to turn his hobby into his profession.

He established himself in a small studio in the Springburn area and from there spent the rest of his life capturing an amazing catalogue of images of the city.

Not only did he record the old buildings for posterity and the new ones that were taking their place but he also captured a unique collection of images of people's daily lives and the society they lived in.

Graham was a founding member of the Old Glasgow Club in 1900, now the oldest club of its kind in Scotland which continues to meet to research and record the history of the city.

After William Graham's death in 1914, his collection of more than 3,000 glass negatives, slides and prints were bought and donated to the Mitchell Library.

Marzaroli, Oscar (1933-1988)

One of the greatest photographic documents of Glaswegian and Scottish daily life was compiled by an Italian film-maker, Oscar Marzaroli.

Born in La Spezia, Italy in 1933, Marzaroli moved to Glasgow with his family in the mid 1930s.

He was educated in both Scotland and Italy before pursuing a career as a freelance journalist in Europe from 1954.

But he returned to Glasgow in 1959 where he continued his work, co-founding a film company in 1967.

Ogam Films built up a reputation for making short films on subjects which included local artists, the lives of people from the Highlands and Islands and urban Glasgow.

While making these films, Marzaroli took many still photographs of his subjects and compiled them into several beautiful and touching books.

Looking at the rural and urban landscape, he captured the ups and downs of everyday life, studying the happiness and sorrow of ordinary people.

Although many of his pictures show beautiful landscapes, it was the daily life of domestic chores and working practices that fascinated him the most.

Over a period of almost 40 years, he built up a collection of images accurately depicting the real lives of Scottish people.

He intentionally documented the real images of Scotland that he had grown to love and respect rather than the tartan and bagpipe Brigadoon portraits that appeared on the lids of shortbread tins.

His books include *One Man's World: Photographs 1955-84* (1984), *Shades of Grey: Glasgow 1956-87* (1987) and *Shades of Scotland 1956-88* (1989).

Urie, John (1820-1910)

The first successful photographer in Glasgow was John Urie.

Born in Paisley in 1820, he was the son of a handloom weaver.

His great grandfather, an early Glasgow printer, was shot in 1685 for perpetuating Covenanter principles despite the 1664 declaration by the Covenanter Convention Society.

Urie moved to Glasgow and by 1850 had established himself as a skilled wood engraver but three years later his interest lay in the new and revolutionary medium of photography.

Urie focused his talents on commercial photographic work.

In many respects the steps of his career were mirrored by the better known Glasgow photographer, Thomas Annan, who broke into photography a few years later.

Annan had been a lithographer and copperplate engraver before becoming a photographer in 1855.

And today, Annan is famous for his pictures of Glasgow's slums before they were demolished in the 1860s and 1870s.

But Urie's work has failed to gain the same lasting interest.

However, his most famous work was when he photographed one of Glasgow's most prominent families in 1857.

He was commissioned by one of the city's leading architects, James Smith, whose eldest daughter was Madeleine Hamilton Smith.

Madeleine later posed for a portrait to give to her secret lover, Pierre Emile L'Angelier.

Shortly afterwards, she was sensationally tried at the High Court in Edinburgh for his murder but escaped execution because of Scotland's unique jury verdict of 'not proven'.

In 1908, two years before his death, Urie published his pictographic volume – *Reminiscences of Eighty Years*.

Leeries

Today the streets and closes of Glasgow are brightly lit with electric lighting tha is computer-controlled or automatically activated when natural light drops below a certain level.

But not all that long ago, lighting up the streets was a manual affair, lamplighters would illuminate the darkness with gas lamps.

The very last gas lamp in Glasgow was ceremoniously lit for the final time in North Portland Street, Townhead, in 1971, by Lord Provost Sir Donald Liddle.

Lamplighters, or leeries as they were known in Glasgow, had been around since 1718 when animal fat wicks were used, dimly illuminating the streets.

They were so few and far between that they were almost useless but by 1765 oil lamps replaced them.

Most of them however, found their way into privately-owned closes but eventually magistrates had them returned to the streets for public use.

By 1780, the council started putting up lamps as a reward to shop owners who had laid pavements outside their premises, resulting in many more pavements and more than 1200 lamps in Glasgow by 1815.

Gas lighting was introduced in 1818, initially with around 1400.

But after the 1866 Police Act, authorizing the council to erect lamp-posts and maintain lighting in private and public areas, the city really began to brighten up.

Leeries were a common site at dawn and dusk for much of this century, plodding up and down the streets and closes in all weathers to bring a degree of safety to the community in the hours of darkness.

People always marvelled at the abilities of the leeries as they skilfully went about their business with ladder and lighting pole, balanced on their shoulders.

But they were also a great source of amusement for youngsters, who used to wait until the leeries had finished in one street and would then shimmy up the lamp post and blow the light out and then announce their mis-deed to the poor fellow who would then have to return and start all over again.

However, in 1893, the council installed the very first electric street lights and gas lamps slowly went into decline.

The nostalgia of the leeries and gas lights have now faded into the past but the council made a bit of a killing when they were taken down, selling the famous lamp posts all over the world, especially to America and Canada.

CHAPTER 11
Transport

The River Clyde

The River Clyde was completely responsible for making Glasgow one of the greatest cities in the world.

Of the 106 miles of the river, only the last 20 that run into the estuary from the city have provided the transportation needs that shaped Glasgow's history.

The city became renowned the world over in the 18th century for its tobacco and cotton industry which derived its success from being the nearest European coastal port to the Americas.

But in those days the river was shallow and large vessels had to off-load their cargoes at Greenock and Port Glasgow and then ferry them up to Glasgow in smaller river vessels.

By the 19th century, the Clyde Trust undertook the huge task of dredging the Clyde, removing millions of cubic metres of silt to deepen and widen the channel.

But in 1854 work was delayed 30 years while engineers blasted a huge slab of volcanic rock, measuring 900 x 300ft, from the river bed near Elderslie.

Around this time, major industries were building up around Glasgow including steel and iron manufacturing.

The timing could not have been better.

Just as the Clyde became navigable all the way up to Glasgow the shipbuilding industry was turning to steel fabrication.

The coastal shipbuilding industry moved up river and by the 1900's Clydeside was producing around 25 per cent of the world's ships.

Priding themselves on producing high quality vessels, the Clyde shipbuilders launched some of the most famous ships ever built.

Horses

Glasgow is now congested with cars and buses but before their arrival it was teeming with horses.

They were the only form of urban transport, especially for the rich in their fine carriages, and all the best houses had their own stables.

Along the grander West End terraces today, many high kerbs can still be seen, built originally to make it easier to get in and out of carriages or on and off horses.

Delivering goods up and down steep hills needed extra horse power with trace horses, usually Clydesdales, hired out to help other horses with the heaviest loads. Coal carts had to be wedged on steep inclines to relieve some of the terrible strain put on the horses while the coal-men struggled up close stairs making their deliveries.

There was no public transport until Robert Frame started a service using horse-drawn omnibuses in 1845. By 1872 two large firms, Menzies and Walker, ran 38 services throughout the city.

The 1100 horses needed for the service were stabled in space-saving three storey buildings with outside staircases.

The Corporation took over the omnibus services in 1894 and horses gradually disappeared from the streets, superceded by electric trams.

Today, only the police can be seen on horse-back in the city centre.

Railplane

The government is desperately trying to improve public transport and encourage more people to use it and reduce congestion and pollution on our roads but almost 70 years ago, a Glasgow inventor came up with what could have been the perfect solution.

It was called the Railplane and its creator was George Bennie.

Son of an engineer, born in Auldhouse in 1892, Bennie came up with a unique design for passenger transport.

Existing rail links were slow and tensions existed between passenger and freight transport needs. Bennie's idea was to build a double track, 30 ft above existing railway lines and sling his revolutionary coach underneath.

The 10-tonne luxury coach was powered by a powerful electric motor turning a propeller, front and back.

And at speeds of more than 120mph, it would be able to transport passengers in perfect safety and comfort from Glasgow to Edinburgh in under 20 minutes. Cheaper, cleaner and faster, it would also allow existing track to be used for much slower freight trains.

On July 8, 1930, in a field in Milngavie, hundreds of people witnessed the railplane's first trip, carrying 50 passengers along 426 ft of track.

Despite great interest in the prototype, the economic climate and railway company pressures ensured Bennie's idea was crushed.

Left to rust in Milngavie, it was eventually scrapped in 1956.

Bankrupt, George Bennie died the following year.

All that is left of his great pioneering ambition is a small plaque in Milngavie testifying to its very short transport career.

Trams

In September 1962, more than a quarter of a million Glaswegians waved goodbye to the most popular, cheap and efficient transport system the city has ever seen.

Despite torrential rain, the streets were lined with people, many of them placing their coins on the track to be flattened for the last time by the 'caurs'.

Glasgow trams originated in the city in 1872.

Privately owned horse-drawn cars ran until 1894 when the city corporation took over the service, using more than 3000 horses to pull the trams all over the city.

By 1898, the first electric trams were introduced and at their height they travelled on more than 130 routes over nearly 200 miles.

Over 450 million passengers annually, staffed by nearly 6000 employees travelled as far afield as Loch Lomond, Clydebank, Govan, Rutherglen, Airdrie and Bishopbriggs.

Powered from electric wires hung from street hooks, they travelled along tracks and therefore could never get lost.

Many car drivers used to follow them in heavy fog, often ending up at tram depots rather than their own homes.

Glasgow was the first city to introduce female conductresses, the clippies, famous for their quick wit and sharp commands. During WWII, 2000 women were employed, more than 300 of them as drivers. But by the 50s private vehicles and buses challenged the trams for the use of the roads and they were eventually removed.

With the state of public transport and congestion in the city today many people would perhaps be glad to see their return.

Trolley-buses

Glasgow was the last city in Britain to introduce trolley-buses despite the idea of this form of transport being discussed as far back as 1912.

And although the necessary power supply was available to operate them by 1935, they did not appear until 1949.

Trolleys first operated from Larkfield Garage at Govanhill on the south side but they were later changed to a new garage built near Hampden Park.

Trolleys combined the best aspects of the other two forms of road public transport, trams and motorised diesel buses.

They used overhead power cables like the trams and could move across the traffic lanes like the buses.

As they made so little noise and often startled unsuspecting pedestrians meandering across the road, they were nicknamed the Silent Death.

In 1954, the corporation decided to stop further expansion of the cheap and efficient electric trams which had been introduced in 1898.

With private vehicles on the increase, the corporation thought that buses and trolleys could adequately cope.

But the great appeal of the trams, which at their height transported more than 450 million passengers annually, never materialised with the trolleys.

In 1959, they reached their peak of popularity with 194 trolleys serving eight routes, the largest service of its kind anywhere in the UK outside London.

But by 1962 the cost of running the trolley-buses was greater than that of the buses.

In 1967 they were eventually withdrawn from service and despite recent calls for their return have never done so.

Tunnels

Of the two tunnels built under the River Clyde only one is still operational.

The Harbour tunnel, built at the end of the 19th century, was closed in 1980 but the Clyde Tunnel remains a very popular route for commuters.

Like its predecessor, it was built at a time when it was unthinkable to consider building a bridge further downstream than the Jamaica Street Bridge because of the shipping traffic.

Plans were drawn up after WWII and the government gave it the go-ahead in 1948 but financial difficulties delayed the start of excavating under the river until 1957.

It's route would link Govan on the south side of the river with Whiteinch on the north.

Despite being only half a mile long, work on the tunnel was slow because of the hard rock and soft silt that the tunnel had to pass through, 20ft below the river bed.

The tunnel has two separate tubes, one for northbound, the other for southbound traffic, each 29ft in diameter, wide enough for two lanes.

A smaller tunnel was built underneath for pedestrians and bicycles.

The maximum gradient of the tunnel is one in 16 and gives the impression that no sooner have you finished your descent than you are rising back up again.

The tunnel was completed at a cost of £10million and became fully operational in 1964.

It had been estimated that around 9000 vehicles would use the tunnel daily but that number has now risen to more than 60,000.

The two domed rotundas on the banks of the River Clyde down river from Jamaica Street Bridge mark the ends of the old Harbour tunnel.

The rotundas at Finnieston Quay and Mavisbank Quay covered the 80ft diameter vertical shafts that led down to three parallel tunnels, each 16ft across.

Two were used for horse drawn vehicles, one for south-bound, the other for north-bound traffic, while the third was for pedestrians.

Six hydraulic vehicle lifts were installed in each rotunda and stairs were provided for pedestrians.

The Glasgow Harbour Tunnel Company started building work in 1890 and the tunnels were opened six years later.

However, it proved a financial disaster and the company went bankrupt the following year.

In 1913 the Glasgow Corporation re-opened them free of charge.

Four years later the pedestrian tunnel was closed but people used the vehicle tunnels.

In 1943 the lifting machinery was removed and the scrap metal was used for the war effort.

But in 1947 the tunnels were re-opened again for pedestrians and continued to be used until 1980 when they were eventually closed and sealed up.

The rotundas were repaired in 1986, the vehicular entrance bays were closed and glassed over and the rest of the structure was maintained in the original style.

During the Garden Festival in 1988 the south rotunda was opened briefly as a discovery centre.

From the 1990s the north rotunda has been used as a restaurant and in 1998 a casino was opened.

Underground
Glasgow's underground system has been running beneath the city for more than 100 years and apart from London is the only city in Britain to have one.

The 'Clockwork Orange' has been taking commuters between the city centre, West End and south-side since 1980 but the original system dates back to 1896.

Opening for one day only in December 1890, the Subway, as it was originally called, became fully operational by the end of January 1896, using a two tunnel system.

Linking 15 stations and using a cable traction system, the first cars ran on bogies, taking 40 minutes to travel the full route.

As there were no points on the system, trains had to be lifted out of the tunnel by cranes when they terminated at Govan.

In 1935 trains were electrified, taking only 28 minutes to complete the full journey.

The busiest route was between Govan and Partick Cross stations, being the quickest way to cross the Clyde using public transport.

Renamed the Underground in 1937, it ran until 1977 before closing for modernisation.

In 1979 the re-vamped system was inaugurated by the Queen and officially re-opened the following April minus the famous 'shoogle' and all too familiar fusty smell.

Stations were lengthened anticipating the three carriage trains introduced in 1992.

At its height the old system carried seven million passengers every year but today that number has doubled.

People
Brown, Sir Arthur Whitten
For many people the name of Charles Lindbergh immediately makes them think of the famous flight he made across the Atlantic Ocean in the *Spirit of St Louis* in 1927. The name Sir Arthur Whitten Brown most likely does not ring so many bells although it should.

Brown was born in Glasgow in 1886 and together with fellow aviator, John W Alcock, they made the first non-stop Atlantic flight some eight years before Lindbergh.

Their historic crossing started on June 14 1919, from St John's in Newfoundland. Flying in a twin-engined Vickers-Vimy biplane, Brown, navigating, and pilot, Alcock, made the crossing in 16 hours and 27 minutes, touching down at Clifden in County Galway, Ireland.

This most remarkable achievement not only got them written into the history books but earned them £10,000, the prize money put up by the London *Daily Mail* for the successful venture.

Although they were the first to do it, Lindbergh, who was the 65th person to make the trip, is still better known than Brown and Alcock because he had flown solo.

Today, passengers passing the visitor centre at the UK's busiest airport, Heathrow, may not notice the famous aviators' statue.

Most are unlikely to stop and think what it must have been like to have made the long Atlantic crossing 80 years ago, a journey which today only takes a few hours.

Both Brown and Alcock were knighted but sadly Alcock died soon after in a flying accident.

Brown died in 1948.

MacBrayne, David

The Highlands and Islands have always been dependent on a reliable shipping service for their every day lives and transport to and from the mainland.

One man who played a major part in providing that service was David MacBrayne.

Born in Glasgow in 1818, he was related on his mother's side to a shipping family – D & A Hutcheson.

In 1851 MacBrayne went into partnership with Hutcheson brothers David and Alexander, forming the steamer firm 'David Hutcheson and Co'. The following year they secured a mail service contract to the Western Isles.

For almost 30 years they developed shipping routes between the Clyde estuary and the west coast, linking island communities and helping to improve local trade. After David Hutcheson retired in 1876 and Alexander two years later, MacBrayne continued to run the business alone.

By the end of the 1880s, MacBrayne had built up a fleet of 28 vessels for his regular ferry and excursion service that braved all but the worst storms. Sons David and Laurence, joined the company in 1902 although Laurence quit shortly after. Three years later David senior retired but retained half the shares in the company.

David junior continued to run the business until 1906 when it was re-named 'David MacBrayne Ltd'.

The following year his father died.

Bought over several times since and called Caledonian MacBrayne Ltd since 1973, its vessels still sail up and down many routes he established more than a hundred years ago.

Mollison, James Allan

Glasgow-born James Allan Mollison was one of the greatest solo pilots during the pioneering early years of aviation history.

He became the first person in history to fly solo across both the North and South Atlantic Oceans from east to west.

He was also the first to fly from Britain across the Sahara to the Cape of Good Hope.

Mollison was born in 1905.

His flying career started in 1923 when he joined the RAF and soon became its youngest qualified flight instructor.

In 1928 Mollison went to Australia where he taught at Adelaide Aero Club and later became a stunt flyer and pilot for Australian National Airways.

His international fame and reputation for bravery and determination was established in 1931 when he flew from Australia to England in record breaking time.

In 1932, the same year he crossed the North Atlantic, he married the famous female aviator Amy Johnson, from Hull, Yorkshire.

The following year they made the first flight across the Atlantic to the USA.

Also in that year, Mollison completed his solo flight across the South Atlantic.

Their marriage aroused great adulation from the public and they competed with each other in solo flights over the next six years until their marriage came to an end.

He married again twice but continued to maintain a hectic lifestyle, renowned as a debt-dodging, drunken womaniser.

When arthritis set in he was forced to give up flying and settled in London where he bought a pub.

He died in 1959.

Stevenson, Robert

Lighthouses have always played an important role in protecting shipping from many of the hazardous coastal areas surrounding the British Isles.

One man in particular, Robert Stevenson, grandfather of the famous author Robert Louis Stevenson, played a revolutionary role in helping save the lives of many sailors over the last 200 years.

Born in Glasgow in 1772, Robert lost his father early on in his life.

His mother re-married in 1786.

Robert's step father was Thomas Smith, first engineer to the Northern Lighthouse Board.

This influenced Robert's choice of career and he became an engineer with the board.

By 1796, he took over from Smith as first engineer.

During his 47 years with the lighthouse board he was responsible for the introduction of the catoptic system where the light is reflected off mirrors and focused more powerfully into two beams with greater illuminating range.

He also introduced the flashing system to the lighthouse with the mirrors revolving around the bulb to create the sweeping motion still used in lighthouses today.

He planned and constructed 23 lighthouses, notably at the Bell Rock off Arbroath and the 523ft high Cape Wrath lighthouse which faces the full force of the Atlantic at the most north-westerly point of Scotland.

Not just a lighthouse engineer, Robert was also a consultant to other engineering projects including many roads, bridges, canals, harbours and railways.

Robert Stevenson died in 1850 but some of his sons and grandsons continued on in the lighthouse business for many years.

Thomson, Sir William Johnston

Scotland has produced many famous engineers over the years and many of them have been gifted in other fields as well.

Engineer, Sir William Johnston Thomson excelled in business, building up one of Scotland's largest public transport systems and also became a civic leader.

He was born in Muirend, Baillieston, in 1881.

When he was only 12 years old, he left school and within a few years he had managed to secure himself an engineering apprenticeship.

After serving his time he emerged as a fully qualified mechanic and went to work for the Arrol Johnston Motor Works at Paisley.

He quickly proved himself to be a gifted tradesman but he also developed exceptional organisational skills.

His employers soon recognised his leadership potential and promoted him to manage one of their departments before his 21st birthday.

But by 1905, Thomson decided to go it alone and set up his own bus company in Edinburgh.

With only £12,000 capital, he started the Scottish Motor Traction Company.

Over the next four decades he worked hard to make sure his company became one of the top public transport organisations in the country.

In 1932 Thomson was elected Lord Provost of Edinburgh, a position he held until 1935.

During that time he was honoured with a knighthood for his services to industry and he was also given an honourary degree of LLD from Edinburgh University.

In 1949 the British Transport Commission acquired his SMT fleet which had grown to more than 3000 buses.

He died the same year.

Structures

Albert Bridge

The Albert or Hutchesontown Bridge is the fifth bridge to cross the Clyde at or near the Saltmarket since the construction of the first one was started in 1794.

The first bridge was a complete disaster.

The trustees of Hutchesontown were legally required to construct a crossing and had appointed the engineer John Robertson to undertake the project.

But in 1795, while the five-arch bridge was still being built, a high flood swept away the foundations and the bridge was completely destroyed.

Eight years later a temporary wooden bridge was built, spanning the river just upstream from the original bridge.

In 1829, however, the foundations were laid for the building of a new stone bridge by Robert Stevenson. It took five years for this new five-arch bridge to be completed.

But after only 30 years it was deemed unsafe when the river was deepened and a weir further upstream was removed.

Four years after it was closed it was demolished and replaced by another wooden bridge.

This remained in use until after the present-day bridge was opened in 1871.

Crossing between the Saltmarket and Crown Street, this three-arch, 410ft long bridge was constructed using a cast-iron superstructure set on abutments and piers of grey granite.

These in turn are supported on massive foundations of concrete-filled cast iron cylinders.

This was the first time that this building technique was used on any of the bridges across the Clyde.

Antonine Wall

The Antonine Wall was the northern-most wall the Romans built to defend their occupation of Britain in the second century AD.

It was 37 miles long, half the length of Hadrian's Wall, and cut across central Scotland at its narrowest point between Bo'ness and Old Kilpatrick.

The Roman Legions constructed the Wall in sections around 142AD.

It was a turf and dirt wall built on top of stone, with a deep ditch to the north and a military road to the south, connecting about 30 small forts and signal towers.

Constructed under the reign of the Emperor Antoninus Pius, the wall was intended to be impenetrable but within 10 years it was already being breached by the northern tribes. The Picts and the Scots got through it many times between 154 and 157AD, after which the Romans abandoned it.

They retreated to Hadrians Wall prior to withdrawing all their permanent garrisons from Scotland in 164AD.

The line of the Antonine Wall can still be seen today, although in most places, only a slight mound and ditch formation remains evident.

Two stone forts were built along the wall at Bearsden and Balmuildy but almost nothing survives above ground.

And although the wall passed very close to Glasgow, there is no evidence that the Romans ever built any permanent structures here.

Artifacts found within the city, of which there have been relatively few, consist mainly of coins and pottery, many of which are on display in the Hunterian Museum at Glasgow University.

Bell's Bridge

The newest crossing of the River Clyde, Bell's Bridge, was built in 1988.

This footbridge is the furthest down river of any crossing with the exception of the Erskine Bridge, built in 1971, the second youngest bridge over the Clyde.

But where the Erskine Bridge was built high above the level of the water to allow shipping to pass easily underneath, this was not practicable with the footbridge.

Although few ships today come up as far as the city, it was still necessary for the bridge's designers to devise a way to allow vessels to pass.

So the bridge was built with three spans. The northern most span is fixed, supported on the quay wall and to a pier in the river. But the other two spans are cantilevered around a second pier closer to the southern bank.

This allows the sections to be pivoted around the pier from a north-south direction to east-west, parallel to the river's banks, which enables vessels to pass through when required.

The bridge was built for the Scottish Development Agency and was completed in time for the opening of the Garden Festival in April 1988.

Its initial purpose was to provide a direct route from the Scottish Exhibition and Conference Centre on the north bank of the river to the Garden Festival on the south.

And it served its original purpose well, aiding the flow of four million visitors who attended the 100-acre festival site at Prince's Dock during the 150 days that it was open.

Caledonian Railway Bridge

The first Caledonian Railway Bridge over the River Clyde was built between 1876 and 1878.

It was made for the Caledonian Railway company to bring their locomotives into Glasgow after they had been refused use of St Enoch Station by the Glasgow and South Western Railway.

Land was bought to build Central Station and work started in the same year as the railway bridge although the station was not opened until the year after the bridge was completed.

It was built by famous Glasgow engineering firm William Arrol and Company.

The granite piers, mounted on 15ft diameter cast iron cylinders that were sunk to bedrock and filled with concrete, are all that remain of the bridge today.

The girders and tracks were removed in 1966.

Just down river from the first bridge, the second and current bridge was built between 1899 and 1905 to accommodate a major expansion of Central Station.

It was during this period that the Central Station viaduct was constructed over Argyle Street between the bridge and the station.

It is still warmly referred to by many as the Heilanman's umbrella.

The new bridge was also built by William Arrol along with engineering firm Morrison and Mason.

Varying in width between 114ft and 205ft, supported by a minimum of eight main girders, the bridge carries up to 10 tracks across its low-arched structure.

Today rail passengers using Glasgow's busiest railway station can still catch a glimpse of the tops of the old piers as they cross the new bridge.

Clyde Navigation Trust building

The former Clyde Navigation Trust building is one of the grandest architectural works in Glasgow.

It was also one of the city's most important, reflecting the importance of maritime trade and industry from which most of Glasgow's wealth and international importance derived.

The Trust built its headquarters at the corner of Robertson Street and the Broomielaw, at that time a bustling hub of ships off-loading their wares into the numerous vast warehouses.

The oldest part of the building was constructed between 1882 and 1886 by architect John James Burnet who also added the magnificent domed corner piece, built between 1905 and 1908.

Among the many stunning pieces of Greek-inspired sculpture that adorns the building's exterior is the colossal statue of Neptune which was produced by Mossman.

There are also impressive statues of Poseidon, Thomas Telford, James Watt and Henry Bell.

The building's grandeur was not restricted to the outside however, with the interior equalling the finest to be found anywhere in the city.

The original building plan involved two more sections which would have rivaled the size of the City Chambers but this was never undertaken.

The Trust had great power during the late 19th and early 20th centuries, comprising councillors, shipowners and Trades House and Chamber of Commerce members.

It was established in 1858 to replace the River Improvement Trust.

But with the slow-down in shipbuilding, it was replaced in 1966 by the Clyde Port Authority which is now Clydeport.

Dalmarnock Bridge

The first bridge over the River Clyde in Glasgow to have a flat road surface was built at Dalmarnock.

It joins Dalmarnock, which became a district of Glasgow in 1846, with the ancient royal burgh of Rutherglen on the south side of the river.

Dalmarnock bridge, the furthest up river of any of the city's bridges, was built in 1891 by the engineers Crough and Hogg, who constructed it close to the site of the old Dalmarnock Ford.

The five spans of this elegant structure are supported on concrete filled wrought iron cylinders that were sunk down 65ft below the river bed into solid bedrock.

The piers themselves are made of a combination of sandstone and granite.

Originally the perfectly horizontal bridge deck was constructed from riveted steel plate girders with a wrought iron fascia.

But in 1997 the deck was replaced by more durable and weather resistant steel beams and reinforced concrete decking but the original cast iron gothic outer detailing was retained.

The bridge is actually the third river crossing on this part of the river.

The first bridge was constructed of wood in 1821.

It was a pay bridge and as well as domestic traffic, it was also used by commercial vehicles to and from the old Dalmarnock Pit.

However, it was eventually replaced in 1848 by another wooden structure.

This one remained in operation until 1887 until it was decided that a more permanent and substantial structure should be built there in its place.

Finnieston Crane

The Finnieston Crane is the last visible reminder of the international might of the Clyde at its height as a major shipbuilding centre.

Standing resolutely alone at the Stobcross (or Queen's) Dock, the huge and aptly named titan crane was commissioned in 1926 by the Clyde Navigation Trust.

The contract to build the crane unexpectedly did not go to the experienced local firm of Sir William Arrol whose company was responsible for building the Caledonian Railway Bridge over the Clyde, the Forth Railway Bridge and London's Tower Bridge.

Instead it was won by the Carlisle firm Cowans, Sheldon & Co.

Completed in 1932, the crane is 175ft high with a 152ft long jib and a lifting capacity of 175 tons.

At the time it was the largest hammerhead crane anywhere in Europe and its services were always in great demand.

It was capable of loading the vast number of railway locomotives and tanks built in Glasgow that were shipped to countries all over the world.

The crane was also used to load the massive guns on to British warships during WWII.

When shipbuilding went into decline the Finnieston crane survived because of its lifting potential, remaining in use long after the great forest of cranes that once lined the Clyde were removed.

During the 1988 Garden Festival, a huge straw built locomotive was suspended from the crane as a nostalgic reminder of its once great importance in helping shape the Clyde's industrial might.

Glasgow Bridge

The second oldest permanent crossing of the Clyde in Glasgow is over the bridge that runs between Jamaica Street and Bridge Street.

It was the third built there in the 300 years since the first was constructed to facilitate crossing of the river downstream from Victoria Bridge as Glasgow expanded westwards.

The foundation stone was laid in 1767 and the seven arch bridge was opened in 1772.

Known as Broomielaw Bridge because of its proximity to the harbour of that name, it was 350ft long and 32ft wide.

It soon became the most important bridge in Glasgow.

But within 50 years it could no longer handle the ever increasing traffic load and it was decided that a new bridge must be constructed in its place.

Thomas Telford undertook the project in 1833 and three years later the new seven arch bridge was completed.

At 560ft long and 60ft wide, it was the most spacious in the UK at that time.

Its usefulness survived a decade longer than its predecessor, failing to meet the demands of traffic both on and under the bridge.

In 1894 new plans were made to build a 100ft wide, four arch bridge but such was the public outcry over the changes that it was altered to an 80ft width.

And the seven arch design of its forerunners was retained along with many of Telford's granite facings.

Today it is called Glasgow Bridge although it is often referred to as the Jamaica Street Bridge.

Heilanman's Umbrella

The famous railway bridge running south out of Central Station has long been affectionately known as the 'Heilanman's Umbrella'.

For many people it was always thought that it got its name because Highlanders were too mean to buy umbrellas and gathered under the bridge to stay out of the rain.

But the real reason was that between the two world wars, there was a great exodus from the Highlands and Islands of people looking for work in the cities.

Those that went to seek employment in Glasgow were told by their relatives before they left to go to the bridge on the Sabbath, the only day most people didn't have to work.

Even more specifically, they were told the shop front where they would most likely meet people from their own village or island.

Therefore on Sunday afternoons and evenings, whether it rained or not, Highlanders would gather where they would be among old friends and neighbours.

This small networking system also allowed the Highlanders to pass on information to each other of any work that was available.

This was not unique among Highlanders new to the city.

The other great influx to Glasgow around this time was the Irish.

They too had their own meeting place to locate friends.

Young Irish men or women fresh off the boats would head straight for the Ship Bank Tavern in the Briggait, tell the man behind the bar where they were from and feel less alienated and more at home.

Kelvin Aqueduct

One of the greatest engineering feats of the 18th century was the construction of the Kelvin Aqueduct at Maryhill.

It was an integral part of the last 11-mile stretch of the Forth and Clyde Canal, which had been under construction since 1768.

Robert Whitworth became the canal's architect in 1786 and completed the Stockingfield Aqueduct over Lochburn Road to the west before work on the Kelvin Aqueduct started in 1787.

By the time it was completed three years later it was not only the largest aqueduct on the canal but the largest functioning aqueduct in the world.

This magnificent structure is 400ft in length, spread over four massive but graceful stone arches, and stands 70ft above the Kelvin valley.

It cost a staggering £8,509 to complete which practically bankrupted the canal project, holding back work for seven years.

Eventually work was resumed after generous donations had been 'raised' from the forfeited funds confiscated from Jacobite supporter's estates by the government.

With the completion of the aqueduct, the final link could be made through to Bowling near Dunbarton.

The huge undertaking of the canal at last made it possible for vessels to travel from the Forth in the east to the Clyde in the west, linking Edinburgh and Glasgow together for the first time.

The canal was eventually closed to commercial traffic in 1963.

But it has recently undergone major renovation work, carried out by British Waterways, to rejuvenate the waterway and path for use by leisure craft and pedestrians alike.

Kelvin Way Bridge

Kelvin Way Bridge is one of the least remarkable river crossings in Glasgow.

But it makes up for it with its magnificent sculptures at each corner.

Spanning the River Kelvin close to the vehicular entrance to the Kelvingrove Art Gallery and Museum, work started on this bridge in 1913.

Designed by Alex B McDonald, the city engineer at the time, it was completed the following year, as were the four sets of bronze sculptures by Paul Raphael Montford.

However, Montford's work was not erected onto the four corners of the bridge until 1920.

Each sculpture has two figures mounted high on pedestals, grouped around a sandstone pillar which has four dolphins and a lamp standard at the top.

The serious of figures represent Peace and War (a woman and a warrior), Philosophy and Inspiration (a bearded sage and a female musician), Navigation and Shipbuilding (a figure holding a tiller and a woman with a model ship), and Commerce and Industry (a female with a purse and a man with a large hammer).

During WWII a bomb was dropped on the bridge but it was not seriously damaged.

Ironically, the statue that was most affected was the one in commemoration of War.

It was repaired by the Estonian-born sculptor Benno Schotz who became the Queen's Sculptor in Scotland.

He had studied his craft at night school while working in the Clydebank shipyards during the day.

He was one of the most renowned sculptors in the country at the time of his death in 1984.

King George V Bridge

King George V bridge was the last of the old style bridges to be built over the River Clyde.

It spans the river from Commerce Street to Oswald Street and when it was built it was the farthest down river over the Clyde.

It was designed to compliment the elegance of its immediate up-river neighbour Glasgow Bridge, which is more commonly referred to as the Jamaica Street Bridge.

At first glance both bridges appear to be of a three-arched granite design but this is not actually the case.

The 'arches' of the King George V bridge are in fact constructed from reinforced concrete box girders, faced with grey Dalbeattie granite.

The first plans for building the bridge were proposed four years after the coronation of King George.

However, it was to be a full decade before the bridge's construction actually got under way.

The problem was that the original design proposal, which was to duplicate the style and design of Glasgow Bridge, was vetoed by the Clyde Navigation Trust.

As has been the problem with several bridge plans across the Clyde, they had not taken into consideration the important need for river traffic to pass underneath at that time.

Eventually a new design was agreed upon and the bridge was finally completed in 1927.

It is 80ft wide, has a central span of 146ft and stands 18.5ft above the high water level which allowed the Clyde puffers and dredgers to pass beneath too and from the Broomielaw.

Kingston Bridge

When the Kingston Bridge was built over the River Clyde it was the longest pre-stressed concrete bridge in any British city.

Crossing between Kingston on the south and Anderston on the north, it is an integral part of Glasgow's Inner Ring Road.

Linking the M8 motorway on either side of the river, this is the only stretch of motorway anywhere in Britain that passes through a city rather than around it.

Costing £7million, it was built by engineers W.A. Fairhurst & Partners between 1967 and 1970.

It consists of two five-lane bridges, supported on either quay by piers with a central span of 470ft, 60ft above the river.

The total structure, including the fly-overs and ramps leading onto the bridge, comprises three miles of roads and offers spectacular views of the city and its surroundings.

The popularity of the bridge increased over the first decade after it was opened by the Queen Mother.

But from the 1980s it has become a major traffic bottle-neck for commuters.

And it has been officially recorded as the busiest river crossing anywhere in Europe with 155,000 using it every day, far more than its original design capacity.

Recently the centre spans of the bridge, weighing 50,000 tonnes, were jacked an inch off their piers to allow strengthening work to be carried out – the greatest weight-lifting exercise the world has ever seen.

St Andrew's Footbridge

One of the finest examples of wrought-iron suspension bridge design in Scotland is the St Andrew's Footbridge.

Every aspect of the spanning structure is built from wrought iron including the deck structure, suspension bars and the 20 feet pylons on either bank.

Each pylon support comprises four beautifully detailed Corinthian columns with the wrought iron lamp posts doubling as gate posts to close the bridge at either end.

It spans 220ft across the River Clyde from the bottom of McNeil Street in Hutchesontown on the south side of the river to the south eastern corner of Glasgow Green on the north.

It was built between 1854 and 1855 by the engineer Neil Robson and its design has been little altered since.

The 13ft-wide bridge was built to replace a busy ferry crossing that had long been the only means of crossing the river this far up from the city centre.

However, as more and more people started to live on the south side of the river it was decided that a bridge would better serve the population.

And unlike other bridge proposals around this time, river traffic would not be impeded this far up-river.

The bridge's location made it an ideal and free method to convey workers between the Gorbals area and Calton and Bridgeton.

Fifteen years after the bridge was first opened it had to be closed to allow essential maintenance and repair work to be carried out but it was soon reopened to pedestrian traffic.

St Enoch Underground station

Standing alone in the centre of St Enoch Square is one of the city's grandest buildings in miniature – the former St Enoch Underground station.

Built in 1896 by architect James Miller in a mixture of Jacobean and Baronial styles, it became the architectural mascot of the city's new underground, launched the same year.

The castle-like structure was deliberately built to a small scale so it would not compete physically with St Enoch's Church which stood towards the back of the square.

The church was built in 1780 and was eventually demolished in 1925.

Throughout the history of the underground station, it has been dwarfed by its neighbours.

To the east today stands Europe's largest glass structure, the St Enoch Centre, officially opened in 1990.

This huge shopping complex replaced the very grandiose St Enoch Hotel and Station built by the City of Glasgow Union Railway 20 years before the underground station was conceived.

The hotel and adjoining station had themselves invaded what, until that time, had been one of the most exclusive residential areas in Glasgow.

Both station and hotel were demolished by 1977, the same year the underground was closed for major renovation and modernisation.

The only buildings that remain contemporary to that of the underground building today are the buildings on the west side of the square.

When the new underground system opened in 1980, a new station had been built at St Enoch and the old building was preserved as a travel centre.

South Portland Street Bridge

The South Portland Street Bridge was the first purpose built pedestrian bridge to cross the River Clyde.

In 1833, the original bridge was of wooden construction and was built to link the city with Portland Street on the south side of the river.

Over the years it gradually deteriorated and in 1846 the bridge became too unsafe.

It was decided that work should be started on a new wrought-iron suspension bridge.

Designed by engineer George Martin and architect Alexander Kirkland, it was paid for out of the heritors of Gorbals own pockets.

The pylons, styled as Greek triumphal arches, are built from yellow-brown sandstone topped with massive square-cut ashlar plinths where the suspension chains pass through.

By 1853, the 410ft-long, 15ft-wide suspension bridge, the first of its kind in the city, was completed.

However the construction work proved not to be of the best with one of the masonry towers splitting and later the supporting iron chains were also found to be defective.

In 1871, because of the constant need for repairs the bridge was largely reconstructed by engineering firm Bell & Miller.

Today the bridge, which is usually just referred to as the suspension bridge, spans the river in direct contrast to the far more solid construction of more than a dozen other bridges that cross the Clyde.

At night the bridge is beautifully lit up and over the years has become a very popular location for film and television programmes.

Victoria Bridge

The oldest of Glasgow's bridges crossing the River Clyde is also the site of the very first bridge built across the river more than 650 years ago.

Victoria Bridge, previously known as Stockwell Street Bridge and Glasgow Bridge, links Gorbals Street on the south bank with the Bridgegate on the north.

It is on the site of a medieval wooden bridge built during the 14th century.

Replaced by a stone bridge built by Bishop Rae around 1345, for more than four centuries it was the farthest down-river crossing on the Clyde.

It had eight stone arches and rose steeply to 40ft above water level in the centre.

Only 12ft wide, its strength was somewhat lacking for the amount of traffic and in 1671 one of its arches collapsed and had to be repaired.

From the 1760s cart traffic was all but prohibited due to its poor condition and over the next decade five of the arches were filled to increase its strength.

In 1821 Thomas Telford widened the bridge by adding elegant cast-iron arches to support footpaths on either side but in 1847 it was demolished.

In 1851 work on a new bridge was started.

Completed in 1854, Victoria Bridge was the last of the city bridges to be built using wooden piles, subsequent ones using concrete and iron.

It's five sandstone arches, the largest spanning 80ft, are faced with light coloured Kingstown granite from Dublin.

It is still the finest of all the Glasgow bridges.

CHAPTER 12
War and Death

Cemeteries

Eastern Necropolis

The Eastern Necropolis was opened in 1847 in accordance with the growing population in the east end of Glasgow. It was the third of the four large necropolis burial sites in the city which were not linked to any church or religious group. It was opened 15 years after the first and most famous necropolis next to the Cathedral, which was followed by the Southern (1840) in the Gorbals and finally the Western in Lambhill (1882).

Situated to the south of the Gallowgate in an area known as Easter Camlachie, this large burial ground was built on part of the old Tollcross Estate. Since the middle of the 18th century, the area was also known as the 'Little Hill of Tollcross'. Today it is also called the Janefield Cemetery, derived from the street that borders it to the south. Janefield itself comes from the name of a country house built there in 1764 by wealthy grocer and Glasgow eccentric Robert McNair. He named the mansion Jeanfield after his wife and business partner Jean Holmes.

Measuring just under 25 acres, the Eastern Necropolis is the last resting place for many working class people who moved to the east end during Glasgow's 19th century industrial boom. One of its first and best known memorials is to the Bridgeton poet, songwriter, political satirist and journalist Alexander Rodger.

Born in Bridgeton in 1784, he died the year before the cemetery opened but a public subscription was raised to erect a monument in his honour.

Necropolis

The Necropolis is regarded as one of the grandest Victorian cemeteries in the whole of Europe. Necropolis translates literally as 'City of the Dead' and Glasgow's most important citizens, who died between 1832 and 1867, are entombed there. Overlooking the Cathedral and the Royal Infirmary, it was the city's first planned cemetery.

Glasgow's population was expanding rapidly with many forced to live in squalid, overcrowded conditions.

Thousands died from cholera and typhus every year and poor sanitation in church graveyards, with run-off entering streams and rivers, only added to the problem. It was decided, especially among the wealthier classes, to find a more hygienic solution.

The Merchant's House organisation undertook the building of the Necropolis and it was opened in 1833. Not only a final resting place, it was a tribute to those who had made Glasgow the Second City of the Empire. Many of the tombs and monuments were the work of eminent architects such as Charles Rennie Mackintosh and Alexander 'Greek' Thomson. The well-off in those days were entombed rather than buried to deter the grave robbing and body snatching practices made infamous by the likes of Burke and Hare in Edinburgh.

Today, the Necropolis, standing more than 200ft above the River Clyde, offers a grand view of the city and has been used for many TV and film locations. It also offers visitors a chance to take a step back in time and marvel at the city's most influential men and women of more than a century ago.

Sighthill

Sighthill Cemetery was the second burial ground to be established that was not connected to a church. It opened in 1840 and originally occupied 12 acres of land and later expanded to more than 46 acres on the west side of the steeply rising Springburn Road.

The name of the cemetery derives from its location, standing some 400ft above sea level with commanding views extending as far as the hills of Perthshire. Initially, the burial plots were located by compass bearing and distance from a central point. Eventually this method proved so complicated that it was soon abandoned.

Whereas the Necropolis, which opened seven years before, was reserved for the weathiest and most influential of the city's dead, Sighthill was the last resting place for the middle-classes and was not filled with the large tombs and monuments that have made the former so familiar. However, its most famous monument is the Martyr's Memorial, which was erected in honour of two men, John Baird and Andrew Hardie. They were both hanged and, for good measure, beheaded at Stirling for leading the Radical Rising of 1820. The third leader, James Wilson met a similar fate in Glasgow and was buried in Strathaven, South Lanarkshire.

Baird and Hardie's bodies were removed from Stirling in 1847 and re-interred secretly at Sighthill in front of the obelisk monument that had been erected by public subscription.

The Mossman family, responsible for many of Glasgow's most magnificent statues, also sculpted many of the finest tombstones in the cemetery. Many of the family are interred at the site.

Southern Necropolis

The second Necropolis to be built in the city was the Southern.

Like the first and most famous one on the hill to the east of Glasgow Cathedral, the Southern Necropolis was not associated with any Church. It was opened in 1840 in the Gorbals. Built on an 11-acre site it was extended to the east in 1846 and to the west four years later. The main entrance to the cemetery at Caledonia Road is a rather grand and imposing castellated gateway of a Norman design, built by Charles Wilson in 1848.

It served a much different class of people than the first Necropolis which devoted its space to the wealthy and influential members of Glasgow society.

The Southern Necropolis was built to accommodate the growing number of working class people who, until that time, could only expect to be buried in mass graves. It was the first place in Glasgow to offer them a cheap but dignified burial.

Among the notable people to have found their last resting place in the cemetery are Rab Ha' the Glasgow Glutton, famed for eating a whole calf in one sitting. Wee Willie White, a blind Glasgow street musician, much loved for his tunes on his tin whistle during the early 19th century, was also buried here from funds raised by his admirers.

Some of the more well known occupants include the author Hugh MacDonald and the millionaire grocer and yachtsman Sir Thomas Lipton.

Western Necropolis
The Western Necropolis was the last of the four large unaffiliated Glasgow cemeteries. It opened in the Lambhill area in 1882, the Necropolis near the Cathedral having opened in 1833, the Southern Necropolis in the Gorbals in 1840 and the Eastern Necropolis in 1847.

Among the notable citizens buried here is Sir William Smith, the Sunday School teacher who founded the Boys' Brigade in 1883 at the North Woodside Mission Hall. He died in London in 1914 and when his body was brought to Glasgow to be buried alongside members of his family, 7000 Boys lined the route of the funeral procession.

Another great man to be buried in the grounds was Albert Ernest Pickard Unlimited, as he liked to be called. He was a Yorkshireman who had arrived in Glasgow in the early 1900s and became known as the last of Glasgow's great eccentrics. Famous for his Panoptican theatre – which introduced to the world the unknown comic, Stan Jefferson, who later changed his name to Stan Laurel – Pickard became a very wealthy, influential man in Glasgow. He died on Halloween, 1964, in a fire at his Belhaven Terrace home in the West End. His ashes were scattered in the Garden of Remembrance within the Western Necropolis.

The Crematorium of the Western Necropolis was the first of Glasgow's four crematoria. It was founded by the Scottish Burial Reform and Cremation Society in 1895. The other three crematoria: Daldowie, Linn and Craigton, were opened many years later in the second half of the 20th century.

Disasters
Cheapside Street fire
One of the worst disasters in Glasgow's history was the fire that broke out

in Cheapside Street in the Anderston area of the city on 28 March 1960.

Fire and smoke billowed up into the night sky and was visible for miles around. Fourteen members of the Glasgow Fire Service and five from the Glasgow Salvage Corps lost their lives fighting the blaze, which started in a bonded warehouse that contained more than a million gallons of whisky and rum.

Within minutes of the firefighters arriving at the scene there was a massive explosion which blew the building apart. The firemen and three appliances that had been tackling the fire from the Cheapside Street side of the warehouse were buried by falling masonry.

As the fire spread, it engulfed a tobacco warehouse, an ice cream factory and the Harland and Wolff engine works. Fed by a huge lake of whisky, the fire took a week to extinguish completely.

Apart from the volatile nature of the liquid, the location of the fire made it extremely dangerous to fight. The streets around the warehouse were very narrow and made it difficult for the emergency teams to get close enough to tackle the fire effectively.

Much criticism was later laid on the siting of the whisky warehouse in such a built-up area. Few who witnessed it will forget one of the city's most harrowing modern tragedies.

Clarkston gas explosion

Just before 3pm on Thursday October 21 1971, a massive gas explosion ripped through a shopping precinct near Clarkston Toll on the south side of Glasgow.

Twenty people were killed and more than 100 were injured, many of them seriously. But for the heavy rain, the disaster would have been worse, the weather having kept many shoppers indoors.

A strong smell of gas had been reported the day before and repair work had been carried out by the early hours of the morning of the incident. On the afternoon of the blast, Scottish Gas Board inspectors and workers were checking the repair when the row of shops along the Busby Road erupted with the force of a 300lb bomb.

The car park above the single-storey shopping terrace collapsed with more than 20 vehicles adding to the debris. And a double-decker bus was also caught by the blast with flying glass badly injuring many passengers.

Passers-by started to rescue the injured from the shops until the emergency services arrived. More than 100 police officers and 20 fire brigade units and every available ambulance was called to the scene. The injured were first taken to Victoria Infirmary but when its casualty unit was full, survivors were driven to the Royal Alexandria, Hairmyres and Southern General.

More than a dozen bodies were found on the first day of the explosion while the remaining dead were recovered from the wreckage the following day. Most of the victims were young female shop assistants and housewives.

Grafton store fire

More than a dozen women and girls were killed in a fire that started in Grafton's four-storey clothes shop in Glasgow on May 4 1949.

At the time it was the worst blaze in the city since the lodging house fire in Watson Street in 1905 which killed 39 men. The fire was discovered by an employee when she opened the door to a room next to the lift shaft. She raised the alarm but in just over a minute this fire had spread rapidly through the building, creating an inferno. Shoppers and staff on the ground floor managed to escape but many of those on the upper floors were trapped.

Seven employees managed to escape by climbing out a top storey window, moving along a ledge onto the Argyle Cinema roof and dropping down onto another roof where they were rescued by firemen with ladders. Others were not so lucky.

Many of those who died were found together on one floor where they had tried to escape the blaze but had died of asphyxiation. In total 13 women and girls died, most of them in their late teens or early 20s. Two of the girls were only 15.

It took the fire brigade more than an hour and a half to bring the fire under control. Apart from the blaze and the thick black smoke they were hampered by a huge crowd that had gathered and had to be controlled by military and mounted police.

Great Storm of 1968

The Great Storm of 1968 was central Scotland's worst natural disaster since records began. In the early hours of Monday, January 15, Hurricane Low Q, which had been building in the Atlantic since Friday, turned sharply east and funneled its way up the Clyde Estuary. Wind, gusting to 140mph, tore through Glasgow and central Scotland with such ferocity that it would be several years before all the damage would be put right.

More than 20 people lost their lives that morning, nine of them in Glasgow. And the deaths did not stop after the winds died – more than 30 others lost their lives repairing the damage, 11 of them while carrying out roof repairs.

In Glasgow alone more than 300 homes were totally destroyed and around 70,000 were damaged, leaving nearly 2000 people homeless. Overall, some 250,000 houses in central Scotland were affected, many of the occupants being forced to live with make-shift tarpaulin roofs for years.

Repair costs eventually rose to almost £30million – equivalent to more than £150m today. But the Labour government of the day, lead by Harold Wilson, seemed little concerned. Eventually it grudgingly sent £0.5m – not a gift but an interest free loan.

The disaster had been given little national press coverage, unlike an incident the previous year when the oil tanker Torrey Canyon ran aground near Land's End. Almost immediately £1.5m was handed over along with substantial grants for the environmental disaster, which had posed no real danger to human life.

James Watt Street fire

Glasgow, like any other city, has had to deal with the tragedy of major fires breaking out during its history. But one of the most harrowing was the one that took place on November 18 1968 in James Watt Street, in the Anderston area of the city.

The fire bore a terrible similarity to another dreadful event that had taken place only a few blocks away in Cheapside Street just over eight years before. Both fires started in bonded warehouses and both resulted in the loss of many lives.

The fire in James Watt Street broke out in an upholstery factory situated in an old three storey bonded warehouse. Because it was a high-security building like many others in the area, all the windows had been heavily barred to prevent break-ins. But it also made it impossible for most of the workforce to escape. Only three people managed to escape the inferno.

Another 22 perished as they desperately tried to find a way out of the inferno that could be seen from miles around. Some had been trapped in a lift between floors while others died trying in vain to break out through a padlocked fire escape. The workers' escape had also been hampered by the wooden staircases which were consumed by the fire. In total, 20 fire appliances were brought in to fight the blaze and bring it under control but the building was reduced to a burnt out shell.

SS Daphne

One of the worst catastrophes and losses of life in the history of Clyde shipbuilding took place in July 1883. The *SS Daphne* had been built for the Laird's Line, one of the oldest in Glasgow, having started trading with Ireland in 1814. Construction of the vessel had been undertaken at the yard of Alexander Stephen & Sons' Linthouse yard, near Govan, on the south side of the River Clyde.

The 500-ton vessel was launched on July 3 with its engines in place but the boilers had yet to be fitted.

Tragedy occurred just after the vessel hit the water. It started to roll over and water quickly filled the ship through the large opening on the deck for the boilers to be lowered into place. The vessel quickly capsized, drowning 124 shipyard workers, many of them trapped below deck in the engine rooms where they were still working.

Two statues in Glasgow commemorate this terrible loss of life. One was erected in 1997 near Stephen's shipyard in Elder Park. It stands to the south west of the 1906 Isabella Elder statue, the first monument to a woman apart from Queen Victoria to be honoured in Glasgow.

A duplicate statue was also placed in Victoria Park, directly across the river from the yard, as many of the men who lost their lives came from that area of the city.

Watson Street lodging house fire

Nearly 40 people lost their lives in the early hours of the morning of November 19, 1905, when a fire broke out in a warehouse building on Watson Street near Glasgow Cross in the east end of the city.

The warehouse had been converted into a lodging house for those of little means. Consisting of four floors, a basement and an attic, the premises had been split into many dormitories using cheap wood to partition the old warehouse.

There were estimated to be between 300 and 400 men staying there when the fire broke out on the third floor. It was thought that a carelessly discarded cigarette or a spark from a pipe had caused the fire.

Within a few minutes of the alarm being raised, the fire brigade arrived but the blaze had taken hold. The closely packed flammable material used to make the rooms helped the fire spread quickly throughout the upper floors of the building. No provision had been made for fire escapes and other fire safety precautions had not been installed.

Most of the men on the third floor found they were trapped. Many of the men on the floors above were forced to smash windows in order to get clear. The majority of the occupants did manage to escape the blaze but in total 39 men lost their lives that morning and another 24 were badly injured.

War

602 Squadron

602 (City of Glasgow) Squadron, which formed in 1924, based at Abbotsinch, was part of the Auxiliary Air Force that played a vital role during WWII. Even before the war, 602 made aviation history as it was the first to fly over Mount Everest in Westland biplanes on April 3, 1933, a feat that was made into the film 'Wings over Everest'.

Because 602 trained as much as the RAF, it was ready to take part in WWII right from the start.

The squadron shot down the first enemy plane over Britain on October 1939 and 602 pilots were the first awarded the Distinguished Flying Cross (DFC) for their heroic actions.

During the Battle of Britain, they showed outstanding skill, earning them more than a dozen DFCs.

Archie 'Killer' McKellar, was the first Glasgow pilot to be awarded the Distinguished Service Order (DSO) to go with his DFC and Bar. McKellar made the most kills, 16, of any pilot during the Battle of Britain but was sadly killed just a few days later.

And 602 was the first AAF Spitfire Squadron and also conducted the first night attacks, dive-bombing, attacking V1 and V2 rocket sites and shot down the first airborne V2.

The longest serving squadron in the front line, it held the second highest number of 'kills' and lost the fewest number of pilots.

And most famously, 602 put Rommel out of the war, shooting his staff car in Normandy resulting in his skull being fractured.

A most remarkable squadron, 602's history is now displayed at the museum in Hillington.

Butts, battles of

Two of the most bloody battles to take place in Glasgow happened at an area known historically as the Butts in the east end during the 16th and 17th centuries.

They took place at Barrack Street, named after the first military barracks established in the city in 1795 after Glaswegians complained at having soldiers billeted in their homes. They were built on Glasgow Muir, known as the Butts. This was where, for hundreds of years, targets had been set out on weapon showing days for the military men in the area to carry out exercises.

The first battle took place in 1544 during Mary Queen of Scots' minority rein.

Regent Arran had treacherously slaughtered the Earl of Lennox's garrison which had surrendered the besieged Bishop's Castle in the High Street. In retribution, the Earl of Glencairn raised an army of 800 against Arran's troops on the Butts but he too was defeated.

The Regent, realising the citizens of Glasgow had supported Glencairn, then plundered the city and more than 300 people were slain.

In 1679 the second major battle was between John 'Claverhouse' Graham, Viscount Dundee, (later Jacobite commander 'Bonnie Dundee') and the Covenanters. Having already been defeated at Drumclog by the Covenanters, Claverhouse roused the Glasgow garrison and was this time victorious.

As a mark of contempt, he left the enemy's corpses on the Butts to be eaten by dogs. And like Regent Arran before, Claverhouse exacted revenge on the citizens of Glasgow who had supported the Covenanters.

Bell O' The Brae

The first real battle ever fought on the streets of Glasgow took place at the end of the 13th century. It was fought at a place called Bell O' The Brae – the brow of a hill – situated at the top of the steep incline of the High Street where it levels off at the junction of Rottenrow.

The battle occurred in 1297, a year after the start of the Wars of Independence. William Wallace had just been victorious in a battle against the English at the Barns of Ayr, and having given his support to the Bishop of Glasgow, Robert Wishart, he assembled 300 men and headed for Glasgow to rout the English garrison.

They were stationed at the Bishop's Castle, built around the middle of the 13th century as a Royal Castle, and was a stronghold for Glasgow's bishops during the wars with England. Although captured several times by the English, the attack by Wallace was the first time it had been retaken.

The garrison came out to meet Wallace who turned and was chased down the High Street. But this was a deliberate move by Wallace. When his force reached the Bell O' The Brae he and his men stopped and turned to face the pursuing English. At the same time from the enemy's rear Wallace's uncle, Auchinleck, appeared with another group of men. This clever tactic resulted in an impressive victory for the Scots with Wallace personally killing the English Governor, Earl Percy, during the battle.

Black Friday

One of the worst riots on the streets of Glasgow took place on Friday January 31 1919. The Scottish TUC and Clyde Workers' Committee called 'the 40 hours strike' which was later referred to as 'Black Friday'.

Before WWI the working week was 54 hours but Scottish workers wanted it cut to 30. However, Emmanuel Shinwell, Glasgow Trades Council president, persuaded them to go for 40. A strikers' meeting was called for Monday, January 27, and more than 3000 workers gathered at St Andrew's Halls. By Friday 50,000 had congregated, Scotland's first mass picket.

City magistrates were forewarned of the dangers of keeping trams on the streets as 10,000 strikers marched from the halls to occupy George Square. But this warning was ignored and the riot started after a tram tried to make its way through the square while strike leaders waited inside the City Chambers to have talks with the Lord Provost.

Fighting broke out between the workers and the police with the fighting spreading as far as Glasgow Green. Many people, including women and children were injured. More than a dozen strikers were arrested and taken to Duke Street Prison and were later tried at the High Court in Edinburgh. Manny Shinwell, William Gallacher and David Kirkwood were jailed for several months.

After the riot, soldiers from Maryhill Barracks, armed with machine guns, tanks and a howitzer, occupied Glasgow's streets for a week to prevent any more gatherings. A 47-hour week was eventually agreed between employers and trade unions.

Campbell, Sir Colin John

One of the great military leaders of the nineteenth century was a carpenter's son, born in Glasgow in 1792.

Born Colin Macliver, he took the surname Campbell after his mother's brother, Colonel John Campbell. Sir Colin Campbell spent his whole life in the army and was rewarded Field Marshall rank and created Baron Clyde in 1858.

Regarded a great leader by his men, the sentiment was not often shared by his superiors. Nicknamed 'slowcoach' he never risked his soldier's lives to achieve victory, unlike many other generals of the time. It was his slow, skilled and calculated soldiering that broke the famous siege of Lucknow and the eventual quashing of the Indian Mutiny in 1857. His tactical leadership played a significant part in many other empire building campaigns of Victorian Britain, including the 1842 Chinese expedition and the second Sikh War of 1848-49.

Commanding the Highland Brigade at the outbreak of the Crimean War in 1854, he brought about the victory at Alma and repelled the Russians at Balaclava with his famous 'thin red line' of Scots infantry. This victory was quickly overshadowed, just hours later by the most famous cavalry charge in history, the disastrous charge of the Light Brigade which killed 500 men.

Sir Colin Campbell, Baron Clyde, died in 1863 and is buried in Westminster Abbey.

Cenotaph

The most important of all the memorials in George Square must be the Cenotaph. Today it commemorates all those who have died in 20th century conflicts, but originally it was built as a memorial to all those who died in WWI, in particular the 20,000 from Glasgow who made the ultimate sacrifice in defence of their country.

Designed by Sir John Burnet, it was unveiled by Field Marshall Earl Haig in May 1924, and bears the solemn inscription 'Their Name liveth evermore'.

Scottish-born, Douglas Haig was the commander-in-chief of the British forces in France between 1915 and 1918. He had always maintained a strong belief that the German army could only be beaten on the Western Front through a continued attack. This strategy eventually won through but at a very high cost of men's lives and Haig was much criticised for it afterwards. Three years after the war finished Earl Haig helped establish the Royal British Legion to aid and improve the welfare of ex-servicemen.

Work started on the memorial in 1921 after the bronze statue of William Gladstone was moved from its original position in front of the City Chambers. Its original design intended for a sunken pool to reflect the white granite oblong.

Ernest Gillick designed the two majestic white lions on either side of the monument and also the detailed figure of St Mungo, Glasgow's Patron Saint.

Moore, Sir John

The first statue to be erected in George Square was that of soldier, Sir John Moore, in 1819. Appropriately the statue was sculpted from brass cannons, which turned out to be a fortunate choice.

It received little respect and some harsh treatment from youths of the day. Aside from throwing stones at it, some vandals, on at least one occasion, tied a rope around an arm but failed to bring it crashing down from its eight foot high granite plinth.

Born near Candleriggs in Glasgow in 1761, John Moore went on to have a famous and distinguished career, fighting in the American War of Independence, the West Indies and in Europe. His greatest fame came from his service in the Peninsula War, taking command of the British Army in 1808, and co-operating with the Spanish in repelling the French.

When Madrid fell, he was forced to retreat with 25,000 men to avoid annihilation from Napoleon's 70,000. Retreating in winter through near impassable mountains, they reached La Coruna in the north-west corner of Spain. And on January 19, 1809, with their backs to the sea, they managed to win a great victory over the French with the loss of only 2,000 men. Moore was sadly one of the 2,000 and was buried there the following day.

His death was commemorated in the poem by Charles Wolfe in 1817, 'The Burial of Sir John Moore' and for many years, every Glasgow school boy was made to learn it off by heart.

INDEX

libraries 42, 50
mansions 13, 18, 19, 23, 24, 26, 28, 68, 193
memorials 30
Royal Faculty of Procurators Hall 120
schools 45, 48
shops 220
stations 245
Stock Exchange House 222
synagogues 138
theatres 94, 95, 97, 98
warehouses 214
Western Club 105
Argyle Cinema 252
Argyle Street 7, 35
Argyll divorce case 121
'Armadillo' see SECC
Arran, Regent 255
Arrol, William 239
arson 123, 124
art and artists 44, 49, 70–1, 77, 86–7, 88
  Glasgow School 103–4
art dealers 77, 86–7
art galleries 2, 4, 15, 25, 40, 62–3, 87, 88, 127, 212, 243
Art Nouveau 2, 11, 14, 45, 142, 143
Art Purchase Fund 62
Asian immigrants 140
Assembly Rooms, Ingram Street 15
Athenia, SS 176
Auchentoshan distillery 106
Auchinlea Park, Easterhouse 27
Auldhouse Castle 16
'Aunt Kathleen' see Garscadden, Kathleen
Australia 119, 122, 210, 235
aviators 233–4, 235, 254–5

B

Babbity Bowster 106–7
Baden-Powell, Robert 103
Badger Club 105
Baillie, Canon William 27
Baillie, Matthew 59
Baird, John 3, 24, 249
Baird, John Logie 87, 199–200
Baird Hall, Sauchiehall Street 5
Balfour, Arthur 203

Balfron 3
Balmoral Castle 38
Balmuildy Roman fort 238
bandstands 69
Bank of Scotland 211
bankruptcies 212, 230
banks and banking 1, 3, 4, 5, 14, 50, 193, 195, 211–12, 222
Bannerman, Sir Henry Campbell 203
Barclay, H. & D. (architects) 220
Barclay, William 150–1
Barlernark, Prebendary of 27
Barlinnie Prison 115, 117, 124
Baronial architectural style 245
Baronial Hall, Gorbals 5–6
Barony Church 135, 137
Baroque architectural style 30, 42, 146
Barr, Robert F. 109
Barras market 197
Barrhead Ashvale football team 187
Barrowfield, Lady 18
Barrowland Ballroom 101, 112, 197
Barrowman, Mary 115
Bates, Harry 36
Bath Street 6
Battle of Britain 254
Battlefield monument 141
Baxter, Stanley 74, 95
BBC 33, 77, 80, 200
  John Reith 87
  Music Live 149
  radio 74
  Scottish Symphony Orchestra 12, 102
Beardmore, William 55, 190–2, 206
Bearsden Roman fort 238
Beaux-Arts Style 1
Bedlay Castle 17
beer 110
Belhaven, Viscount 6
Belhaven Church 139
Bell, Henry 169, 239
Bell & Miller (engineering company) 246
Bell O' The Brae, battle of the (1297) 17, 255–6
Bell Rock lighthouse 236
Bellahouston Park 5, 64, 65–6
Bellerophon, HMS 162
Bell's Bridge 238